SIGNS & WONDERS
UPON PHARAOH

SIGNS & UPON

Moreover thou didst see the affliction of our fathers in Egypt and hear their cry by the Red Sea, and didst show signs and wonders upon Pharaoh and upon all his servants, and upon all the people of his land.

Nehemiah 9:9-10

WONDERS

PHARAOH

A HISTORY OF AMERICAN EGYPTOLOGY

JOHN A. WILSON

THE UNIVERSITY OF CHICAGO PRESS / CHICAGO AND LONDON

Library of Congress Catalog Card Number: 64-23535

The University of Chicago Press, Chicago and London
The University of Toronto Press, Toronto 5, Canada

To the Memory of
James H. Breasted
George A. Reisner
and
Herbert E. Winlock
who showed
Signs & Wonders in
the Land of Egypt

PREFACE

When the enemy was in sight, the army took its positions, and when Bonaparte had given his last orders, he pointed to the pyramids and said: "Go ahead, and remember that from the top of these monuments forty centuries are watching you!"

From Vivant Denon's account of the Battle of the Pyramids, on July 21, 1798.

The United States, one of the newest of civilizations, has long had a deep regard for the study of past cultures, and a concern for the preservation of man's great achievements of art and thought. We have also had a special interest in the civilization of ancient Egypt from which many of our own cultural traditions have sprung—and a deep friendship for the people who live in the valley of the Nile. In keeping with this tradition, and this friendship, I recommend that we now join with other nations through UNESCO in preventing what would otherwise be an irreparable loss to science and the cultural history of Mankind.

From the late President John F. Kennedy's recommendations to Congress for the use of American government credits to preserve Egytian monuments threatened by the construction of a High Dam at Assuan, April 6, 1961.

It is a long distance from Napoleon Bonaparte to the late President Kennedy. What is the record of America's long interest in ancient Egypt? This book examines the development of curiosity about that old culture and the beginnings of professional concern for understanding the culture more thoroughly.

Today the United States holds a respected place in Egyptological scholarship—as in other ancient Oriental fields. It was not so one hundred years ago, when there was no American to match the scholars of France, Germany, and Great Britain. Americans were concerned with their own future in their own land, were engrossed in the struggle between the North and the South, and had only a slight curiosity about Egypt as a land which figured, rather unpleasantly, in the Bible. Authors like Mark Twain and Charles Dudley Warner and wealthy tourists, who might spend a winter on the Nile, did nothing to dispel the feeling that Egypt was a strange and different land which could do nothing for the American but satisfy a restless curiosity. What were the pyramids and the sphinx to a people who still had not learned their own incredible West?

Fifty years ago the situation was radically altered. Two Americans, Breasted and Reisner, won international recognition and occupied the first two chairs of Egyptology established in this country. In the years between 1894 and 1914, the pursuit of Egyptology shifted from the pleasant and leisurely avocation of the wealthy amateur to the serious and dedicated vocation of the professional. A similar change was taking place in parallel archeological fields, but the concern of this book is limited to the study of ancient Egypt. Archeological scholarship was becoming mature.

A focus on the Americans may suggest that this is a chauvinistic presentation. There is no intention here to suggest that the Americans were in any way superior to their foreign colleagues. The concentration on persons who came from the United States has been a pleasant task, because I enjoy working out the scholarly tradition to which I belong. Further, the story is fascinating because it shows an unexpected flowering sixty or more years ago. The United States had no tradition of Egyptology to maintain, as did France, with the Napoleonic expedition, Champollion, Mariette, and Maspero; as did Germany, with Lepsius, Brugsch, and Erman; as did Great Britain, with Thomas Young, Birch, Wilkinson, and Petrie; as did Italy and Austria and Russia. Americans of the nineteenth century, like Gliddon, Edwin Smith, Berend, Groff, and Wilbour, did not form a tradition of scholarly sequence and consequence to compare with our European counterparts. Then, in the early twentieth century, there suddenly appeared Breasted and Reisner, with Winlock to follow. In a psychological sense, the book cannot explain this explosion of competence, but it can chart it as a phenomenon of which we may be proud.

The details of the story are not always clear. Much of the characterization of an individual and his work appears only incidentally in the remarks of others, and two different accounts may paint two contradictory pictures. Those who put down reminiscences at the end of a long life tell a highly personal story based on memory, which is often treacherous. I shall here have to follow my own personal judgment of the truth. The story is not always noble. This is an account of the coming of age of a field of study, and adolescence has its fine impulses and activities, but it is not a comfortable period.

Structurally the treatment notes the centuries of neglect of the monu-

ments and then divides into six time zones, as characterized by Egyptological work. Within each of these historical periods I try to give the more
general political and atmospheric development of Egypt, then the process
of the study of ancient Egypt, with reference to archeological progress
elsewhere in the Near East, and then a focus on the American part in the
scene. Although this may seem to be an anecdotal and episodal record of
the Americans who were interested in Egypt's ancient past, its purpose is
to give the intellectual setting which controlled and directed their interest.
The six periods are, with some overlap:

from Napoleon's expedition into Egypt to Champollion's decipherment
of the hieroglyphs, 1798–1822;

Mohammed Ali's new nationalism, the opening up of Egypt for Western development, and the consequent arrogant plundering of the monuments, 1806–54;

the Egypt of Ismail Pasha and the Suez Canal, with archeology controlled by a Frenchman, Mariette, but still undisciplined, 1854–82;

the Egypt of Lord Cromer, the British Diplomatic Agent; the period
of the elegant connoisseur who lived on a houseboat on the Nile, but
scholarly control beginning under the insistence of Petrie and Erman,
1880–1908;

the invasion of the professional, with American scholars moving into
the foreground, 1894–1914;

Egyptian nationalism asserting its demands against Western exploitation,
while foreign archeology was producing such discoveries as the tomb of
Tut-ankh-Amon and the burial of Hetep-heres, 1914–36.

The detailed treatment ends about 1936, both because that date marked
increased independence for Egypt and because the depression enforced a
marked decline in the volume of archeological work. In any case, we stand
too close to the most recent developments to see them in historical perspective.

The popular nature of this book is illustrated by the fact that I have
resigned myself to the absence of footnotes. Instead, the several chapters
are followed by the more important references—I have not attempted to
document each statement—and by such skeletal biographical notes on individuals as may seem helpful.

The bibliographical references do not pretend to be exhaustive, but they
do cover the chief sources used for the writing. In addition, this book
includes my own memories and impressions out of forty years. They are
of course as unreliable as such objectivity always must be.

For the brief biographies I have had to rely upon such obituary references as may be provided in the literature, with a heavy dependence upon

Warren Dawson's *Who Was Who in Egyptology*. Practically all of the persons treated lived a long time ago, and there is little reference there to anyone now living. In the Index, the page references to these biographical sketches are given in italics. The Index itself does not attempt to be exhaustive.

Like all historical writings, the book is colored with personal prejudices. Since I am a warm admirer of Breasted, Reisner, and Winlock, I may be unfair to their predecessors, who were not governed by the same standards nor motivated by the same passions. I shall try to present them as creatures of their day, having standards in conformance with their times, and to credit them for accomplishments within that setting.

More people helped me in the writing of this book than I can adequately record. I do want to express my gratitude to John D. Cooney of the Brooklyn Museum, the late William C. Hayes of the Metropolitan Museum of Art, Richard A. Parker of Brown University, and William Stevenson Smith of the Boston Museum of Fine Arts. Mr. Cooney's many helpful suggestions are not specifically acknowledged in the text. My wife excavated references to several persons and episodes and always was a willing audience to my ideas about the book. I should be grateful if readers would correct my errors of fact and omission.

I hope that this book will be of interest to those many people who have expressed such curiosity about ancient Egypt and about the type of scholar who works in the field. In particular, I have been thinking of those students who have asked: "Did you know Breasted? And Petrie and Reisner and Winlock? What were they like?"

The courtesy of those persons and institutions who permitted the use of illustrations has been noted in the list of Illustrations, and it is a pleasure to express my gratitude for their generosity.

In the text some borrowings were direct quotations, and some abstracts of the borrowed material. The record of persons, institutions, and publishers who sanctioned the use of published material is long, and the absence of footnotes makes specification of their good will a matter of grateful detail. For the most part, the Bibliography records my obligation.

I am indebted to Warren R. Dawson for frequent reference to his book, *Who Was Who in Egyptology*, and for permission to quote from his *Charles Wycliffe Goodwin, 1817–78: A Pioneer in Egyptology*, and to Charles Breasted for quotations and general guidance from his book on his father, *Pioneer to the Past: The Story of James Henry Breasted, Archaeologist;*

to the Museum of Fine Arts, Boston, for permission to quote and abstract from their *Bulletin* (XII, 72; L, 19–27), and from Dows Dunham,

The Egyptian Department and Its Excavations; to the Brooklyn Museum for permission to quote and abstract from Charles E. Wilbour's letters, *Travels in Egypt,* and from their *Bulletin* (XI, 11–15); to the Metropolitan Museum of Art, New York, for authorizing similar use of material from Herbert E. Winlock, *Models of Daily Life in Ancient Egypt from the Tomb of Meket-Rēᶜ,* Herbert E. Winlock, *Materials Used in the Embalming of King Tut-ᶜankh-Amūn,* and their *Bulletin* (XVI, 36–52; XVII, 37–48; XXI, 12–14; XXIII, 11–19, 32–44; XXIV, 3–14); to the Peabody Museum, Salem, Massachusetts; Mount Auburn Cemetery, Cambridge, Massachusetts; The Johns Hopkins University; the University of London; and the Oriental Institute of the University of Chicago for information promptly supplied; and to all of the above for illustrative material with permission to publish;

to the Egypt Exploration Society for permitting quotations and abstracts from *Studies Presented to F. Ll. Griffith,* Warren R. Dawson, *Who Was Who in Egyptology,* and the *Journal of Egyptian Archaeology* (Vols. XII, XIII, XIX, XXI, XXII, XXIII, XXXV); the American Philosophical Society for authorizing quotations from their 1942 *Yearbook* (pp. 358–62; 369–74), on Petrie and Reisner; to the Archaeological Institute of America and the journal *Archaeology* for permission to abstract an article on Egyptian architecture in the United States in that journal (III, 164–79); and to the *Encyclopaedia Britannica* for permitting a quotation from their article, "Archaeology";

to E. J. Brill, Leiden, for permitting the use of an illustration from J. Vandier d'Abbadie, *Nestor l'Hôte;* to Cassel and Company, Ltd., London, and Cooper Square Publishers, Inc., New York, for authorizing quotations and abstractions from Howard Carter and A. C. Mace, *The Tomb of Tut.ankh.Amen* (Vol. I); to the University of Chicago Press for permission to abstract from William B. Hesseltine and Hazel C. Wolf, *The Blue and the Gray on the Nile;* to Christy & Moore, Ltd., literary agents of London, for information abstracted from Ralph A. Bagnold, *Libyan Sands;* to Constable Publishers, London, for authorizing quotation from Theodore M. Davis, G. Maspero, and G. Daressy, *The Tombs of Harmhabi and Touatankhamanou;* to Doubleday & Company, Inc., for permitting a quotation from *The Bible and the Ancient Near East: Essays in Honor of William Foxwell Albright;* to Macmillan & Co., Ltd., London, for sanctioning quotations and abstracts from A. H. Sayce, *Reminiscences;* to John Murray, London, for authorizing quotations and abstracts from Sir E. A. Wallis Budge, *By Nile and Tigris;* to the University of Oklahoma Press for permitting similar use of Joseph Lindon Smith, *Tombs, Temples, & Ancient Art,* edited by Corinna Lindon Smith (quotations from pp. 23–24, 31, 32, 41, 61, 189, 211; abstracts from pp. 10–12, 25–28, 30–33, 37–42, 54–75, 87, 133–34, 144–51); to Charles Scribner's Sons for permission to quote and abstract from Charles Breasted, *Pioneer to the Past* (particularly pp. 30, 64, 77, 78, 349, 366, 370, 376); to Walker and Company, New York, for sanctioning general reliance upon Stanley Mayes, *The Great Belzoni: Archaeologist Extraordinary;* and to the Yale University Press for permission to quote from *The Brooklyn Museum Aramaic Papyri*, edited by Emil G. Kraeling.

May those who read this book show a similar charity for the author, forgiving his prejudices and enthusiasms and correcting his errors.

CONTENTS

ILLUSTRATIONS

(Following page 54)

PLATE 1

a. Vivant Denon accompanied the detachment of Napoleon's army which pursued the Mamelukes southward. In January, 1799, he made this sketch of the temple of Edfu. Over the centuries, debris had choked the temple nearly as high as its outside walls, and a village perched upon the roof. (From Denon, *Voyage dans la Basse et la Haute Égypte,* Pl. 58.)

b. About one hundred and thirty-five years after Denon's visit, Edfu from the air showed the work of clearance and maintenance begun by Mariette and continued by the Service of Antiquities which he founded. (Courtesy of James H. Breasted, Jr.)

PLATE 2

In the latter part of the nineteenth century, the second court of the temple of Medinet Habu at Thebes still had columns remaining from its service as a Christian church. At the upper right, the Copts removed part of the architrave to form a transept and thus gain the cruciform shape. (Photograph by Bonfils, from the Bettmann Archive.)

PLATE 3

a. The gifted French artist, Nestor l'Hôte, was a member of Champollion's copying expedition and in 1828 made this sketch of a temple of Ptolemaic and Roman times. Soon after, this temple was dismantled in order to build a sugar factory. (From J. Vandier d'Abbadie, *Nestor l'Hôte (1804–1842),* Plate XXXI, 1. By permission of the publisher, E. J. Brill, Leiden.)

b. The temple of Wadi es-Sebua in Nubia was later used as a Coptic church, with the pagan sculptures plastered over and covered with Christian paintings. A picture of St. Peter replaced the ancient Egyptian gods in the sanctuary. Now most of the plaster has fallen away, and the older carving has reappeared. The result has been a composition in which Pharaoh Ramses II is apparently offering flowers to St. Peter. (Photograph by an expedition of the Royal Prussian Academy of Sciences, 1908–10.)

PLATE 4

A contemporary picture shows the young Napoleon viewing a mummy in its wooden coffin. The gentlemen in the civilian hats are presumably some of his savants. The pyramids appear in the background, but the precise setting may be apocryphal. (From the Bettmann Archive.)

PLATE 5

Another contemporary picture shows Napoleon and his staff on camel-back. The desert terrain and the faces muffled against heat and driven sand suggest that this may have been on his campaign into Palestine. (From the Bettmann Archive.)

PLATE 6

a. Napoleon's scholars gathered material which was published in the great Description de l'Égypte, *of which this is the Frontispiece. A portal in the style of the pharaohs is embellished with the crowned N below, royal cartouches containing the Napoleonic bee in the two lower corners, and a list of military triumphs on the two sides, framing a picture in which several hundred miles of Nile landscape are compacted into a single view.* (From the Description de l'Égypte, Vol. I.)

b. Muffled in his robe, the Middle Kingdom official Senebefni now sits in the Brooklyn Museum as number 39.602, while his wife It-noferu-sonb holds her modest place before him. This was one of the pieces which Napoleon brought back from Egypt as gifts for Josephine. (Courtesy of the Brooklyn Museum.)

PLATE 7

a. Jean François Champollion, "le Jeune," holds a table of some of the hieroglyphs which he deciphered. (From H. Hartleben, *Champollion: sein Leben und sein Werk,* Frontispiece.)

b. Giovanni Battista Belzoni, adventurer-archeologist, in Arab dress. (From a painting in the National Portrait Gallery, London.)

PLATE 8

Bernardino Drovetti, Consul-general for France in Egypt, is shown in Thebes, surrounded by some of his agents in the search for salable antiquities. (From le Comte de Forbin, *Voyage dans le Levant* [1819].)

(Following page 86)

PLATE 9

Water color by Belzoni, showing how he removed the colossal head of Ramses II from the Ramesseum in western Thebes. (From Belzoni, *Narrative of Operations . . . Six New Plates.*)

PLATE 10

The French literary figure, Maxime du Camp, who visited Egypt in 1850 in the company of Gustave Flaubert, was one of the first enthusiasts for photography. With the equipment of the time, he took remarkably good pictures, as this exposure of a colossal head at Abu Simbel shows. (From the Bettmann Archive.)

PLATE 11

Commander Gorringe lowering an obelisk to a horizontal position, preparatory to loading it into a ship in the Alexandria harbor for its journey to New York, where it now stands in Central Park. This photograph was taken just after the heavy weight had come crashing down upon its supporting cradle. The American flag is being planted near the point of the obelisk. (From H. H. Gorringe, *Egyptian Obelisks,* Plate IX.)

PLATE 12

a. Colonel Mendes Cohen of Baltimore formed a major private collection in the 1830's. This wooden statuette of a girl dates from the New Kingdom and is now a part of the Cohen Collection in The Johns Hopkins University. (Courtesy of The Johns Hopkins University and Professor Hans Goedicke.)

b. Officers of New England sailing ships returned from their journeys with curios from strange places. In 1823 Lieutenant Thomas Tanner presented these three Egyptian pieces to the East India Marine Society in Salem, Massachusetts, where they formed part of the first museum collection of Egyptian objects in the United States. (Courtesy of the Peabody Museum, Salem, Massachusetts.)

PLATE 13

a. In 1832 Dr. Jacob Bigelow designed an Egyptian gateway for Mount Auburn Cemetery in Cambridge, Massachusetts. It was first constructed in wood, then rendered in granite in 1843. (Courtesy of Mount Auburn Cemetery.)

b. In New York City, the Halls of Justice, popularly known as the "Tombs," showed the use of the massive Egyptian architectural style for a prison. (From the Bettmann Archive.)

PLATE 14

The hillside of western Thebes was honeycombed with tombs of the ancient nobles, with the modern fellahin living in and around the cavelike structures. Gardner Wilkinson's house stood on a ledge at the upper right; its remaining tower is here marked with an X. (Photograph by Bonfils, from the Bettmann Archive.)

PLATE 15

The temple of Luxor, as seen from the Nile. At the left appears the minaret of the mosque of Abu'l-Haggag. Along the corridor of the highest columns were the houses of Mustafa Agha and Edwin Smith. (Photograph by Bonfils, from the Bettmann Archive.)

PLATE 16

a. Auguste Mariette, who brought a measure of control to excavations in Egypt, is here inspecting one of his finds, an Egyptian family group. (From Mariette, *Voyage dans le Haute Égypte*, Vol. I, Pl. VIII.)

b. A sailing dahabiyeh, of a size to accommodate a single family, has its sails down and its crew at the oars, as it prepares to pull away from the shore. (Photograph by Bonfils, from the Bettmann Archive.)

(Following page 118)

PLATE 17

a. Shepheard's Hotel in Cairo, a picture of Victorian elegance, with its famous entrance terrace. (From the Bettmann Archive.)

b. The barracks beside the Qasr en-Nil Bridge in Cairo, unadorned symbol of the security control which the British army held over Egypt for three generations. (Courtesy of the Royal Air Force; British Crown Copyright reserved.)

PLATE 18

A group of Egyptologists in the temple of Karnak. Rochemonteix, Gayet, Insinger, Wilbour, and Maspero. (From Wilbour's *Travels in Egypt*, facing p. 240. Courtesy of the Brooklyn Museum.)

PLATE 19

a. A limestone plaque with carved sketches of Akh-en-Aton and Nefert-iti, which Wilbour bought at Tell el-Amarna in 1881 for a little over a dollar. Now Brooklyn Museum number 16.48. (Courtesy of the Brooklyn Museum.)

b. Charles Wilbour's sailing dahabiyeh, the "Seven Hathors." (From Wilbour, *Travels in Egypt*, facing p. 400. Courtesy of the Brooklyn Museum.)

PLATE 20

The desert bay at Deir el-Bahri in western Thebes. In the foreground is the terraced temple of Queen

Hat-shepsut of the Eighteenth Dynasty, with the temple of Mentu-hotep of the Eleventh Dynasty beyond it. On the distant shoulder framing the bay lay the hiding place of the royal mummies. (Courtesy of the Metropolitan Museum of Art, New York.)

PLATE 21

a. Flinders Petrie was rarely photographed at work. This photograph shows him looking down into a pit which his workmen are clearing. (Photograph courtesy of University College, University of London.)

b. Sir Flinders and Lady Petrie at Jerusalem when he was eighty-six years old. (Courtesy of Harold W. Glidden.)

PLATE 22

a. Theodore M. Davis' expedition found this chair of Princess Sit-Amon in the tomb of her grandparents, Yuya and Tuya. This is the chair in which the ex-empress Eugénie seated herself, commenting on its Empire style. The Cairo Museum number is 51113. (From J. E. Quibell, *Tomb of Yuaa and Thuiu* [Cairo, 1908], Plate XXVIII.)

b. This is the controversial coffin, inclosing its controversial mummy, found by the Davis expedition in a tomb which was published as the burial place of Queen Tiy of the Eighteenth Dynasty. The photograph shows the confusion at the time of discovery; pieces of rock have fallen from the ceiling, and there is a general welter of confusion and disintegration. (From Theodore M. Davis et al., *The Tomb of Queen Tîyi*, Plate XXX.)

PLATE 23

a. The western slope of the Valley of the Kings at Thebes. In the lower center is the entrance to the tomb of Ramses VI. The tomb of Tut-ankh-Amon was discovered under and slightly to the right of this. (Courtesy of the Oriental Institute.)

b. At the end of an excavation season Sir Robert Mond gave a fantasiyeh—*an entertainment of music, dancing, and juggling—for his workmen and guests. Sir Robert sits in the center, Walter B. Emery behind the table, and Dr. and Mrs. Breasted at the right.* (Courtesy of the Oriental Institute.)

PLATE 24

The Breasted expeditionary party at Abu Simbel in 1905–6. Dr. and Mrs. Breasted and their son Charles are in the center. (Courtesy of the Oriental Institute.)

(Following page 150)

PLATE 25

a. At Abu Simbel, Breasted crosses a plank from the head of one colossus to another, to join the photographer. (Courtesy of the Oriental Institute.)

b. The Kagbar Rapids in the Third Cataract, showing the rocky barriers within which the Breasted expedition of 1906–7 suffered shipwreck. The air is full of wind-borne sand. (Courtesy of the Oriental Institute.)

PLATE 26

The working party for the tomb of Tut-ankh-Amon at lunch in a neighboring tomb. Breasted, Burton, Lucas, Callender, Mace, Carter, and Gardiner. The empty chair was for Carnarvon, who had not yet arrived. (Courtesy of the Oriental Institute.)

PLATE 27

a. Howard Carter, with the walking stick, supervising the removal of a small bust of Tut-ankh-Amon to a tomb which served as the laboratory for cleaning and consolidation of the finds. (Courtesy of the Oriental Institute.)

b. Visitors wait outside the tomb of Tut-ankh-Amon. Lord Allenby, with the boutonniere, is at the right; Breasted, bareheaded, is talking to Lady Allenby, seated. (Courtesy of Lindsley F. Hall.)

PLATE 28

a. A characteristic view of George A. Reisner, as he looked in 1935. (Photograph by Leslie F. Thompson, courtesy of the Oriental Institute.)

b. The carrying-chair of Queen Hetep-heres, as reconstructed on the basis of fallen and disintegrated fragments. The Museum of Fine Arts number is 38.874. (Courtesy of the Museum of Fine Arts, Boston.)

PLATE 29

a. An early morning photograph of the pyramid plateau at Gizeh. The long central shadow points directly toward Harvard Camp. (Courtesy of the Oriental Institute.)

b. An air photograph of Chicago House at Luxor, shortly after it was built in 1931. (Courtesy of the Oriental Institute.)

PLATE 30

At Deir el-Bahri the myriads of pieces of the smashed statues of Queen Hat-shepsut were sorted, studied, and pieced together. In 1929, Herbert E. Winlock (foreground) was working at this task. (Courtesy of the Egyptian Expedition, the Metropolitan Museum of Art.)

PLATE 31

a. Fragments of a red granite statue of Hatshepsut, as pieced together. The granite pieces of the original can be distinguished from the grey torso, taken from a cast in Europe, and from the white plaster reconstruction. (Courtesy of the Metropolitan Museum of Art, Museum Excavations, 1926–29; a contribution from Edward S. Harkness and the Rogers Fund.)

b. The same statue, restored and exhibited in the Metropolitan Museum in New York. The museum number is 29.3.3. (Courtesy of the Metropolitan Museum of Art, Museum Excavations, 1926–29; a contribution from Edward S. Harkness and the Rogers Fund.)

PLATE 32

a. One of the first classes of Egyptians in Egyptology, about 1925, at Cairo University. Breasted, in the center, is a guest. Golenischeff, at the left, and Graindor, at the right, professors at the University, sit beside Breasted. (Courtesy of Labib Habachi.)

b. Junker, Reisner, Breasted, and Borchardt in the garden of the Continental Hotel in Cairo in November, 1935. (Photograph by Leslie F. Thompson, courtesy of the Oriental Institute.)

1 CHANGE AND DECAY

An ancient Egyptian temple is today a silent and lonely place. Of course it may be filled with a crowd of chattering visitors, led by a stentorian guide. A gang of workmen may be shouting in unison, as they haul some great block of stone away. Overhead the circling hawks may shrill their displeasure at the invasion by the tourists. Yet the monument, looming up in its battered and crumbled ruin, stands withdrawn, distant, mute, and shrouded with sorrow. There is no loneliness like the loneliness of a mighty place fallen out of its proper service to man.

Once the temple was the busy heart of a great religious faith. The soaring walls were carved with scenes and inscriptions, vivid with bright paint —garishly so, to our modern taste. In that central sanctuary the priests shouldered the sacred boat of the god and brought him forth in a solemn procession. As they passed through the columned hall and reached the Station of the King, the Pharaoh himself saluted his divine father and joined the procession. When they issued from the central portal of the temple, a waiting crowd broke into shouts and songs and dances. The great god had deigned to appear before his people.

On the other side of the river priests had been up before dawn to climb on top of the cliff, where they would vie with each other to catch the first glimpse of the sacred procession as it approached their western shrine. As they idled their time away, they chiseled their names and titles on the cliff, in commemoration of the honor which had been allotted them. Down below was a ledge of rock, with the tombs of three nobles. Squatting there in the warmth of the morning sun were three tomb priests, dutifully at their posts on this feast day. They were not bored: the Feast of the Valley came only once a year, and there was an abundance of gossip. Nobody had to work on that day. Women and children had long been waiting at the approach to the temple in the Valley to add their shrill noise to the festivity. These were the proper services which temples should render to man. This is why they stand today so silent and lonely.

Why are the temples and tombs so sad? When did man cease to honor them and delight in them? When did man begin to tear them to pieces with a savageness of hate and distrust? Why is the ruin so uneven, with some monuments stripped down to their foundation blocks, whereas others still rise in impressive dignity?

The answer is not simply the story of the two thousand years since the days of the pharaohs. The answer goes back into the days of the pharaohs, since the entire three-thousand-year career of these monuments saw neglect, decay, and pillage.

THE YEARS OF THE LEAN AND ILL-FAVORED CATTLE

The ancient Egyptians lived in houses of mud brick, but they built their temples and tombs in stone for the everlasting service of a god or the perpetual maintenance of a dead man. Temples and tombs were "houses of eternity" and were based upon endowments which were intended to keep them active for all time.

Yet "all time" was a heavy burden for the future to bear. In periods of weak government, economic foundations broke down. Further, it was too much to expect that treasure buried in desert tombs would defy human greed. Tomb robbery is almost as old as tombs themselves, and each generation is more interested in its own memorials than in those of its ancestors. Pyramids and tombs of the Old Kingdom show architectural provisions against robbery and sometimes carried curses against violators. An early lament observes that the wisest of men in the past could not protect their tombs: "Their walls are broken apart, and their places are not—as though they never had been!"

There were periods of pious restoration and repair, such as the reign of Seti I about 1300 B.C. or the Twenty-sixth Dynasty about 600 B.C., but generally speaking monuments lasted a few centuries and then began to fall into ruin. Impatient pharaohs would tear down the shrines of their ancestors to get building stone for their own temples. Any modern restoration is likely to find this re-use of old stone in later buildings. At Karnak, when an Eighteenth Dynasty pylon had to be taken apart and reconsolidated, the archeologists found a beautiful little Twelfth Dynasty shrine which had been taken to pieces and used as stuffing for the inner body of the pylon.

About 1130 B.C. the proud Egyptian Empire was disintegrating. The pharaohs were weak; foreign trade had been drastically cut down, and there was a period of extreme inflation in the cost of food. For a stretch of about twenty years in this period we have documents about the wholesale robbery of the tombs of kings, queens, and nobles at Thebes. The record of an official investigation carries the report:

These are the tombs and sepulchers in which rested the blessed ones of old, the women, and the people of the land, on the west of the city: —it was found that the thieves had broken into all of them, that they had pulled out from their coffins and sarcophagi their occupants, thrown out upon the desert, and that they had stolen their articles of household furniture, which had been given them, together with the gold, the silver, and the ornaments which were in their coffins.

That investigation was at pains to say that only a few of the royal tombs had as yet been pillaged, but in the extract above it is admitted that "all" of the tombs of the nobles had been thoroughly ransacked. As the years went on and the government made only token gestures to halt the looting, the burials of the kings and queens were also ransacked. Indeed, the scandal could not have continued so long without official connivance. The pious activity of the few could not stem the tide of greed for gold and silver and jewelry. In the following century, the priests quietly took the mummies of the pharaohs and the queens from their robbed resting places and stacked them up in a secret hiding place for final security. As we shall see in a later chapter, they remained hidden there until eighty years ago.

Yet, despite robbery, neglect, and re-use, the ancient monuments belonged to the ancient Egyptian system as long as the old religion prevailed. How and when did the religion break down?

"The Years That the Locust Hath Eaten"

There were active services in the Egyptian temples on into Roman times. Those successors of Alexander the Great, the Ptolemies, lived in Egypt as pharaohs and cultivated the land for its own prosperity and their own power. There was much religious building under the Ptolemies, and the Romans at first continued that attention to the temples. The state of Egypt, however, was different under the Romans.

Egypt was a land with great agricultural wealth and a strategic location, but it was also a country with a rebellious spirit. The Roman Army held the land in a tight control. Augustus placed three legions in Egypt, and his personal command of the army meant that he himself had a firmer rule of the land than of other Roman provinces. No Roman Senator was permitted to visit Egypt without the personal permission of the Emperor. Bustling Rome needed the wealth of the land of the Nile, so Egypt was bled white by taxes. Tiberius may have protested that he wanted his sheep sheared, not flayed, but exorbitant taxes continued to mount. It came to the point where tax-collectors might seize the mummy of a dead defaulter to force his relatives to pay up. Entire villages were deserted when the inhabitants found themselves unable to pay their taxes. The large Roman army was there to back up the fiscal bleeding and to crush any protest. Under this pitiless oppression, men found no comfort in the ancient religion, and in the second century A.D. great masses of the people went over to Christianity, to monasticism, to otherworldliness. Many of the temples and tombs fell into neglect. When Theodosius (A.D. 379–95) proclaimed Christianity to be the religion of the Empire, persecution of the pagans became both a religious and civil duty. The old monuments were destroyed, violated, or converted to other use.

Basically, then, the Arab conquest of Egypt in A.D. 640–41 made no real difference with regard to the ancient monuments. They had been pagan abominations to the Christians; they became pagan abominations to the Muslims. Even the tradition about the destruction of the Library of Alexandria needs to be understood in historical setting. The great library and research academy which the Ptolemies had set up in Alexandria was, according to tradition, wiped out by 'Amr ibn el-'As, the conquering Arab. The story runs that 'Amr was asked whether the scrolls in the library should be saved. He answered that if they agreed with the "Book of God," they were superfluous, since the Book existed; and if they disagreed with that Book, they should be destroyed. So all were burned. The tradition is probably based on truth, but the Library was then only a ghost of its past glory. Julius Caesar had raided the collections for his own purposes. Diocletian had ordered the burning of books on alchemy. When Egypt became formally Christian, pagan and philosophical and heretical works were attacked. There was little of importance left for the Muslims to destroy. To be sure, the Alexandrian Library is not one of the ancient monuments in which this book is interested, but the dwindling of its importance over eight centuries is a good parallel to the concern which was paid to the relics of the pharaohs.

Thus some of the monuments were razed to the ground, and their stones were used for the construction of other buildings. Elsewhere the essential structure was used for new churches or houses, but the pagan pictures and inscriptions were mutilated and covered with plaster. It was particularly common to destroy the potential life of an ancient picture by hacking up the face or the eye. Let us consider a few examples of the fate of the monuments of the times of the pharaohs.

The city of Thebes was always a rebellious community, and about 29 B.C. the Roman Prefect Cornelius Gallus crushed a revolt and destroyed the town completely. When Strabo visited the site of the once mighty capital, he saw only a few small scattered villages. The later inhabitants built their houses and churches inside the temple of Luxor, in order to take advantage of the support of its great stone walls and columns. One hundred and fifty years ago, the essential village of Luxor lay inside the temple. Today the mosque of the local Muslim saint, Abu'l-Haggag, still lies within the forecourt built by Ramses II. According to rumor, when the government wanted to clear the entire temple, the saint appeared in a dream to one of the faithful and insisted that he should not be moved.

In ancient Egypt the god Amon made an annual trip from his temple at Karnak two miles south to his temple at Luxor. He went by boat, and the happy occasion gave Thebes its great popular festival once a year. Carvings in the Luxor temple show the gay holiday atmosphere, with crowds lining the banks of the waterway and cheering joyously.

Today the gay annual festival of Luxor is the Feast of Abu'l-Haggag, when a boat sacred to this saint is put on a cart and towed around the temple of Luxor. Carts decorated with flowers and streamers and carts loaded with children follow the sacred boat. Men, women, and children shout the name of the saint. Legend says that Abu'l-Haggag's boat has never needed repair, miraculously maintaining a strong, sound wood. One can step from the street into the temple and see a very similar scene carved more than three thousand years ago. There is little doubt that the boat feast of Abu'l-Haggag is a lineal descendant of the boat feast of Amon. Somewhere in between these two, there probably was a boat feast for a Christian saint, with the people in the same holiday mood. Local religion has a way of accommodating itself to the simple pleasures of the people, even though the dogmatic faith has changed drastically.

There is a pleasant tale about Abu'l-Haggag which I shall try to relate as it was told to me in his mosque. Centuries ago Luxor was a Coptic village, ruled by a Christian queen, Tarzah. In a dream she had been warned to beware of strangers, so her guards forbade unknown visitors to enter the town. Then one day a Muslim from Baghdad, Yussuf Abu'l-Haggag, mounted on a camel, mysteriously appeared inside the circle of guards and appealed to Tarzah for hospitality. That was an appeal which no Arab could deny, for a day or two or three. She was willing to permit him a place large enough for him to sleep, but she set hard conditions: he might have no more ground than that which might be taken by the hide of a camel. During the night Abu'l-Haggag sliced the skin of his camel into a single long thong, and in the morning the entire village of Luxor, lying inside the ancient temple, was encompassed by the camel's hide. The logic of his wit was so captivating that Tarzah proposed that he marry her. He consented on the condition that Luxor become Muslim. Today the boat procession on his feast day is said to start at the point where he fastened the strip of camel string and then to make the same circuit of the temple that he did.

Classicists will recognize the parallel in the story of the founding of Carthage, when Dido was granted no more land than could be contained by the hide of an ox and was able to inclose an entire hill by cutting the hide into one long strip.

The advantage of seeking support and shelter for mud-brick villages by using high stone walls was obvious all over Egypt. Settlements tended to stay in a single place in order not to encroach upon the agricultural fields. The lofty temple of Horus at Edfu became so completely covered with debris that an Arab village was able to occupy the roof of the temple, until it was finally cleared out by Auguste Mariette only a century ago.

Across the river from Luxor lies Medinet Habu, the mortuary temple of Ramses III. After the Twentieth Dynasty there were probably no more religious services in this temple. The various temples of Medinet Habu were inclosed in a high mud-brick wall, however, so the complex was useful as a closed center for the administration of western Thebes. Such service by pharaoh's agents protected these monuments from depredation in the search for building stone. Just outside of the inclosure two temples were quarried down to their foundation blocks. Later the Christians located the town of Djeme inside the inclosure wall, went into the great temple of Medinet Habu, plastered over the pagan carvings, cut new doors and windows into the structure, and erected a Coptic church in the second court. Actually the Copts unwittingly preserved the essential structure of the temple, the wall carvings, and the painted surface. Now that the plaster has been removed, the ancient scenes in the second court have a delightful freshness of color. Both the church and the town were probably abandoned by the ninth century A.D. In 1891 the Service of Antiquities cleared the second court and removed the remaining elements of the Christian church, unfortunately with very little record.

An amusing remnant of Christian re-use may still be seen in the temple of Wadi es-Sebua, built by Ramses II in that area of Nubia which will soon disappear beneath the waters of a new lake. In a niche in the holy of holies there once stood statues of gods. Framing the niche were two carvings of Ramses II, offering flowers to the deities. When the Copts used the temple for a Christian church, they cut away the statues and plastered over all the scenes. On the plaster they painted their own religious pictures. Now the plaster has fallen away, except at the back of the niche, where a fine figure of St. Peter may be seen. Solemnly on each side the old pharaoh Ramses II has reappeared, now offering flowers to the Christian saint.

The beautiful terraced temple of Queen Hat-shepsut at Deir el-Bahri in western Thebes experienced two changes which defaced the monument and yet preserved its essential core. In Ptolemaic and Roman times the temple had become sacred to two traditional wise men of older Egypt: Ii-em-hotep, of the Third Dynasty, who was deified as the patron god of physicians, and Amen-hotep, son of Hapu, of the Eighteenth Dynasty, who was a magician god. Inscriptions in the upper terrace of the temple show that the priests serving these two gods ran a religious health center, with the sick coming in hope of cure and carving brief grateful texts. Later on, when Christianity came to Egypt, Coptic monks took over, as the name Deir el-Bahri, "the Northern Monastery," shows. Although the monks defaced the pagan inscriptions, they did maintain the architectural structure, so it has survived to our times.

At the First Cataract, the great temple on the island of Philae was a late center for the worship of the mother goddess, Isis. It flourished under the Ptolemies and the early Romans, for whom Isis became a supreme deity. Although Christianity made great advances in Egypt and Nubia in the third and fourth centuries, the cult of Isis at Philae remained powerful. Even after Theodosius proclaimed Christianity to be the religion of the Empire, including Egypt, inscriptions show that many of the people of Upper Egypt and Nubia stubbornly carried out the festivals of Isis. Finally Justinian (A.D. 527–65) closed the temples, carried away the statues to Constantinople, and threw the priests of Isis into prison. Philae then withered in neglect, although the temples were not used as quarries for building stone elsewhere because it was an island.

The three great pyramids lay across the river from Egyptian Babylon and the Arab cities of Fustat and Cairo. They were always the object of curiosity and of greed. Apparently the Great Pyramid had been penetrated during the times of the pharaohs. Certainly it was a center of tourists' interest in ancient times: Herodotus writes that the blocks of its outer casing were covered with inscriptions, probably the records of pious visitors. Down into Roman times the pyramid stood open, was accessible to visitors, and was used for burials of Egyptians who wished to take advantage of strong walls and a holy setting. Later the monument was deserted, with its opening clogged up. In the ninth century, Ma'mun, the son of Caliph Harun er-Rashid, forced a passage through the masonry in search for treasure. The records make it almost certain that the Fourth Dynasty burial was already gone by that time and that he found only the later, lesser burials. Most particularly, in the thirteenth century and after, the beautiful limestone casing blocks, which had inscriptions, were carried off for the building of the new city of Cairo. It was the fate of many monuments to be used as handy quarries.

The official religion and the religion of the masses might change to

Christianity and then to Islam, but the ancient monuments remained impressive to the people. They were so big, so lasting, that they must have some magic power which would help the poor. Many of the temples are marred with shallow vertical scrapings. These run on a level where an individual might stand, and using a sharp point, gouge away the soft sandstone or limestone into a bowl. The origin of these scratches is uncertain. I have guessed that the poor people over the ages believed that a temple might have some good magic within it, so they scraped away some of the stone, took it home, and perhaps introduced it into the food of invalids. The virtue within a mysterious and mighty monument might be curative.

Over the ages the women of Egypt carried on ancient superstitions without regard to the changes in official faith. At Gizeh, east of the Third Pyramid lies an important Fourth Dynasty tomb, that of a noble named Debehni. For centuries this has been regarded as the burial place of a Muslim saint, Sidi Hamed Sam'an. Pious women and children encamp here on Fridays to worship the saint and to get the virtues of such an association. A picnic place is never the tidiest of spots. Modern scholarly visitors are advised to view the tomb on Thursdays, when the debris and the infestation of vermin may be at their weekly minimum.

In the western cliff south of the village of Tuna el-Gebel, in Middle Egypt, the heretic Pharaoh Akh-en-Aton had a boundary stela carved to mark one of the limits of his capital city, now known as Tell el-Amarna. Above the inscription is a scene which shows Akh-en-Aton, his wife Nefert-iti, and their children worshiping the sun disk. Today this stela draws the women of the region, for they credit the monument with great powers for fertility. When they want more children, they visit this "saint" and make small sacrifices on the spot. Akh-en-Aton and Nefert-iti, who produced only a string of girl babies, have become the patron forces for women who long for a string of fine sturdy boys.

"I Will Scatter the Egyptians among the Nations"

Antiquarian interest and imperial looting contrived to carry off many Egyptian monuments in Roman and Byzantine times. We have already seen that Justinian, when he closed the temples at Philae, took the statues to Constantinople. There had previously been a flow of objects to Rome. As an example of the imperial desire for an Egyptian monument, let us take two obelisks. As modern experience has shown, these are the most cumbersome and vexatious pieces to take down, ship, and re-erect.

In the open square before the Aya Sophia Mosque at Istanbul a striking soaring piece is the granite obelisk of Thut-mose III, of the fifteenth century B.C. According to tradition, Constantine the Great (A.D. 306–37) had the piece, 97.5 feet tall, transported from Thebes to Alexandria. There it lay until Julian (A.D. 360–63) offered the people of Alexandria a colossal statue of himself if they would forward the obelisk to Constantinople. The tradition continues that the ship carrying the unwieldy monument was driven ashore near Athens by a storm, where it was rescued under Theodosius and set up in its present place about A.D. 390.

In Rome there is a baker's dozen of obelisks, seven of them authentic pieces from Egyptian antiquity and the remainder Roman imitations of a highly regarded form. The finest of them stands in the Lateran, before the church of San Giovanni in Laterno, and is 105.5 feet tall. Thut-mose III had had it cut out of the Assuan quarries and taken to Thebes, but he did not erect it, and it lay in the south part of the temple of Karnak for thirty-five years. Then Thut-mose IV had it set up in pious honor of his famous grandfather. Again tradition credits Constantine with its transport from Thebes to Alexandria. His son Constantius then took it to Rome, where it was erected in the Circus Maximus about A.D. 357. The centuries were not kind to it. In A.D. 1587 it was found fallen, broken into three pieces, and buried in debris. Pope Sixtus V had it repaired and re-erected in its present location, the tallest of all standing obelisks.

Through the late Renaissance and on into the eighteenth century there was a trickle of curiosities from Egypt into Europe. Classical collections often included a few antiquities from the land of the Nile. John D. Cooney points out to me that the Egyptian collection of the Comte de Caylus was bequeathed to Louis XV about 1755 and that the British Museum received similar pieces about the same time. This small, steady collectors' interest must be remembered as a corrective of the flat generalization that Napoleon's expedition rediscovered ancient Egypt.

Ezekiel thundered out the prophecy: "Thebes shall be split asunder, and Memphis reduced to gravel." To a great degree his prophecy came true. The tombs and temples out on the desert sands were attacked by wind and sand, but especially by man—later Egyptians of the days of the pharaohs, Romans and Byzantines, Copts and Muslims. Further, the preponderance of the evidence on ancient Egypt should have come, not from the desert, but from houses, palaces, storehouses, and villages located on the fertile soil. This material has long since disappeared under the accumulation of the alluvial deposit and has disintegrated under agencies of water and organic chemicals. The wonder is that so much has survived down to our day. A people that built for eternity over three thousand years ago might suffer greatly in that ambition and still leave a stunning heritage of architectural and artistic glory for us to rediscover.

2 THE DAWN (1798–1822)

In the late eighteenth century Egypt slumbered soddenly, still in the Middle Ages. Europe and America were changing rapidly. The Industrial Revolution had already brought to the West the spinning jenny and the power loom. The steam engine and the use of coal for power were changing economics and society. Small factories were springing up everywhere. The political currents were even more exciting: the American and French revolutions had expressed violently new ideas about the rights of man. The world could never be the same again.

None of this ferment affected Egypt. The country was nominally a dependency of the Turkish Sultan, but it was ruled with arrogant brutality by foreign mercenaries, the Mamelukes. They were interested only in maintaining their power and collecting taxes from an inert populace. Their military power seemed to them absolute, because it had never been successfully challenged, and they were vigorously hostile to any change which might endanger their privileged power.

Such a country was of little interest to Europe and of no interest to the young United States, intently trying to establish its new sovereignty. Any knowledge about Egypt was based on the Bible and the classical authors, supplemented by a few fantastic books of travel. Ideas about ancient Egypt had a large factor of the preposterous. The fertile mud of the Nile, when emerging from the inundation, was thought to produce life spontaneously. Said Lepidus in Shakespeare's *Antony and Cleopatra:* "Your serpent of Egypt is bred now of your mud by the operation of your sun. So is your crocodile." Dried and pulverized mummy was believed to be an effective drug in medicine. By the thirteenth century there was a brisk trade in exporting mummy powder to Europe. Perhaps the bitumen had some effectiveness, but people forgot this very early and transferred the healing reputation to the embalmed flesh, just as the word *mummiya* originally meant "bitumen," but came to be applied to the preserved body. Sir Thomas Browne wrote: "Mummy is become merchandise, Mizraim cures wounds, and Pharaoh is sold for Balsams." Indeed, the European demand created a scandal in the seventeenth century, when the mummy merchants of Alexandria began to use recent corpses—never embalmed and quite possibly dead from some pestilence—to pulverize and send abroad. Human greed might have surmounted scandal, however, if the Governor of Alexandria had not imposed a restrictive tax on these dealers early in the eighteenth century.

Another demand, a small one, was that of the European painters in oils. They used a pigment called "mummy," made of bitumen and animal remains from Egyptian tombs, because it was reputed not to crack on the canvas.

Equally fantastic were the ideas of the Europeans about the Egyptian hieroglyphs. Generally speaking, ancient Egypt was both remote and incomprehensible; by definition, hieroglyphic was priestly carving, and priests are always suspected of cabalistic mysteries. Therefore, the hieroglyphs must be supercharged with secret symbolism; they could not be read as a Westerner might read Arabic or Chinese. About 1762 a distinguished British physician, William Stukeley, the Secretary to the Society of Antiquaries, wrote:

> The hieroglyphics of the Egyptians is a sacred character; that of the chinese is civil or a common way of writing. . . . The characters cut on Egyptian monuments, are purely symbolical. They are nothing than hymns & invocations to the deity. . . . To give a few instances. A feather so often appearing, signifys sublime. An eye is providence. . . . A boat, the orderly conduct of providence in the government of the world. A pomegranate imports fecundity, from the multitude of its seeds. . . . I believe the true knoledg of the hieroglyphics was immersed in extremest antiquity. So that if any skill of interpreting them, remain'd with the priests, to the time of *Cambyses;* after that time, the just understanding of them was lost. . . . The perfect knoledg of 'em is irrecoverable, with the most antient preists [sic].

With such an attitude of mind among literate people, it is not surprising that there was no initiative to find the key to hieroglyphic and that the scholarly world was slow to accept Champollion's decipherment in 1822.

Such a small interest in ancient Egypt meant that there was little market for the antiquities. In 1778, when forty or fifty Greek papyri appeared on the Cairo market, only one of them was sold. It is alleged that the Egyptian finders thereupon burned up the remainder for their aromatic odor. Although modern experiment discounts the legend that burned papyrus has a pleasant smell, there is no reason to doubt that papyrus might be burned to meet Egypt's lack of fuel or kindling. At Thebes in 1817 the locals used pieces of mummy cases and mummy wrappings in their little ovens.

Two hundred years ago, and as recently as eighty years ago, Egyptians buried ancient stone or bronze figurines under the thresholds of their houses as protective forces or used a slab carved in hieroglyphic, a good-luck symbol, as the home threshold.

Most distressing in a wholesale way was the use of ancient monuments as quarries. To the Muslim the temples and tombs were the hostile forces which Prophet Mohammed had denounced; they were also pagan to the Christian. So they lay there, great masses of already hewn stones, available to the nearest builder for his walls. The amount of ancient structure which went into Old Cairo and more recent Cairo must have been appalling.

Who in the eighteenth century cared about ancient Egypt?

JEFFERSON'S FRIEND IN CAIRO

Apparently that remarkable man, that amateur archeologist, Thomas Jefferson, was interested in ancient Egypt. We learn of this through letters written from Cairo by an American in 1788.

John Ledyard was a Connecticut Yankee whose first impulse had been to convert the Indians. He went to Dartmouth two years after that college was opened for his missionary training. The lad was restless and kept disappearing from college on rugged journeys. He finally shipped as a sailor across the Atlantic, begged his way to London, enlisted in the British marines, and accompanied Captain Cook's expedition around the world from 1776 to 1780. Under ship's discipline he performed creditably.

In 1785 he made the acquaintance of Thomas Jefferson in Paris and was encouraged to plan the exploration of the northwest coast of North America. When nothing came of this, he went to St. Petersburg, received a visa from Catherine the Great, and set off for Siberia. His observations on the land and people were admirable, but apparently he strayed too close to the Russian fisheries and seal industries in the Pacific, because he was arrested, brought back to Moscow, and expelled from the country.

In London Sir Joseph Banks encouraged Ledyard—then thirty-seven years old—to undertake a pioneer exploration on behalf of the African Association: to go up the Nile as far as Sennar, which lies south of modern Khartum, to cross Africa, and then to go down the Niger to the Atlantic. Practically all of this was terra incognita.

In the early summer of 1788, Ledyard left London, and in Paris he visited Jefferson and Lafayette. As we shall see, Jefferson must have expressed a keen interest in ancient Egypt and urged the young man to report to him about the antiquities. In the heat of August he sailed into the harbor of Alexandria and wrote Jefferson his first impressions. "Alexandria at large presents a scene more wretched than I have witnessed. Poverty, rapine, murder, tumult, blind bigotry, cruel persecution, pestilence!"

That set the tone for his reports from Egypt. To him, "the mighty, the sovereign of all rivers, the vast Nile," as he saw it in the Delta, was a paltry stream no larger than the Connecticut. Both the city of Cairo and the indignities heaped upon a foreign Christian appalled him. "Sweet are the songs of Egypt on paper. Who is not ravished with gums, balms, dates, figs, pomegranates, circassia, and sycamores, without recollecting that amidst these are dust, hot and fainting winds, bugs, musquitoes, spiders, flies, leprosy, fevers, and almost universal blindness?" In his journal he wrote: "I find the situation of a Christian, or, what they more commonly call here, a Frank, to be very humiliating, ignominious, and distressing."

There is no record that he visited the pyramids or took any trouble to see antiquities. The one gleam of curiosity about ancient Egypt arose out of his previous comparison of Siberian trading media with those of the American Indians. Mummy beads caught his attention: "I have seen a small mummy; it has what I call wampum-work on it."

On November 15, 1788, he wrote Jefferson in Paris that he would be leaving Cairo in two or three days on his great expedition. Then came these weary words.

> Perhaps I should not have pleased you, if I had written much in detail. I think I know your taste for ancient history; it does not comport with what experience teaches me. The enthusiastic avidity with which you search for treasures in Egypt, and I suppose all over the East, ought in justice to the world, and your own generous propensities, to be modified, corrected, and abated. . . . I cannot tell you why I think most historians have written more to satisfy themselves, than to benefit others. I am certainly very angry with those, who have written of the countries where I have travelled, and of this particularly. They have all more or less deceived me. . . . I have passed my time disagreeably here. . . . The humiliating situation of a Frank would be insupportable to me, except for my voyage. . . . I assure myself, that even your curiosity and love of antiquity would not detain you in Egypt three months.
>
> From Cairo I am to travel south-west, about three hundred leagues, to a black king. Then my present conductors will leave me to my fate. Beyond, I suppose I go alone. . . . Do not forget me. . . . I shall not forget you.

John Ledyard never left Cairo. Within a few days of writing that letter, he was dead, apparently from dysentery. Jefferson's hope of penetrating the secrets of Egypt was not to be realized by an American.

NAPOLEON'S EXPEDITION

Then, at the very end of the century, on July 1, 1798, a young man, twenty-nine years old, Napoleon Bonaparte, landed in Egypt. He had persuaded the French government that England could be wounded by a military force which lay athwart the line to India. At any rate, he did invade the land, with an explosive train of consequences.

For one thing, the supremely confident Mamelukes thought that they could dispose of the infidel invader as easily as their predecessors had disposed of the Crusaders. With superior numbers and with sabered knights mounted on horseback they could roll these French foot soldiers back into the sea. They did not understand the firepower of an infantry square or the mobile and massed use of cannon, which Napoleon knew brilliantly. There is a tragic gallantry in knightly cavalry charging and charging against a grim professional army, but gunpowder has no use for romance. The medieval army of the Mamelukes was mowed down by the French fire, first in the Delta and then at the Battle of the Pyramids. They retreated into Upper Egypt, and the French forces, after securing the northland and Cairo, pursued them and continued to defeat them.

The troops under General Desaix were poorly dressed, poorly supplied, and poorly experienced in the guerrilla tactics which the Mamelukes followed. Nevertheless, they doggedly followed as far as the First Cataract and forced the enemy to retreat into the Nubian wilderness. At Philae, on its island in the cataract, within the doorway of the first pylon of the temple of Isis, they left this inscription: "L'An VI de la République, le 15 Messidor, une Armée Française commandée par Bonaparte est descendue à Alexandrie. L'Armée ayant mis, vingt jours après, les Mamelouks en fuite aux Pyramides, Desaix, commandant la première division, les a poursuivis au dèla les Cataractes, où il est arrivé le Ventôse de l'an VII." Of the carvings and scratchings of names and dates on the ancient monuments, scholars are inclined to class the old and historically interesting additions as graffiti and the names and dates of ninetenth-century tourists as tasteless excrescences. This inscription is a graffito.

With emphasis, the Orientals had been taught a lesson—the Westerners must be respected, after all; they certainly had superior power. Abruptly the attitude of the Orientals toward the West changed; they might still be hostile and resentful, but they did want to know about these successful and energetic invaders.

For our purposes, Napoleon introduced into Egypt two elements which were revolutionary in different ways. One was the printing press, which could produce documents in Arabic quickly and cheaply. The long-range effect of this cannot be overestimated. The ability to read and write, the dissemination of ideas, and the urge to be an author instead of a mere calligraphic copyist abruptly became goals for the upper and middle classes. The cannon and the printing press—they were very different, but each was very subversive to a world which had been stagnant.

A second force which Napoleon brought into Egypt was a body of scholars. There were well over a hundred of them—mathematicians, astronomers, chemists, engineers, mineralogists, naturalists, botanists, surgeons and physicians, artists, a musician, writers, and antiquarians. He turned them loose on a different world, which they were to study and describe. Most of them were young men, eager to make a sound reputation. In 1806 it was estimated that nearly a quarter of them had lost their lives: five killed in battle, five assassinated, ten dead of the plague, five dead from dysentery, one drowned, and five dead in Europe from the lasting effects of the experience. Yet they had responded magnificently to the challenge of their assignment. Nineteen superb volumes appeared from 1809–28, the famous *Description de l'Égypte*, with beautifully illustrated descriptions of minerals, fish, architecture, antiquities, and so on. Under the weight of an appalling ignorance of Egyptian monuments, the plates of ancient scenes show a praiseworthy artistic conscience. These volumes and the incidental publications by members of the expedition, such as that by the observant Vivant Denon, thrust ancient Egypt upon the attention of Western scholars. Egyptology was born.

The *Description de l'Égypte* had first been proposed by another of Napoleon's innovations, the Institut d'Égypte. The General encouraged his young scholars to base a research institute upon Cairo and was graciously pleased to accept the vice-presidency himself. A leaven of ideas, including the idea of research, was thrust into the Orient.

The British were not happy about finding Napoleon in Egypt. Nelson succeeded in defeating the French fleet at Abukir only a month after the landing and thus cut off Napoleon's army. Then the British enlisted Turkey on their side in the attempt to push the French out of Egypt. The beleaguered army had to strengthen its coastal defenses against a British attack from the sea. In 1799 Lieutenant Pierre F. X. Bouchard was busy looking for stone to consolidate the ramparts. Near Rosetta his men dug out a slab of stone with writing on it: Greek down in the bottom third, strange scratches which turned out to be the demotic script of Egyptian in the middle, and hieroglyphs in the broken upper third. Here was a bilingual text by which one could test whether hieroglyphic could be read or not.

What does it matter that the British, when they forced the French to evacuate Egypt in 1801, demanded the Rosetta Stone as part of their terms, so it now rests in the British Museum, instead of the Louvre? Napoleon's army had not only aroused curiosity about Egyptian antiquities; it had also provided an essential key to the mind and spirit of the ancient Egyptians.

The United States was not too preoccupied to pay attention to the Napoleonic expedition and its cultural consequences. That Brooklyn lawyer, Robert Livingston, one of the founding fathers of the country, became Minister to France in 1801. On his initiative, the American Academy of Arts in its first year elected Napoleon Bonaparte and Vivant Denon as honorary members, in recognition of the opening up of Egypt to scholarship.

In the summer of 1799, Napoleon had hurried back to France, leaving his army to consolidate its conquest of Egypt and to hold off the British and Turks. He had to travel swiftly and lightly, to avoid British vessels prowling the Mediterranean. He had not forgotten Josephine, however, and brought back with him seven objects as gifts for her. These formed part of the decor of her château at Malmaison. One of the pieces was a handsome statue of a seated Egyptian, a fine product of the Middle Kingdom. A century ago this was put on sale and was purchased by one of the most distinguished British collectors, Lord Amherst of Hackney. In 1921 a different kind of lord, William Randolph Hearst, bought it at auction. Then his treasures also went on auction, and in 1939 Josephine's statue became one of the fine pieces exhibited at the Brooklyn Museum. Around its career might be written the history of three continents.

The withdrawal of the French army left a vacuum in Egypt. Military defeat had discredited the Mamelukes and left them disorganized. Further, their dead hand was now unacceptable to a land which had experienced new contacts and ideas. However much the French soldiers may have shocked the Egyptians by their free and easy manners, however much the invading infidels may have been hated, the air was changed. Into the vacuum rushed a Balkan soldier of adventure, Mohammed (or Mehemet) Ali, who was thirty-eight years old in 1806, when he was confirmed by the Sultan as Pasha of Egypt. In 1811, in a single act of calculated treachery, his troops massacred more than four hundred Mamelukes. He became undisputed master of Egypt. In the next chapter we shall deal with the politics of Mohammed Ali and with the despoiling of monuments which took place under his regime. Here we shall make only one note. The population of Egypt in the stretch from 1798 to 1821 was calculated at 2.5 million. When we consider that the present population in an arable territory only modestly greater than 1821 is in excess of 26 million, we have a picture of an impoverished land in the early 1800's, with a thin agriculture, a people ravaged by disease, and little incentive toward betterment. This was the legacy of five centuries of Mameluke rule. The sharp wind from the West was to make great differences.

CHAMPOLLION'S DECIPHERMENT

It is often said that the Rosetta Stone was the key to the decipherment of the hieroglyphs. The argument is that a successful breaking of the system depends upon a bilingual text like this decree of Ptolemy V in 196 B.C. That is largely true, but is not the whole truth. Modern analytic methods have deciphered ancient languages without the help of a bilingual, as in the cases of Hittite and of Cretan Linear B. Only a third of the upper section of the Rosetta Stone, the hieroglyphic section, had survived. It does not diminish the great achievement of Champollion to state that he had other aids and clues besides the Rosetta Stone.

Ancient Egyptian began as a picture writing, with the basic principle that the picture of a bee might be read "bee" and that of a leaf "leaf." Perhaps borrowing from cuneiform, it then added the rebus principle that a picture of something might stand for its sound, rather than itself, so a picture of a bee followed by that of a leaf might be read as the English "belief." It indicated no vowels, and we know from the latter stage of the language that the vowels were subject to change, like our "mouse," "mice," or "spring," "sprang." It therefore clarified series of concepts by determinatives, so the words "walk," "run," and "come" might all be determined with the picture of walking legs, the words "palace," "temple," and "granary" with the picture of a house. Because the picture writing was particularly used for the carved texts in temples and tombs, religious conservatism attempted to hold it unchanging, both in the use of the pictures and in an archaic style and syntax. Hieroglyphic therefore was in use from 3000 B.C. to A.D. 250.

The making of pictures is slow, and the needs of government clerks, tax-collectors, and letter-writers produced a flowing script which might be written rapidly with a reed pen on papyrus, leather, wood, or other portable material. The earlier stages of this script are called hieratic; the later, from 700 B.C. onward, are called demotic. Demotic was the middle text on the Rosetta Stone, so this is a bilingual, with two forms of Egyptian and one of Greek, rather than a trilingual.

When Christianity took over Egypt, the pagan writings died out, and the old Egyptian language was written in Greek letters, with a few alphabetic characters added where the Greek did not meet the phonetic need. This form of the language is called Coptic. There is a modestly extensive Coptic literature, and the language could be read in Champollion's time because it still survived in the liturgy of the Coptic or Egyptian Christian church.

There was another helpful factor, and that is that the ancient Egyptians in their hieroglyphic writing inclosed the names of kings and major queens within a flattened ring which we call a cartouche. It was clear that this emphatic separation of a small part of a text was significant, and it could be theorized that the one element which would be given such differentiation would be the name of a king.

In 1819 an obelisk and its base were brought to England from the island of Philae. The base had Greek texts honoring a Ptolemy and two Cleopatras. The obelisk itself was carved in hieroglyphic, with both names incased in cartouches. The two writings were thus successfully compared.

These different aids were present, but there was still that heavy obstacle, the belief of many scholars like Stukeley that the hieroglyphs were not a writing like other scripts of the world, but were heavily symbolic.

There was progress. Two years before the Rosetta Stone was found, a Danish scholar had concluded that the cartouches must contain royal names. Three years after the stone was found, a Swede was able to publish a very sound analysis of the demotic section of the text, which is more fully preserved than the hieroglyphic part. Then one of those highly gifted Englishmen, Thomas Young, entered the scene. He was a physician and physicist, with an amazing gift for languages. One account credits him with abilities in eight Oriental languages. In physics he discovered the principle of the interference of light, enunciated the undulatory theory of light, and gave the word "energy" its physical meaning, as in an expression such as "atomic energy."

In 1814 Thomas Young published a translation of the demotic text on the Rosetta Stone, and five years later he contributed an article to the *Encyclopaedia Britannica* in which he demonstrated the relationship among hieroglyphic and hieratic and demotic, the relationship between hieroglyphic and Coptic, and identified the hieroglyphic names of some gods. He fell just short of success: "You may, perhaps, think me too sanguine in my expectations of obtaining a knowledge of the hieroglyphical language in general from the inscription of Rosetta only; and I will confess to you that the difficulties are greater than a superficial view of the subject would incline us to suppose." From 1819 on he was increasingly engaged with his studies in physics. The breakthrough was left to another.

Jean François Champollion, called "Champollion the Younger" to distinguish him from his older academic brother, was eight years old when the Rosetta Stone was found. He also was gifted in languages and was barely of age when he was named Professor of Ancient History at Grenoble. The young man was something of a hothead. He was a democrat, anticlerical, and anti-imperial, which was dangerous in Napoleon's day. For some years, until he settled down to unravel the hieroglyphs, Champollion's political writings and acts lost him jobs and threatened his personal freedom. He had spent a year in Paris following the false lead that hieroglyphic was merely a symbolic language. This handsome and brilliant young man then went off on his own analysis. He seems to have been aware of the work of others, but essentially he worked it out for himself—playing the demotic against the Greek, the hieroglyphic against the demotic, the hieroglyphic against the Greek, checking against Coptic, comparing the positions of the p-o-l in the cartouche of Ptolemy with the positions of the l-o-p in the cartouche of Cleopatra. With a genius which was chiefly methodical, he broke the system open. He compared the hieroglyphic and hieratic versions of the Book of the Dead. His famous "Lettre à M. Dacier relative à l'alphabet des hiéroglyphes phonétiques," read before the French Academy in 1822, was the unlocking of the door. From that time on, with increasing facility, the words of the ancient Egyptians could be read. We need no longer be dependent on outside sources, like the Bible and the classical writers.

To be sure, the material employed was so slight and the misconceptions were so strong that the scholarly world was slow to give Champollion the great credit he deserved. Within the narrower range of those devoting themselves to Egyptian, it was not until 1837 that the German Lepsius wrote a letter to the Italian Rosellini which affirmed that the Frenchman Champollion's system was the one true and acceptable analysis.

A few stubborn souls held out, including an immigrant to the United States, Gustav Seyffarth. He left a post at the University of Leipzig and came to this country in 1854. Two years later, at a lecture in New York, he permitted himself to be billed as the "discoverer of the key to the hieroglyphs" and then proceeded to expound the most fantastic theories about the language, emphasizing Champollion's alleged errors and his own successes. He was unmoved by the fact that each new text published immediately conformed to Champollion's principles.

The notion that the ancient Egyptians were cabalistic esoterics devoted to hiding their mysteries from others dies hard. I have it only on verbal authority, but it is said that only a score of years ago a cultured European gentleman assembled a group of scholars in Egypt and advised them that

their reading of hieroglyphic was only superficial. Deep under the surface meaning of mundane events in the world of politics, the ancient
Egyptian priests had imbedded their true and essential meanings, which
had absolutely no relation to the surface translation. He presented an
example, translated into his different levels. It may be only malicious
rumor that alleges that this earnest seeker for the truth found, under the
veil of a sedate historical inscription, the secret text—a recipe for onion
soup! This occult knowledge has gone with its discoverer to his grave.
The less imaginative scholars present were not moved to follow it up.

3 DESPOTISM AND DESTRUCTION (1806–54)

MOHAMMED ALI, THE MEDIEVAL MODERNIST

Alexander the Great had been born in Macedonia, conquered Egypt, and was succeeded there by a Macedonian dynasty, the Ptolemies. Mohammed Ali was born at Kavalla, less than fifty miles from Alexander's birthplace, conquered Egypt, and left a Balkan dynasty as rulers of the land. The resemblance ceases there. Alexander was in his day trained as a modernist, but was fascinated by the Orient, and sought to make himself a ruler on the pattern of the pharaohs or the Persians. Mohammed Ali was always an Oriental in his psychology, but he was fascinated by Western technology and sought to rebuild Egypt along modern lines.

Mohammed Ali was short and broad-shouldered, with a rounded beard which in time turned from reddish to gray. At a distance, he might have looked like a Santa Claus. At closer range, he was not so benign, because his eyes were always probing restlessly. He was utterly ruthless in getting what he wanted. He had come to Egypt with Turkish troops to oppose Napoleon and remained there after the French evacuation. He welded his Albanian soldiers into a loyal bodyguard and played the Egyptians off against the Mamelukes and the Mamelukes off against the Turks. By 1806 he was strong enough to force the Turks to recognize him as Pasha of Egypt; he defeated a small British invasion in 1807, and he treacherously massacred most of the Mamelukes in 1811. He was undisputed master of Egypt at forty-two.

The long-suffering Egyptians had endured eighteen centuries of tyrannical foreign rule. Despite Napoleon's proclamation of liberation for the Egyptians, despite his printing presses, there was as yet no nationalism in the land, except insofar as the Balkan tyrant, Mohammed Ali, identified himself with Egypt and its betterment. He ruled by massacres and assassination. To the Westerner he turned a cordial face, for he wished help from Europe. We shall see that he closed his eyes to conniving foreigners for offenses which would have cost the life of an Egyptian.

Mohammed Ali worked vigorously for what he considered the good of Egypt. Using the *corvée* system of forced labor, he put thousands of fellahin to digging irrigation canals. He claimed to have introduced 38 thousand new water wheels. He brought the cultivation of cotton into Egypt, for its weal and ultimate woe. He encouraged into being hundreds of small factories—for cloth, sugar, glass, machine tools, small engines, and arms. In the thirty-five years from 1813 to 1848, 327 young Egyptians went abroad to study engineering, industry, agriculture, and medicine. In thirty-seven years of British occupation, from 1882 to 1919, the comparable figure was only 74. The economic plight of the fellahin was probably as bad under Mohammed Ali as under the Mamelukes. Yet, with security and the extension of agriculture, the population increased from 2.5 million to 4.5 million in the years from 1821 to 1846.

With Egypt tight in his control, his ambition ranged afield. In Arabia there had arisen a fanatically puritanical sect, the Wahhabis. From 1801 to 1804 they had captured Mecca and Medina, and they controlled the holy cities so tightly that the pilgrims suffered. Turkey was too far away to change the situation but was happy to have the Pasha of Egypt step in, and Mohammed Ali was very willing. Although Mecca and Medina fell in 1812, the Wahhabis were resilient fighters, and it required the military genius of Mohammed Ali's talented son Ibrahim to complete the conquest in 1816. It was a victory of glory for orthodox Islam, but it had been expensive for Egypt, and it brought no great revenue.

The revenue might come from the south. The ancient Egyptians had turned covetously toward those lands from which came fabled treasures—myrrh, ebony, ivory, gum, apes, and giraffes' tails. It was rumored in Mohammed Ali's day that the Nubian hills still had gold. Most of all, the control of the slave trade would be highly lucrative. Mohammed Ali sent his son Ismail to conquer the Sudan. We are not concerned with the details of the campaign, which succeeded at a tremendous cost of Sudanese lives. Along with the expedition went three interesting Westerners.

Frédéric Cailliaud was a French mining prospector who had served Mohammed Ali in the search for mineral resources. Attached to Ismail's rag, tag, and bobtail army, he might find new mines to prospect. But he now became famous as an archeological explorer. His keen interest in the Sudanese monuments led him astray to the pyramid fields of the Meroitic Kingdom, where he made plans and drawings which were admirable in the conditions under which he traveled. His enthusiasm made realities of fabled Napata and Meroë.

Two Americans from Massachusetts were in command of Ismail's artillery. George B. English, who preferred to be called Mohammed Effendi, was a romantic adventurer. In 1820 he held a commission in the United States Marines. Then his ship put in at Alexandria, and he heard the call of the East, resigned his commission, became a Muslim, and served the Pasha. With him was Luther Bradish, a Massachusetts lawyer who had gone on a trade mission to Turkey. Some odd streak of restlessness must have sent him on this rugged detour to the Fifth Cataract. We shall meet him briefly in 1821, as he returned through Egypt.

EXPLORATION AND EXPLOITATION

Another American appears only as a name and function. Two British travelers came to Egypt in 1812 with the purpose of going up the Nile as far as feasible. They received from Mohammed Ali one of those authoritative *laissez-passers* known by the Turkish word *"firman,"* and engaged as a guide an American named Barthow, who had lived in Egypt for several years. We know nothing else about him. They went up the river as far as Qasr Ibrim, within thirty-five miles of Abu Simbel, the glory of which was still to be discovered. What were Barthow's qualifications to show Egypt and Nubia to a Member of Parliament and an English clergyman? He probably could speak Arabic and sail a boat.

A very remarkable explorer met that party in Nubia on its return toward Egypt—he called our unknown "Captain Barthod, an American"— and credits them with being the first Europeans to examine the antiquities between Philae, which Napoleon's expedition had reached, and Qasr Ibrim. This traveler, John Lewis Burckhardt, a Swiss, was the ideal explorer. He journeyed afoot and observed everything—native customs, crocodiles, birds, and rocks. Very carefully he wrote down the place names in Arabic as he heard them.

On March 22, 1813, three weeks after his encounter with the British-American party, Burckhardt, or "Sheikh Ibrahim," as he presented himself in his travels, made a tremendous discovery. He had heard descriptions, apparently from the local Nubians, of a temple at Abu Simbel ("Ebsambal" in his writing). This was the smaller of the two temples there, that of the goddess Hathor and of Queen Nefert-ari. He came at it from above, descended a great sand slope spilling down between two cliffs, and made careful notes. Then came the discovery.

> Having, as I supposed, seen all the antiquities of Ebsambal, I was about to ascend the sandy side of the mountain by the same way I had descended; when having luckily turned more to the southward, I fell in with what is yet visible of four immense colossal statues cut out of the rock . . . now almost entirely buried beneath the sands, which are blown down here in torrents. . . . [Under a hawk-headed figure, surmounted by a sun disk,] I suspect, could the sand be cleared away, a vast temple would be discovered.

How right he was! Under the sand slope was the great temple of the sun god and of Ramses II, unknown to the West and unreported by the local Nubians. Of the four great seated colossi, each more than sixty feet high, only the face of one and the crowns of others were visible. It would be four years more before the Italian strong man Belzoni would follow up Burckhardt's lead and penetrate the great temple.

Back in Cairo, Mohammed Ali's cordiality to Westerners was beginning to stir up a regrettable situation for the antiquities of Egypt—or a splendid opportunity, if one is inclined to think of it in that way. Almost any foreigner of influence might obtain a firman to study the monuments, which meant to carry them off. In particular, the consuls-general of the great powers enjoyed such privileges that they spent inordinate time and attention on becoming collectors and dealers. It seems that nearly all such agents in Cairo were involved, but two of them stand out most prominently, Henry Salt for Great Britain and Bernardino Drovetti for France. They hired tough men to go out and get antiquities under a firman from the Pasha, using violence or bribery as occasion seemed to demand. We shall refer to some of their methods in discussing Belzoni below.

One vigorous example of the day is related in a little book by a Frenchman, M. Saulnier *fils*. He had heard of a ceiling in the temple of Dendereh, which had been carved in Greco-Roman times with a circular zodiac, and he engaged an engineer, M. Jean Baptiste Lelorrain, to go out, rend it from the temple, and bring it back to France. Lelorrain presented himself to Mohammed Ali and received a firman, here translated from the French, which had been translated from the Turkish.

> Decree. In conformance with the explanation and request made by the French traveler named Lelorrain, who wants to go as far as Wadi Halfa, to satisfy his curiosity and make researches and excavations on certain ancient buildings, our present order is issued and transmitted to him, so that he may be able to travel without fear for the already mentioned purpose, and so that, without presenting any obstacle to his researches made on the ancient monuments, the governors of the provinces and the other officials attached to the administration of the land shall give him aid and protection.
>
> If Allah is willing, let there be conformance to these dispositions.
>
> Given on the 20th day of the month Rabiya at-Tani, 1235 [January 27, 1821].

This general *laissez-passer* has no reference to the Dendereh zodiac or any acquisition of antiquities. When Lelorrain arrived at Dendereh in March, he found British travelers there. Either then or later, the French and British consuls-general in Cairo had accepted a gentleman's agreement, the French to have the east bank of the Nile and the British to have the west. Denndereh lay on the west bank. Lelorrain did not tarry, but continued up river. In Luxor he let Salt's agents understand that he was planning a trip to the Red Sea but because of ill-health would rest for some time in a small village. He then hurried to Dendereh and found that he was the only European there. He had a dragoman, a rais or foreman, and twenty workers. In three weeks he had cut the zodiac out and brought it to the Nile. It was now May, and the rais of the boat protested that he could not sail north because of low water at Dishna. Lelorrain suspected the real reason for the captain's reluctance. While work had been going on at the temple, "M. Bradich, *agent des États-Unis*," had passed by and had probably reported to Salt's agents. This must be Luther Bradish, returning from the military expedition in the Sudan. We wish that we could protest that this American's motive was to protect a monument against plunder, but that was not in the spirit of the times. When Lelorrain heard that the rais of the boat had been promised a thousand Turkish piastres to delay departure for three weeks, he matched that amount, and the cargo reached Cairo in June. The British Consul-general, Salt, had already protested to Mohammed Ali. The Pasha asked whether he had issued a firman for Lelorrain's researches, and when an affirmative answer was given, decided in favor of the Frenchman. The zodiac embarked in Alexandria in July. It is now one of the prizes in the Louvre.

Back in Paris the man who had commissioned the enterprise, M. Saulnier, ends his little report with a pious protest which is characteristic of European thought of the day—indeed, of the nineteenth century. He refers to the recent power of the Wahhabis of Arabia, those bigoted purists of the desert. If the Wahhabis should succeed in dominating Egypt,

> they will violently destroy the first fruits of a revived civilization, and perhaps, like the soldiers of Cambyses, like those of Omar, like the first Christians, they also would destroy these ancient monuments, all covered with representations of humans and animals, which their cult forbids even more severely than Islam.
>
> It is from this peril, which is not entirely imaginary, it is from all the destructive forces described above that the circular zodiac of Dendereh has happily been snatched, to be placed under the protection of European civilization.

The peril of the Wahhabis had become remote in 1821; that plea is a smug fraud. Unfortunately, other perils mentioned by Saulnier were real. Mohammed Ali was building, and the monuments were still quarries for construction stone. A fine temple at Armant in Upper Egypt was later destroyed to build a sugar factory. The plea that things are only safe in

Europe has had some justification in the past, as in the case of the Elgin Marbles, which were snatched twenty years earlier from the ruins of the Parthenon, where they were being burned for lime. The real problem is whether the preserving purpose was merely the sanctimonious cloak for acquisitive greed.

BELZONI, THE ADVENTURER-ARCHEOLOGIST

On Easter Monday, 1803, the audience at Sadler's Wells Theater in London was privileged to see the "Patagonian Sampson" lift and carry a human pyramid of eleven men across the stage. Giovanni Belzoni was at least six feet six inches tall and powerfully built. He was a handsome giant. His fine, strong features might be set off with moustaches or a beard, according to the role he was playing at the time; his eyes were mild and even a little dreamy. At twenty-five he had left his native Padua in Italy and come to England to gain a fortune by feats of strength. As the years went on, he played a cannibal chief in a pantomime and performed conjuring feats, but he was ambitious for other things. He was in Malta, on his way to Istanbul to exhibit his skill and strength, when he met a man calling himself "Captain Ishmael Gibraltar," an agent of Mohammed Ali who was recruiting technicians for Egypt.

In England Belzoni had designed and controlled hydraulic displays for public entertainment; he was confident that he could build irrigation machinery for Egypt. It needed no great persuasion from the oddly named captain to change his plans. In the spring of 1815 Belzoni set sail for Alexandria. There was delay in reaching Cairo, where a tenth of the population had been killed by the plague. His Cairo landlord, one of Mohammed Ali's ministers, had arranged an audience with the Pasha. When Belzoni boldly promised a pumping machine in which one ox would lift as much water as the present machines could raise with four, Mohammed Ali asked him to make a full-scale model and put him on an allowance of £25 a month.

Belzoni spent nearly a year on his machine, and it sounds as though it were a jerry-built contraption. When he did exhibit it to Mohammed Ali in competition with six traditional water wheels, however, his one ox, treading in a revolving drum, did clearly pump more water than the combined opposition. Yet the Pasha's advisors did not like it; they counted their prestige in numbers; and they were unwilling to think of using only one man and one ox in place of six men and six oxen. Mohammed Ali was sensitive to this pressure, and Belzoni's great initiative came to naught. He was at a loose end.

The tall, moon-faced Henry Salt had just come to Cairo as British

Consul-general. Before he came out, a Trustee of the British Museum had asked him to send home antiquities. Burckhardt, just back from his arduous Arabian trip, told Salt and Belzoni about a colossal head in the Ramesseum at Thebes. The archeological career of the Italian strong man began. In June, 1816, he started up the river, armed with a firman from the Pasha and apparently in the employ of Salt. He reached Luxor in the July heat and set out immediately to examine that great head of Ramses II.

Less than two years later Shelley would publish his sonnet on the transitory nature of earthly glory:

> My name is Ozymandias, king of kings:
> Look on my works, ye Mighty, and despair!

If Belzoni's colossus was not the inspiration for the "shatter'd visage," it must have been at least one of the elements that entered the poet's mind. "Ozymandias" is derived from "User-maat-Re," the throne name of Ramses II, and also in the Ramesseum were "two vast and trunkless legs of stone."

Moving the head was an engineering problem. Only hand labor and crudely made tools would be available, and the annual inundation was due in a month. Ramadan, the Muslim month of fast, was at hand. The existing piece was nearly nine feet high, nearly seven feet across the shoulders, and consisted of the upper part of the body above the waist. It weighed seven and a quarter tons.

Belzoni had a carpenter construct a heavy wooden platform onto which the colossus might be levered and then pulled by man power on rollers. The head lay in the first court, and it is typical of the recklessness of the day that the bases of two ancient columns had to be smashed to provide a road for the rolling weight. It took seventeen days to reach the river, moving not at all on those days when laborers failed to appear, moving as much as four hundred yards on a good day. The officials who controlled the labor supply sometimes held the men back, both in the hopes of extra bakshish and of a reward from Salt's rival, Drovetti. Belzoni used entreaty, bribes, and in one case, force.

Leaving the colossal head beside the Nile to await a favorable stage of the flood, Belzoni went up the river as far as Abu Simbel, where he could not employ enough labor to clear the entrance to the great temple which Burckhardt had discovered only three years before. The people there distrusted money and could not be hired for pay. Belzoni would return and succeed the next year.

Back at Luxor, Belzoni found that Drovetti's agents had appeared, to try to thwart his collecting. One of them advised him that his throat would be cut if he continued to compete with the French Consul-general. But these bullyboys made a tactical error in not bringing an honorable and costly present to the local Turkish governor. Two bottles of anchovies and two of olives were a miserable gift. The *Kashif* was furious and threw his influence on Belzoni's side; a boat and laborers were made available; the head was levered over four palm boles onto the boat. In November it started north toward Cairo and Henry Salt, and after another year, to the British Museum. Within that time Belzoni's achievement became known, and by the standards of the day, he was accepted as an archeologist.

The standards of the day were certainly not high. Belzoni found a dozen carved blocks on the island of Philae, components of a scene from a ruined temple. He felt that they were too thick for easy shipping, so he left money to have them cut thinner before he should return. When he did come back months later, they were lying ready for him, but someone had ruined their sculptured surface with a hammer and had written in charcoal on one of the stones "*operation manquée.*" The French words were a clear indication that Drovetti's hirelings had been there. French, British, Italian, or Greek—they were willing to destroy or mutilate antiquities to gain the upper hand.

Belzoni turned his attention to the Valley of the Kings at Thebes and uncovered four tombs, with mummies and mummy cases. If a blocked-up doorway confronted him, he fashioned a battering ram and knocked a hole in it, without regard to any seal-impressions which might be on it or to any objects which might have been immediately behind it. When he first penetrated a passage of a tomb, he said, "Every step I took I crushed a mummy in some part or other." In October, 1817, he discovered the most magnificent structure in the Valley, the tomb of Seti I, its sloping 328-foot passage covered with beautiful carvings in superb preservation. Down in the burial chamber was a thing of wonder and beauty: a sarcophagus carved out of a single block of alabaster, with the sculptures filled with blue paste. Nothing like it had been seen before. It was empty —the Pharaoh Seti I had been removed to hiding nearly three thousand years earlier.

There was an interlude here, while Belzoni tried to resolve a disagreement with Salt. Although a generally mild-tempered man, the Italian was intensely proud of his growing reputation, and he resented the fact that in Cairo and London the Consul-general received the acclaim for the work of his agent. There had been no written compact between them, but in April, 1818, they signed an agreement that Belzoni "under the auspices of" Salt would return to Thebes, bring back the sarcophagus of Seti I and other objects for the Consul-general, with the reward to come from the sale of the sarcophagus to the British Museum, and the Italian to receive half of anything over £2,000. The former portrait painter and the former music-hall strong man thereby drew up a legal document full of pitfalls.

Back in Thebes in the hot weather, Belzoni took wax impressions of the carvings in the tomb of Seti I, at marked cost to the painting. It was months before he undertook the highly delicate task of bringing out the slender and fragile sarcophagus. When this precious piece reached London, the Trustees of the British Museum were unwilling to meet the high price set on it. It went without a buyer until 1824, when Sir John Soane paid £2,000 for it. In strict accordance with their agreement, Salt got all of this, Belzoni received nothing.

One more Belzoni adventure. William John Bankes, an enthusiastic British amateur of archeology, had seen on the island of Philae an obelisk with a hieroglyphic inscription and a base with a Greek text. He had suggested that a name in a cartouche might be the hieroglyphic writing of Cleopatra. That was prior to Champollion's decipherment. Now, late in 1818, Bankes was back in Egypt, being entertained at Thebes by the wily Drovetti, with Salt and Belzoni present. The obelisk at Philae was mentioned, and Drovetti learned of Bankes's previous interest in the piece. The falcon-eyed consul for France thereupon relinquished his claim to the obelisk in favor of the English gentleman. Bankes and Belzoni made off for the First Cataract; at the same time Drovetti sent an agent post-haste in the same direction. The *Agha* of Assuan told Belzoni that Drovetti's men had been trying to remove the obelisk without success; and when the Italian reached the island of Philae he was handed a note in French, just delivered there, that the obelisk was to be respected as the property of Drovetti. Thus did the French Consul honor his offhand "gift."

Fortunately Bankes was able to present the *Agha* with a gold watch, a splendid ornament to the dignity of that official. The work began immediately. Belzoni had the workmen lever the twenty-two foot obelisk down to the river on rollers, dig out the inscribed base, and work it also down to the bank. The workmen built a stone jetty out into the water. Slowly the heavy obelisk was maneuvered onto the jetty toward the boat. When its full weight rested on the pier, the loosely piled stones dispersed right and left, and the monument settled ponderously into the Nile. This looked like disaster, and Bankes went off in disgust on a trip to Nubia. Belzoni's reputation was at stake, and he used the traditional means of Egypt. Stones were put in the water to serve as fulcrums; the obelisk was levered up, rolling over and over, until it was once more on land. With the same bridging of the palm boles that Belzoni had used for the colossal head at Thebes, the monument was worked onto the boat. Ultimately it became an adornment of Bankes's estate in Dorset, where its hieroglyphic carving soon began to suffer from the northern weather.

Here we are not concerned with Belzoni's subsequent career. He is important as an exponent of the swashbuckling activities of his day, although he was a cut or two above average. Untaught, inexperienced, without a tradition of careful method, he went straight toward his objective. He did not have the excavating genius of Caviglia, the passionate curiosity of Cailliaud, or that devoted interest in the ancient Egyptians for themselves which was to characterize Wilkinson. On the other hand, he did not suffer from the acquisitive greed of Salt and Drovetti; he was clearly a better workman than d'Athanasi, and he did not use gunpowder in his work, as did Vyse. Commonly a mild and good-humored man, he was out for glory and recognition. What he did was in the hope of praise from the London press and the British public. We do owe him a debt for spectacular accomplishments, which put ancient Egypt more solidly in the public consciousness.

THE EARNEST COPYISTS

Champollion's decipherment had unlocked the door to the reading of hieroglyphic inscriptions, but copying before his accomplishment had been innocent of any knowledge of the writing and was almost unusable. The admirable drawings by members of Napoleon's expedition had been hastily made under miserable conditions, and for scholarly purposes the inscriptions were a mishmash. It was time to lay before the European savants the wealth of material present in Egypt. The relatively enlightened attitude of Mohammed Ali toward Western investigation made an epigraphic expedition possible.

In August, 1828, a joint French-Tuscan mission set out for Egypt, headed by Champollion and his Italian colleague, Ippolito Rosellini. They had an excellent staff for the time: a dozen architects and draftsmen. For ten months they copied and made notes, from Alexandria to the Second Cataract. Their two sumptuous sets of plates, Champollion's *Monuments* and Rosellini's *Monumenti*, frequently overlapping, gave rich grist to the scholars' mill. It is easy to criticize their copies today: sometimes they are inexact for modern use; frequently they restored line or color; repetitive elements—such as a line of marching men—were apparently completed at home. Yet they were pioneers, and their volumes are still highly useful because there has been so much destruction since their day.

Yet this rich fare only made the home scholars hungrier for more. Perhaps there was also some element of competitive national pride. From 1842 to 1845 a Prussian expedition under the direction of Karl Richard Lepsius carried out an even more intensive epigraphic work, going up the Nile as far as Meroë in the Sudan. Lepsius was a meticulous scholar, well versed in hieroglyphic, and had the advantage that for several years men had been able to penetrate the Egyptian writing. He had skilled and sensitive draftsmen whose copies caught both substance and spirit of the ancient scenes and inscriptions, even though they also finished off in ink at home what they had sketched in pencil in the field. It is an exaggeration to say that Lepsius' expedition rounded out the archeological exploration of ancient Egypt; the discoveries of later times have added importantly to our knowledge of places and monuments. Nevertheless, no modern working library of Egyptology is complete without the twelve superb volumes of elephant-folio size by Lepsius, *Denkmäler aus Aegypten und Aethiopien*. The admirable Lepsius became a dominating figure in Egyptology.

England contributed Gardner Wilkinson, who ultimately would be knighted for his contributions to the knowledge of ancient Egypt. No library of distinction in the 1840's would have been complete without Wilkinsons' *Manners and Customs of the Ancient Egyptians* and Edward W. Lane's *Manners and Customs of the Modern Egyptians*. Wilkinson went to Egypt in 1821. On a rock shelf above the tombs of the nobles in Thebes, he built himself a home, using one of the tombs as the rear core of the house. For the most part, it was furnished in Egyptian style, and it contained his working library. High above the noisy and dirty village, it enjoyed the cooling breeze from the north. He made it seem so different from the rest of Thebes that the locals still avoided it eighty years later as a haunted place.

Of all possible locations at Thebes, Wilkinson had located his house at the most thrilling. Straight down, he looked upon the tawny desert, filled with the tumbled rubbish of ancient tombs, overlaid by the little brick walls of the fellahin who lived in the tombs. Just below him was the Ramesseum, from which Belzoni had snatched the colossal head. Over there to the right were the twin statues which Westerners called the Colossi of Memnon, as well as the great sprawling temple of Medinet Habu. Farther away began the black land watered by the inundation, with its fields of grain and palm trees. Then the ever-changing, ever-interesting Nile cut its pulsing course across the land. On the far side there could be seen the columns of the Luxor temple and the soaring pylon and obelisks of mighty Karnak. In the distance the desert hills rose up, with three marked red peaks to the southeast. It was a panorama of never-ending fascination, of a different color at every hour of the day.

Wilkinson carried out excavations at his own expense, but he set definite limits to his task. He specialized in tombs, rather than temples; he made no pretensions to high abilities in reading Egyptian, and he was not interested in buying antiquities on the market, a strange trait in his day. It is alleged that his workmen stole boldly from his excavations and sold to the British and French agents and to tourists, and this is quite credible, since his eyes focused on the wall scenes which he dug out, rather than on the objects buried in the debris. Yet his spirit and production were admirable. He analyzed the life of the ancient Egyptians in categories—history, social classes, architecture and furniture, hunting and fishing, arts and crafts, and so on—as illustrated by the scenes in tombs and temples. On successive pages one can see a military guard from the Ramesseum, an Asiatic woman from Theban Tomb No. 100, Negro slaves from Tomb No. 78, a warship from Medinet Habu, and a large boat from Kom el-Ahmar. Champollion's and Lepsius' plates had been organized topographically; Wilkinson's figures were arranged by subject. Visibly ancient Egypt could appear as an organism which had connected sense and purpose. One might say that Wilkinson took the mummy wrappings off the ancient Egyptians and made them human beings who had loved and labored, fought and played, like other peoples in less remote lands.

Another Englishman exhibited some of the same fidelity to what he saw in Egypt. Robert Hay was a landed gentleman who fell in love with the land along the Nile when he was twenty-five and visited it frequently for the next fourteen years. He was a good draftsman, and he copied with conscientious accuracy wherever he was. Although he never published these copies, they have been deposited in the British Museum, where they are still of high value to scholars.

Hay was also a discriminating collector. Many of his papyri and smaller objects were bought by the British Museum after his death. The bulk of the collection—1,084 objects—was bought and presented to the Boston Museum of Fine Arts in 1872, forming the nucleus of that fine display.

THE EAGER COLLECTORS

A witty French cleric said to Mohammed Ali: "Your Excellency, I am convinced that one may not present himself properly in Europe on return from Egypt without having a mummy in one hand and a crocodile in the other." With the encouragement of the Pasha, the European world was descending upon the Nile, and none wanted to return without spectacular souvenirs.

As we have seen, it was easy to secure a firman from Mohammed Ali to excavate, to copy, or to "conduct researches," which seems to have been another term for collecting antiquities by purchase. It would be an inexperienced traveler who relied solely upon the firman from Cairo; in the provinces the local *kashifs*, *aghas*, *omdehs*, and sheikhs expected those gifts which go under the term "bakshish," and some of the more substantial of them issued their own local firmans. Labor was unattainable without this cultivation of the local officials, but when they were pleased with the applicant's bakshish, labor was plentiful and cheap. In the standards of the day, a lucky nobleman might excavate a mummy and some minor jewelry in an afternoon.

The government at Cairo, however, did not remain indifferent to antiquities which had come from a pre-Islamic and therefore infidel culture. After all, these pieces obviously had value to the West, and collections might be assembled for tourists to see in Cairo. About 1830 it was announced that all permits to excavate would be withdrawn after one year so that all digging thereafter could be carried out exclusively for the Egyptian government, which would then set up a museum for the edification of tourists. This prohibition had some flexibility. It clearly did not stop Wilkinson at Thebes, nor did it apply to the consuls-general of powerful nations. France and Egypt were on friendly terms, so every indulgence might be shown to the vigorous activity directed by Drovetti. Curiously, the reverse reason benefited Salt: since Great Britain was always ready to thwart the ambitions of Mohammed Ali, the Pasha did his best to cultivate the British Consul-general and the stream of influential English visitors. The aggressive rivalry between Drovetti and Salt would have created international scandal in later days. In their own time they regularly received firmans and won the gratitude of the European world for the flow of interesting antiquities which left Egypt. Salt was better provided with funds than his rival, but Drovetti had had a longer experience in the country, and his agents were more vigorous and unscrupulous. Saulnier wrote that they had accepted a gentleman's agreement to divide the land right down the middle, Salt taking the left bank and Drovetti the right. If this is true, the agreement was not always respected, but it will explain why Belzoni had so much trouble excavating in Karnak, which was on the French side, and why the Philae obelisk was the subject of counterclaims, as that island lies in the river. Drovetti was jealous even of his own fellow citizens and did his best to persuade Champollion not to come to Egypt. The motives were probably mixed: the young scholar would be a competitor for Drovetti's acclaim back in Paris, and he might also report on the highhanded methods used by the French agents.

Certainly patriotism was a lesser force than personal ambition or pecuniary greed. The collections made by the British Consul-general were sold to England and France; those made by the French Consul-general went to France, Italy, and Germany; those made by the Consul-general for Sweden and Norway went to England, France, and the Netherlands. Up to 1858 a diplomatic post in Egypt had obvious financial advantages.

The Egyptian fellahin, who had lived for centuries among disregarded and despised antiquities, thought that the collectors and excavators were mad. Why should the Europeans fight so bitterly over old stones? Why should they go out in the heat of the day and watch laborers whom they had hired at great cost? Why should they carry away broken slabs of stone? To that last question there would be an obvious answer: the stone must have gold in it, and the Westerner must have the secret of extracting the gold. There was also some contempt, not simply for the Western waste of money on worthless trifles. A pleased excavator might be seen to run his fingers over the carving of a statue with an ecstatic expression on his face; therefore, he must be an idolator to caress a heathen figure. Because the word went around among the Westerners that a forged stone statue had a salty taste, an Egyptian seller might see the foreigner test the figure with his tongue, and the conclusion was that the infidels kissed the statues. Altogether, the contact with these strange amateurs did not give the Egyptians a high opinion of the foreigner's common sense or religion.

If the Egyptians were a little slow to see where their financial advantages lay, the Armenians, the Greeks, and the Italians were not. They became agents for the consuls-general and dragomans for wealthy visitors. They set themselves up as local dealers. A French visitor in 1819 said wryly: "In Upper Egypt I have often seen Italians who call themselves physicians; they bury the Aghas, they unbury statues, and they profit by the exchange."

We of today fall into the easy habit of thinking that the forgery of Egyptian antiquities is a fairly recent occupation and that something acquired before 1900 would probably be genuine. Unfortunately, forgery is nearly as old as Egyptology. We have seen above that a writer of 1830 told about collectors tasting stone statuettes to put their authenticity to proof. Two Frenchmen, writing in the late 1840's, described the growing vocation of forgery in Egypt. One of them claimed that the attempted withdrawal of firmans for excavation about 1830 had cut down on a lucrative trade and employment, so the Egyptians turned to making fraudulent antiquities.

A piece of jewelry which came to the New-York Historical Society with the Abbott Collection in 1860 is a particularly splendid forgery, a necklace and earrings purporting to have been the property of Menes, the first king of the First Dynasty. It was good enough to have fooled Dr. Abbott, who was a collector of discernment, but Mrs. Williams, in studying the collection, firmly supported earlier suspicions of the jewelry and believed that it was made in the stretch between 1833 and 1843.

This was not the only fabricated piece in the Abbott Collection. A fine New Kingdom statue of a seated scribe had a head which was out of setting: it was too large, and the face had a tense expression. In 1949 the Brooklyn Museum examined the sculpture under violet ray, and it became clear that the head and body of the statue were of different stone. After the head had been removed and cleaned, it proved to be an ancient head which had been recut in the early nineteenth century to fit the body. Since the statue was described in the 1840's as being headless but had come to this country with a head in 1852, there must have been a hasty joining of head and body at some time in the interval, without a careful examination of the two pieces. Perhaps Dr. Abbott had been sold the two with the statement that they belonged together but had never noticed the head was of recent manufacture.

The American Gliddon, writing in 1841, tells a ghoulish story which may be apocryphal, but which certainly illustrates the gossip of Cairo in his day with regard to the demand for ancient Egyptian pieces and the means taken to meet that demand. According to this yarn, an Italian carpenter died out in the country and was buried in the desiccating sands of the desert. Later his body was dug up again, wrapped in ancient mummy cloth, and sold about 1828 at a high price to a British amateur collector as the only example of a bearded mummy.

THE FIRST AMERICAN COLLECTIONS

The United States was certainly preoccupied with internal problems in the half-century we are considering. From the Louisiana Purchase through the Mexican War to the discovery of gold in California, the attention of the young nation was directed westward, rather than eastward. Washington's Farewell Address had advised against alliances with other nations, and the Congress of Vienna had only deepened American suspicions of European governments; in effect, the Monroe Doctrine said to the Old World: "You keep out of our affairs, and we'll keep out of yours." Industrial development was changing the country rapidly, and the cleavage between the Hamiltonian patricians and the commoners was widened by Jacksonian democracy. Tension was increasing between the free-state and industrial North and the slave-holding and agricultural South. The future was still more important than the past. What was ancient Egypt to such a people?

It was surely an exaggeration when the first consul of the United States in Egypt said that when he came to the country in 1832 the name *Amerikan* was unknown. We have already met John Ledyard, Luther Bradish, and Captain Barthow there. But it was only an exaggeration: before 1830 there were only isolated individuals; by the 1840's there was a small, steady stream.

As far as I have been able to discover, the first Egyptian objects to be displayed in the United States came to the Peabody Museum in Salem, Massachusetts. These collections were started by the East India Marine Society in 1799 and reflect Salem's seafaring interests. It was the Yankee ship captain, adventuring in faraway places, who brought home curios from exotic ports. The first ancient Egyptian object was a mummified ibis, presented in 1803 by a Captain Apthorp. Ten years later Captain Nathaniel Page gave a carved wooden bird, and in the period from 1822 to 1826 seafaring collectors presented amulets, *shawabti*-figures, and scraps of mummified bodies. If the Egyptian collection in Salem cannot be called large or important, it seems to have been the first.

Ancient Egyptian architecture also made an early appearance in the New England setting. In 1832 Dr. Jacob Bigelow designed a monumental gateway in Egyptian style for the Mount Auburn Cemetery in Cambridge, Massachusetts. It was first executed in wood then rendered into granite in 1843. Later Dr. Bigelow presented to the Cemetery a sphinx as a memorial to the dead of the Civil War. The eternal massiveness of Egyptian construction found a responsive chord in our own funerary architecture.

Indeed, there is a surprising amount of architecture in the Egyptian style in the United States. The obelisk form appears in many old cemeteries not only as markers for individual graves but also at gates, as in the Westminster Cemetery in Baltimore. The obelisk was not confined to cemeteries, however. As early as 1792 a memorial to Christopher Columbus in obelisk form was set up in Baltimore, and the following century saw the building of the Bunker Hill Monument in Boston and the Washington Monument in the nation's capital. Pylons and floral capitals in Egyptian style invaded such cemeteries as the Granary Burying Ground in Boston and the Grove Street Cemetery in New Haven.

If the massive Egyptian style seemed suitable for asserting immortality in burying grounds, its implications of permanence seem less happy when applied to prisons. The most famous of these was the New York Halls of Justice, popularly known as the "Tombs," a massive structure with battered walls which imitate temple style and with a portico of heavy floral capitals. Similar doom for the convict was expressed by prisons in Trenton and Philadelphia.

One can see psychological reasons for thinking of massive architecture in cemeteries and prisons. Yet the Egyptian influence in the first half of the nineteenth century pervaded a wide range of structures: the First Presbyterian Church in Nashville, Tennessee, where the congregation faced a perspective of painted Egyptian columns; the austere Medical College in Richmond, Virginia; a customs house in New Orleans; and a railroad station in New Bedford, Massachusetts.

Nor should we forget the Great Seal of the United States, accepted by Congress in 1782. One may see it on the back of a dollar bill: "Reverse. A pyramid unfinished. . . . On the base of the pyramid the numerical letters MDCCLXXVI. And underneath the following motto, 'Novus Ordo Seclorum.' " A new order there was; but possibly under the influence of Masons high in the new government, there was an adaptation of ancient motifs.

Of course mummies were a first focus of our attention. In 1823 a merchant of Smyrna named van Lennep presented an Egyptian mummy and its coffin to "the good people of Boston." We do not know the reason for his generosity. Obviously there was one admirable place to exhibit a mummy, and the specimen was turned over to the Massachusetts General Hospital, where it presided over the operating theater for many years. When doubts were raised about its genuineness, Dr. John C. Warren wrote an article describing and authenticating the mummy and its case.

Two mummies became part of the curiosities exhibited at Peale's Museum and Gallery of the Fine Arts in New York in 1826. Sixteen years later they passed into the collections of that great showman, P. T. Barnum, and were destroyed in a fire in 1865.

Early in the 1830's an Englishman acquired in Egypt some mummies and their burial equipment. These went to his nephew, Michell (or Mitchell?) Chandler, who conceived the idea of going to the United States and making money by exhibiting them from town to town. In this gypsy-like life, he came to Kirtland, Ohio, on July 3, 1835. That was the current seat of the prophet Joseph Smith and his followers, the Latter-day Saints. The meeting of the veiled mystery of ancient Egypt and the new Mormon revelation could not fail to be productive. The Latter-day Saints purchased from Chandler at least two documents: a late version of the Book of the Dead on papyrus and a hypocephalus, an inscribed cartonnage disk that the Egyptians used to place under the head of a mummy for its protection.

Joseph Smith used his translation powers and found the texts of particular interest to the Mormons, claiming that both scenes and inscriptions related to the autobiography of Abraham while in Egypt. He published his translations and interpretations in a little book called *A Pearl of Great Price*. There were certain passages which he did not translate, but he wrote austerely that the time was not yet ripe for them to be revealed.

Nine years after these pieces had been bought, there was an attack on the Latter-day Saints in Nauvoo, Illinois. Joseph Smith was assassinated; the Mormon headquarters was destroyed, and the Egyptian pieces were carried off to a museum in Chicago, according to the story. When the great fire swept that city in 1871, these texts with their curious history were allegedly destroyed.

It is impossible now to go back and check the cursive hieroglyphic on the Book of the Dead and the hypocephalus. One has difficulties with veiled mysteries. From the illustrations in *A Pearl of Great Price*, the Book of the Dead showed one scene of the embalming of a mummy and one scene of the deceased before the god Osiris, while the hypocephalus carried the scenes normal on such a piece and was prepared for a man named Sheshonk or Shishak.

In 1832 a citizen of Baltimore, Colonel Mendes Cohen, sailed his own boat from Damietta, in the Delta, to the Second Cataract and back. He returned with 680 antiquities, and as late as 1849 this was described as the only ancient Egyptian collection in this country. Some time after his death, his heirs gave the collection to The Johns Hopkins University, which acknowledged the gift in 1884. There must have been other such gifts, most of them unrecorded. We know, for example, that Dr. Henry Anderson gathered a small assortment of antiquities in Egypt in 1848, which he gave to the New-York Historical Society within the following thirty years.

In 1950–51 the Egyptological staff of the Boston Museum of Fine Arts was trying to relieve the congestion in the basement storerooms. One major obstacle was a great block of granite weighing two and a half tons. It proved to carry the name of a pharaoh in a cartouche which could be read as Philip. This could only be the feeble-minded half-brother of Alexander the Great, Philip Arrhidaeus. A little research showed that it must have come from the central sanctuary in the temple of Karnak. How did a piece of such importance reach Boston and lie undetected for generations?

In 1835 a young Bostonian, John Lowell, Jr., was traveling abroad and was detained in Luxor by illness. He spent his time in acquiring a respectable collection of antiquities. In March he wrote in his diary: "I rode to Karnac to day to see an immense block of granite that the shêkh & some 50 men are slowly transporting to the boat. It is a fragment of an enormous block of red Syanite granite forming part of what perhaps constituted a sanctuary to a little temple in that immense pile of buildings at Karnac."

It was indeed part of the holy of holies at Karnak, and Lowell is otherwise noted as the founder of the Lowell Institute. In 1875 his heirs presented this extraordinary piece to the Boston Museum. At the time it was not identified, and it remained in the basement as a massive nuisance. How many other basement storerooms and estate attics would repay excavation for antiquities?

A melancholy case is that of "Dr." Henry Abbott. This British medical man had practiced in Cairo from 1830 to 1852. His house there was a showpiece; his hospitality was famous, and visitors admired his Egyptian collection fulsomely. When his family moved to the United States, he thought of selling his collection here for their benefit and arrived with fine pieces. In January, 1853, the exhibit was opened at the Stuyvesant Institute, on Broadway in New York, with admission set at fifty cents. It was billed as "the Greatest Attraction in the City." The project was a failure. Although the admission was reduced to twenty-five cents, public interest was insufficient, and no competent buyer appeared for the collection. Dr. Abbott had to return to Egypt in 1854, leaving his exhibit against his mounting debts. When it was rumored that these fine pieces might leave the country, there was scholarly protest, with a dignified memorial signed by several Harvard professors. It was not until 1859–60, two years after Abbott's death, that the collection was bought for the New-York Historical Society, where it remained until 1937. Abbott had asked $60,000, but the Society was able to acquire the collection for $34,000. In 1937 these 1,121 pieces went to the Brooklyn Museum, where they form one of the strong bases for the fine Egyptian exhibit.

THE DISCOVERY OF OTHER CIVILIZATIONS

Egypt was not the only ancient civilization which was rediscovered at this time. Mesopotamia and Syria-Palestine were parts of the Ottoman

Empire. While it is true that the Turks offered no welcome to the West such as Mohammed Ali gave in Egypt, there were Westerners in parts of the Turkish domain, frequently with cultivated interests and time on their hands.

Henry Rawlinson was British Vice-Consul at Baghdad, a young man in his late twenties with energy and curiosity. In a mountain pass between Iraq and Iran, at a place called Behistun, Darius I had carved a great inscription five hundred feet above the floor of the plain. With a sheer drop below it, it was practically inaccessible. In the years following 1835, Rawlinson scrambled up the cliff face and made copies and squeezes of these texts. He makes the dry statement: "The climbing of the rock to arrive at the inscriptions, if not positively dangerous, is a feat at any rate which an antiquary alone could be expected to undertake." Rawlinson's deed was heroic. The texts of Behistun were in cuneiform and proved to be trilingual—Akkadian (or Assyrian), Elamite, and Old Persian. A German had already identified the cuneiform writings of the names of Darius and Xerxes, Old Persian might be compared with modern Persian, and now three different languages could be compared with each other. The Behistun inscriptions were for cuneiform what the Rosetta Stone was for hieroglyphic.

There was also the physical side of Babylonia and Assyria to be discovered. Paul Émile Botta was appointed French Vice-Consul at Mosul in 1842. Almost immediately he began to investigate the great mounds within his district, excavating Kuyunjik (Nineveh) in 1842 and Khorsabad in 1843. The Louvre owes some of its finest Assyrian sculptures to his curiosity and energy. Another Englishman in his late twenties, Austen Henry Layard, also plunged into the Assyrian territory, with excavations at Nimrud in 1845 and at Kuyunjik in 1847. His racy accounts of his adventures and finds stirred much interest in Mesopotamia.

An American was the pioneer in Palestine. Edward Robinson was a sedate clergyman of middle-age, a professor at Union Theological Seminary in New York. In 1838 and again in 1852 he traveled through Palestine in the company of an American missionary, Eli Smith. This was the first scientific study of the Holy Land and was made with topographic care and dispassionate research. His *Biblical Researches*, published in 1841, holds the honor of being the foundation stone for biblical studies in the field. Robinson stood out alone in his day, a peak of archeological propriety amidst the tumbled foothills of preconceptions and prejudices.

Finally, we might record as an expression of minor scientific curiosity that Lieutenant W. F. Lynch of the United States Navy made an exploration of the Jordan River and the Dead Sea in 1848. Throughout this account that navy keeps probing into the area of the eastern Mediterranean.

GLIDDON'S AMERICAN LECTURES

The American public may not have shown enough interest in the Abbott Collection, but only a few years earlier they did respond remarkably to a series of popular lectures on ancient Egypt. That passionate docility with which Americans sit for edifying lectures seems to have been an early trait.

George Gliddon was one of our first consuls in Cairo. He came to the United States in 1842, at the age of thirty-three, to give a series of lectures on ancient Egypt. He began, of course, in Boston. His lectures were so successful that he continued around the country until 1844. That was before the day of lantern slides, and the illustrations for the talks comprised paintings hung on the walls, one table piled with Egyptological books, and one with antiquities. Mr. Richard K. Haight of New York had met Gliddon in Egypt in 1836, and now he generously bought books for him, including the first set of Lepsius' *Denkmäler* to reach the United States. A. C. Harris, the redoubtable British merchant at Alexandria, sent him some antiquities, and Colonel Mendes Cohen loaned his collection. The audiences ran up to two thousand persons at a single lecture.

As an aside, we must recognize that Gliddon did not have a success at every appearance. In 1850 he presided at the examination of an Egyptian mummy and announced that the name on the coffin showed that it was a woman. When the body was unwrapped, it proved to be a male. This aroused skepticism and amusement in his audience and in the press.

Gliddon began each of his series of "illustrated and popular lectures" with a statement that Napoleon's campaigns in Egypt had started a train of discoveries, which "have called forth in this second quarter of the XIXth century the lavish expenditures of enlightened Governments, Societies, and individuals, the enthusiastic investigation of the most illustrious Savans of the age, and the intellectual admiration of all civilized communities."

Gliddon's talks were so well received that he published them in 1843. The slender volume, *Ancient Egypt*, sold to the remarkable total of twenty-four thousand copies. To be sure, the book was priced at only twenty-five cents, but the sale was still extraordinary in a day which looked to the lusty future rather than the dusty past.

Champollion's decipherment was not long past, and the young lecturer's first interest was in this achievement. The first three chapters dealt with the Rosetta Stone, the priority of Egyptian writing over other systems, and the language and scripts of ancient Egypt. Chapter Four was concerned with chronology, including the dates of the Flood and of Abraham; Chapter Five with geography and ancient races; Six laid down the flat dictum that civilization was introduced into the Nile Valley by Caucasians from Asia; and Seven gave the order and dates of the kings of the last sixteen dynasties. Let us look at one paragraph of his lectures.

> There is nothing in my essays or lectures which militates with the most orthodox views of Holy Writ, and there is nothing further from my purpose than to give umbrage to any one, in free, but temperate and deferential inquiries. My observations will tend, on the contrary, to confirm Biblical authority; and if at first sight my still-apprenticed method of introducing a subject, causes a momentary apprehension that I am departing from legitimate views, I am desirous that the results should be found conclusive and satisfactory. Consequently, if I do not take the Deluge at 2348, B.C., I am not differing from the Bible, but simply from Archbishop USHER. These are the reasons which induce me to preface Egyptian History by a brief chronological inquiry.

This statement was followed by a lengthy and tightly knit exposition of dates as offered by different modern authorities. This was rather heavy fare for a young nation. The success of Gliddon's lectures and the remarkable sale of his book give us a new appreciation of the public readiness to accept a strange and different field of culture.

His lectures took him as far west as St. Louis. We salute him as the first of a long and distinguished line of lecturers barnstorming the United States on the subject of ancient Egypt. Did the good man travel by stage or railroad? Did he put up at inns all over the country, or did the local patricians give him hospitality? Did he have a lecture agent? What were the societies or clubs before whom he spoke? Later lecturers would like to compare notes with him.

Gliddon was ahead of his day in other ways. He was appalled by the wanton attack on the monuments, both by the constructors of stone buildings and by the avid collectors, such as Salt and Drovetti—was there an element of jealousy here? He wrote in 1841 that Mohammed Ali had opened up the country for exploitation without setting adequate safeguards against pillage of the monuments. If the pirating of Egypt's treasures was to continue, the land would be stripped of its best pieces with insufficient record, while the objects would be scattered across the museums of Europe. This was just and high-minded criticism. Gliddon was, unfortunately, fifty years ahead of his colleagues.

In 1850 Auguste Mariette came out from Paris on a commission to buy Coptic manuscripts. He paid little attention to his commission but went off to Sakkarah to test a statement by Strabo about a burial place of sacred bulls. He discovered the Serapeum just where he hoped that it would be. Mariette became the leading archeological figure in Egypt for a generation. With him we pass to a different period.

4 EXTRAVAGANZA (1854–82)

Ismail and the Suez Canal

Egypt was ruled by two ardent promoters in the nineteenth century: Mohammed Ali from 1806 until his decline in 1841 and Khedive Ismail from 1863 until his deposal in 1879. In each case the rule was by personal dictatorship, the planning was from the top without consultation of any legislative or advisory group, and the masses of people were merely a labor asset for exploitation. In each case the Western powers, led by Great Britain, intervened to thwart the ambitions of the ruler of Egypt—the territorial expansion of Mohammed Ali and the extravagant expenditure of Ismail. Each acted as an Oriental despot to bring Western innovations into Egypt. In the case of Ismail, the irony is that he had been educated in France, tried to follow the imperious methods of European business entrepreneurs, but belonged to no supporting group which might have justified his prodigal activities.

There was an interval between the rule of Mohammed Ali and his grandson Ismail in which the only notable figure was Said Pasha. This younger son of Mohammed Ali had distressed his father because he was fat and lumbering, but the French had befriended him, particularly the consul, Ferdinand de Lesseps. When Said, perhaps to his surprise, found himself the ruler of Egypt, he leaned heavily upon the advice of his friends. Railroads were introduced into the land, and an idea as old as the pharaohs, an idea that Napoleon had entertained and then abandoned, the idea of a canal across the isthmus of Suez, was taken up with vigor.

The patient determination of de Lesseps in his dream of a canal is another story. Despite Said's approval, it was Turkey that had to give a firman, and the British influence in Istanbul was hostile to a French-built waterway in Egypt. France did not supply adequate diplomatic support or money. When the firman finally was granted, the cost to Egypt was great: she had to supply a *corvée* of sixty thousand laborers, and she lost the revenue she had had from a transit trade between Europe

44

and the East, since an international company was to operate the Canal and reap the profits. Work began in 1859.

Ismail became Pasha in 1863 and was promoted to the title of Khedive in 1867. Since he was pro-French, he ardently supported the Canal project. Since he had lived in France, he was much more sensitive to Western criticism than his grandfather would have been. Criticism centered on the use of forced labor for the Canal and the misery of the conscripted fellah. Ismail abolished the *corvée* to appease the West. He was certainly no financier, and the Compagnie Universelle du Canal Maritime de Suez protested in desperation at the loss of the free labor which Egypt had contracted to supply. With confidence, Ismail submitted the problem to Napoleon III for arbitration. To his chagrin, Napoleon ruled in favor of the Compagnie, and the Khedive had to pay an indemnity of $15 million. Ismail was bitterly disillusioned. He dismissed his French advisors and retreated into lavish expenditures to promote the economic activity of Egypt. Between 1862 and 1875 the debt which Egypt owed abroad rose from $16 million to $443 million. He built sixty-four sugar mills, eight thousand miles of irrigation canals, nine hundred miles of railroads, four hundred and fifty bridges, established a postal service, and increased the number of schools from less than two hundred to nearly six thousand. The Civil War in the United States had sent the value of Egyptian cotton booming. Even so, the sudden expansion undertaken by Ismail could not be financed on a sound basis.

The formal opening of the Suez Canal was in November, 1869, when Empress Eugénie sailed from Port Said to Suez. Ismail had a beautiful and imperial patroness. He turned Cairo inside out with sumptuous festivity. An opera house was built in six months to display Egypt's awareness of higher culture. To be sure, Verdi did not succeed in meeting the deadline for the Canal ceremonies, and the opera *Aida* had its *première* two years later. But there was opera in the new house from the beginning.

The legends about the opera *Aida* deserve comment. Ismail asked his Conservator of Antiquities, Auguste Mariette, for a theme. Mariette's mind harked back to ancient battles between the Egyptians and the Ethiopians, then to Shagaret ed-Durr, a Negress who had ruled Egypt briefly at the time of the Seventh Crusade, and then settled on the dusky little concubine who was one of Ismail's favorites. The plot of undying love between a heroic Egyptian and an Ethiopian slave princess captured Verdi's interest, after he had previously rejected the commission. Rarely has an opera satisfied every condition—except that of delivery on date.

Imperial magnificence must have some backing, and Ismail was alone. In 1875 he was unable to pay interest on his loans. He sold shares in the Suez Canal to Great Britain for less than $20 million, but he still could not stave off the creditors. Under pressure from England and France, he was forced to accept foreign financial control: an Armenian acceptable to the West as Prime Minister, an Englishman as Minister of Finance, a Frenchman as Minister of Public Works, and as controller of the collection of the debt a young Englishman from the Indian civil service, Major Evelyn Baring, who is better known under his later title, Lord Cromer. The hand of the West tightened on Egypt, only gradually and reluctantly to loosen its grip two generations later.

Ismail tried to regain some authority, encouraged a protest by the army, and talked about setting up representative government. But the forces against him were too strong, and in July, 1879, he was handed a curt note: "The French and English Governments are agreed to advise your Highness officially to abdicate and to leave Egypt." He turned his rule over to his son Taufik and went into exile. No representative of a foreign government was at the Cairo station when this visionary but misguided builder left his country.

MARIETTE'S MONOPOLY

The Louvre officials must have been taken aback in 1850 when they received word from their young emissary in Egypt that he had run out of money and urgently needed more. Since Auguste Mariette had been sent out to buy Coptic manuscripts and had spent the money on excavating, they might well have summoned him home for a dressing-down. Yet his discovery of the Serapeum was sensational, and they patiently supported him for four more years. The burial place of the sacred bulls had been holy for many centuries. A long avenue of sphinxes led to a tremendous vault, within which the mummified bulls had been laid to rest in huge granite sarcophagi, each weighing more than sixty tons. There were even classical statues added by votaries in Roman times.

The ponderous Said was still Pasha, and de Lesseps had the ruler's ear, urging that Mariette be appointed as director of a service of antiquities. Said had no interest in these pre-Islamic materials, but he did want to win the friendship of the French. In 1858 Mariette was appointed Conservator of Egyptian Monuments, a post which later became Director-general of the Service of Antiquities. He was the first to hold such an office in the Egyptian government; he occupied it until his death in 1881, and he set a tradition for nearly a century that a Frenchman would be in charge of Egyptian antiquities. In his day he dominated the scene.

It was typical of Mariette that he went straight to his personal objective without regard to the advice or opinions of others. By nature he was so constituted, but his Egyptian experience only hardened his self-sufficiency. He came into a field which had been suspicious and competitive, where any new discovery might be visited by subversive agents from a rival collector or dealer. He became highly secretive not only about his plans but even about his successes. He would try to hide a new discovery until the work was finished and the materials were safely in storage in Cairo.

He was responsible directly to the ruler—first Said and later Ismail—and he depended directly upon the ruler's mood for financial support. Every year there must be striking new finds to catch the Pasha's interest. That is a fine way to build up materials for a museum, but it is no way to run a scientific service. There was no museum as yet. Mariette kept harping on the idea, but Said was not impressed. It was accident and courageous vigor that won the argument.

The one class of antiquity which does excite everybody is gold. Early in his service, Mariette's workmen at Thebes excavated a tomb and discovered a beautifully decorated sarcophagus of a queen. Mariette happened to be away at the time. The local governor, the Mudir of Qeneh, heard that there was gold, hastened to Thebes, took over in the name of the government, ripped open the mummy case, discarded the mummy, and went off in triumph with the striking jewelry. Mariette came immediately, invaded the Mudir's boat, and seized the jewelry by personal force. He realized that he must be the first to tell the Pasha or it would be all up with his position. He hurried to Cairo, gave his version of the story, and presented Said with a scarab for himself and a necklace for one of the royal wives. Said was pleased and impressed. He ruled that Mariette had acted properly, and he agreed to the erection of a museum.

There followed year after year of success. Mariette's work concentrated on some of the most exciting places in Egypt: the Serapeum and the mastaba tombs at Sakkarah; the handsome temple of Seti I at Abydos; three of the greatest temples in the Theban area, Karnak, Deir el-Bahri, and Medinet Habu; and the great Ptolemaic temple to Horus at Edfu. These were big, so they conformed to the desire of the age for the colossal. Many of these temples were filled with squalid modern villages, and Mariette used his authority to move out the inhabitants and raze their buildings. The temple at Edfu had such an overlay of wretched mud huts that it could be seen only with great difficulty. Since Mariette's day, it has rightly been one of the showplaces of Egypt. His regime enjoyed a steady annual progress in the uncovering of temples and the discovery of tombs, but this was mostly Mariette's work. As controller of the antiquities of Egypt, he permitted no one else to engage in major excavation.

While Khedive Ismail was still pro-French, Mariette prepared an attractive exhibit of ancient Egyptian objects for the Paris Exposition of 1867. Empress Eugénie was so taken with these materials that she sent her own emissary to Ismail to drop the hint that she would be graciously pleased to accept the whole exhibit as a gift. The Khedive probably was willing, but he had some awe of the forthright and single-minded Mariette, and he told the envoy that in such matters his man at the Museum was more powerful than he, so permission must be obtained from M. Mariette. Mariette refused to relinquish these treasures, even to his native land. Eugénie was not happy about this, and Ismail blamed Mariette. Relations between the Khedive and his Conservator of Monuments were correct but cool until the French Empire fell in 1870, and there was no further need to cultivate the friendship of Napoleon III and his empress.

By modern standards, Mariette's excavation methods were atrocious. He had no systematic method for the removal of earth, no careful recording at all stages, and there was inadequate supervision of the poorly paid workers. At the end of the century, the exacting Flinders Petrie used to give his disciples caustic lectures about Mariette's field work. Further, the Frenchman sought no friends except the ruler, and he alienated both those who wanted to exploit the monuments of Egypt by denying them that privilege and those who wanted to support his work of conservation by his solitary gruffness. No Egyptian and no European—except perhaps for a single Scotsman, Alexander Rhind—practiced or learned field Egyptology while Mariette dominated the scene.

Nevertheless, he brought to an end the era of ruthless exploitation characterized by Salt, Drovetti, Belzoni, and Vyse. He was a conservator of the monuments for the good of all Egyptian materials. To him goes the credit for clearing up some of the most important temples in the land. And he fought doggedly and successfully for a national museum. His successor, Gaston Maspero, said that he fitted his time. Indeed, with all his faults, he was better than his time.

Two Scotsmen

There were four problems of excavation which the mid-nineteenth century did not recognize. The simplest of these is the fact that as you remove earth, you have to put it somewhere else. If you place your dump only a few yards away, you may have to move it again as your problem extends. If you put it a little farther away, some future excavator may have to tackle it to reach his objective. A second problem is that of stratigraphy, or the overlay of later materials on top of older. Connected with this is the tangle created by constant re-use of an old installation by later peoples, as people of the Twenty-second Dynasty might use an Eighteenth Dynasty tomb for burial or the Copts put a church into a pharaonic temple. The early archeologists simply cleaned out a place without adequately recognizing the different periods of use. A third and major problem is that really showy and valuable pieces are much rarer than the run-of-the-mill pots, broken figurines, scattered beads, amulets, and miscellaneous debris. Since the early diggers were after showpieces, they tended to ignore the majority of the objects they uncovered. The location of materials in association is of critical importance for the historical understanding which would come out of the observation that such and such a mummy case had been found together with such and such scarabs, pottery, crumbled wood, and broken inscriptions. No one today would run a dig without constant supervision, not so much to check pilfering by the workmen from the excavation as to see the location and associations of things as they appear out of the ground. That means constant recording at every stage, and the nineteenth century recorded sketchily and often only after the completion of a dig.

This might be summed up in the fourth problem, which is that archeology, although undertaken for the purpose of historical reconstruction, actually destroys. For centuries a certain assortment of pieces has slumbered beneath the ground in the location and in the relation to each other in which ancient man left them. Archeology takes them out of that setting, and they will never again be put back for re-examination. The questions which one generation will ask the excavator are not the same as those asked by a later generation. Only a step-by-step methodology, with constant recording of every step, can provide a reconstruction of the full record on paper. Related to the problem of archeological destruction is the fact that buried materials may last indefinitely, particularly when they are buried in sterile sand. Once they are uncovered and fully exposed by excavation, destructive factors attack them: climate, sandblasting by strong winds, water seepage from below, and especially human activity, whether appropriation for building stone, wanton malice, or sale of carved pieces.

It would not be until the late 1880's that Petrie insisted on proper method, with the recognition that everything found was significant, whether artistically or financially valuable or not. It would not be until the late 1890's that the Egyptian government recognized an obligation to reconsolidate temples and tombs which had been exposed to forces of destruction. It would not be until the middle 1900's that Reisner would bring field recording to a final perfection and Griffith and Breasted would cry out that Egyptology had a deeper obligation to strengthen and record the things it had already uncovered than to uncover more monuments for slow decay. In the middle of the nineteenth century there was only one shining light of archeological method and conscience, the Scotsman, Alexander H. Rhind.

It is interesting how often when the health of a young European broke down, he visited the milder climate of Egypt and became an Egyptologist. Such was the case of the young Scottish lawyer who came to Thebes in 1855. He had no qualifications or training to become an excavator, but he became the best of his day because of his curiosity and because of a Scotsman's dogged patience. He plotted the exact locations and associations of the things he found and so was able to disentangle the first and second uses of a tomb. It was shocking to him that carved blocks would be ripped from temples and tombs to enrich some museum. He wrote firmly that casts, photographs, or facsimilies should be enough to serve the purposes of a museum so that the monuments might be left intact to tell their story.

Rhind specialized in Theban tombs, and he left us a sufficiently detailed publication of what he found and how he found it. This was new. He was critical of his predecessors and their attitudes. Of d'Athanasi he wrote: "His long residence at Thebes must in practical exploring have given him unusual opportunity and experience; but it is curious to know that, on the spot, he was as reticent and secret in his proceedings as the Arabs themselves." He was not happy about the excavation methods and attitudes of the generation of d'Athanasi and Belzoni.

> Of nearly all of these researches there remain only the most imperfect records: of the great majority there are absolutely none. Prosecuted with ardour more than forty years ago, the mode of procedure was by no means of a satisfactory nature. Mr. Salt and Signor Drovetti entered at the same time actively on the pursuit, and their official influence, as Consuls-General for England and France, obtained for them the necessary permission and facilities from the native government. Various of the ancient sites were fixed upon, and in particular the Necropolis of Thebes was, so to say, mapped out between the working parties employed by these two gentlemen. But nearly all of their explorations were conducted under the supervision of agents whose instructions, while it is only just to believe that they had in some respects broad scientific ends in view, would seem, by some oversight, to have been to attend to accumulation of relics, rather than to the circumstances under which these were found.

Rhind was here too gentle with the plunderers who had preceded him, but it is important that he was concerned with scientific value in an age when almost everybody else was still after financial profit or spectacular display.

He has some interesting things to say about forgeries in his day. The fellahin of Thebes were limited to relatively simple and obvious productions—we shall see in the following section that Rhind himself might be fooled by these. In Cairo, where the forgers were both Egyptian and European, there were bolder frauds. For example, a forger might acquire two sets of Canopic jars, those vessels into which the viscera of mummified ancients were placed. If one set were inscribed and the other not, there would be a careful copying of the inscription from one set onto the other so that the sales value might be increased many times.

This young hero spent only two seasons excavating at Thebes, made one later visit to Egypt, and died just before his thirtieth birthday. He was a model excavator and recorder in his day. It is tragic to note that he had little influence upon Egyptology.

A very different person was Piazzi Smyth. By definition he was a scholar, since he was Professor of Astronomy at Edinburgh and the Astronomer Royal of Scotland. He became a crackpot whose weird ideas still leave a troublesome legacy to the Egyptologist. Working first at home and using the figures of others and then surveying the Great Pyramid himself in 1865, he came to some fantastic conclusions. In effect, they implied that the ancient Egyptians had a mathematical knowledge and an engineering skill far beyond any people up to modern times. He found the mathematical value *pi* present in the construction of the Great Pyramid. He worked out to his own satisfaction a unit of measurement and architecture for the Great Pyramid, which he called the "pyramid inch," equal to 1.001 of our inches. For him the empty sarcophagus in the King's Chamber was unimportant as a place of burial because he believed that it had been designed as a standard measure of capacity for all peoples in all times.

This could be dismissed as unimportant lunacy, if there were not good people today who believe that the ancient Egyptians had some powerful and lost knowledge, believing particularly that the Great Pyramid was designed by God as an instrument of prophecy. A massive tome, published in 1924, states solemnly that the use of the "pyramid inch" within the inner passages of the Great Pyramid shows clearly that the Egyptians were prophesying at terminal points the birth of Christ, the beginning and end of World War I, and so on. These passages end with the King's Chamber, for which the initial and terminal dates were calculated as

September 16, 1936, and August 20, 1953. In an edition written after 1936, it was necessary for the authors to explain this final period of all prophecy: it was "the period during which the nations of the New World Order, of which the English-speaking peoples form the nucleus, are brought safely through the dangers and difficulties which beset them; and as the period during which the forces of war and disorder will be ultimately subdued by Divine Intervention." Would that it had been true!

There was one happy result to the aberrations of Piazzi Smyth. They later brought Flinders Petrie to Egypt to test these theories.

AN AMERICAN NAMED SMITH

How can one judge Edwin Smith, the man from Connecticut, who was the first American living in Egypt and professing to be an Egyptologist? On one rating, he was a serious and accomplished student of Egyptian writing. On another, he was a whining scoundrel. Probably each of these ratings has an element of exaggerated truth, and he was a man of modest attainments who was sometimes subject to evil impulses. From letters that he himself wrote he does not appear in a very favorable light.

Breasted, who edited the Edwin Smith Surgical Papyrus for publication, calls him a "scholar" and "one of the pioneers of Egyptian science." Breasted examined Smith's attempt to translate the surgical treatise which bears his name and found it an extraordinarily successful attempt to understand a difficult document. The able scholar Goodwin, with whom Smith corresponded, praises his "very extensive" acquaintance with hieratic texts. While Lady Duff-Gordon was living in Luxor, she wrote to her husband to send out some books for a friend of hers, an American Egyptologist who was living there. It is quite clear that he could read hieroglyphic and hieratic with some skill and that he was well aware of the importance of the medical papyri he owned.

A good French Egyptologist, Théodoule Devéria, visting Luxor in 1862, gives a curious picture of this "Theban hermit" who lived among the tombs not to become a saint, but to read a medical papyrus. Smith lunched with Devéria but had forgotten his French. He exhibited to the French scholar a unique series of forged scarabs, inscribed with a complete register of royal names and made in Luxor by a "too intelligent Arab."

Devéria writes that Smith was tired out from the preceding days when he had accompanied the Prince of Wales. This refers to a spectacular feat, when Smith and the British Vice-Consul entertained the British Prince by going down a ninety-foot shaft and bringing up thirty mummies and coffins. The physical deed was daring and exhausting, but the modern wonders a little: How is it possible to produce thirty mummies on order, even for royalty?

The most damaging description of Edwin Smith comes from the book of a British naturalist who spent a season of research in Egypt. His heavily jocular report might be dismissed as a scandalous yarn, except for the fact that this Mr. Adams had as his companion A. H. Rhind, that accomplished Scotsman, making his last visit to Thebes. The writing is Adams' at a later date, but it must rest on Rhind's testimony.

> Touching scarabs and their stone representatives, the following rather amusing incident came to my notice during our sojourn in Upper Egypt. A certain individual, who shall be nameless, called upon Mr. Rhind, to make the acquaintance of a brother Egyptologist. This "smart man," as he would be called in his own country, was in the habit of paying regular visits to every boat containing white faces. He gave it out (and perhaps he was stating facts) that he had come across the Atlantic, and settled down in the land of the Pharaohs for the purpose of devoting his entire attention to the study of the hieroglyphic writings. Now, this person was on bad terms with his landlord, and after talking over some intricate points, in which Birch of the British Museum had differed from the German translators, and such-like difficult questions in connection with the construction of the mysterious language, our visitor changed the subject, and informed my friend that having finished the study of many antiquities, papyri, and so forth, in his possession, he would (sic) "to oblige a brother student of ancient lore," let him have whatever he chose, at the exact same price originally paid by the present possessor. Indeed, he said he was afraid to keep them, being the only Christian in town; moreover he had been constantly annoyed by the natives, and even his life threatened, unless he left the society of the "true believers"; even his landlord had proceeded to eject him, but he took the law in his own hands, and "go, he would not!" The result was an attempt at assassination, which, however, eventuated only in somebody having been seen at night before the student's window brandishing a cutlass. The above story, as told to us by the excited narrator, wore very much the aspect of what seemed religious intolerance and persecution, examples of which are still not uncommon among Christians as well as Mussulmans in many semi-civilized countries, and wherever one or the other happens to predominate. We therefore extended considerable commiseration towards our visitor, and by way of comforting him, purchased several of his scarabaei, etc., after which he took his departure. It was ten P.M. when the Egyptologist withdrew, and we were making

preparations for bed, when the cabin-door opened, and who should glide into our presence but our late visitor's landlord! Mustapha was this Ethiopian's name—a good-natured, obliging man, who knew a little English, and was a stanch and ardent friend of Mr. Rhind. He had dogged his tenant to our boat, and most probably overheard all he had told us. With excitement vividly depicted on his sable face, "I come," said he, "to warn you against Mr. Smid." "Mr. S.," he went on to say, flashing his eyes Othello-like, "make scarabaei; he shut his door and tell no one, but I look through a hole, and see him file and polish sometimes all night. He make little idols and rings, and sell them to the Howagee (traveller or trader) who come up the river. I tell him this one day; he get angry. I tell him leave my house, he not go." This set my friend to examine his purchases, when, to his disgust, he found not one of the works of art was real, but so closely counterfeited as not to be known from the original except by a connoisseur. There was a cunning blacksmith at Thebes who fabricated antiquities to please the unlearned, but this specimen of erudition, and of all others, Egyptian learning, in combination with handicraft, is rare indeed. How far the learning was a blind to secure good-paying customers, and as a means of introduction to unsuspecting antiquarians, did not appear, as our friendship with him ceased from that day.

How does the historian handle a libelous statement like that? The landlord's charges may be discounted as malicious, in a situation that bred malice. Yet, when we put it alongside the statement by Devéria, when we read that Naville charged Smith with helping the locals to forge antiquities, the weight of testimony is heavy. Let the witness speak for himself in letters he wrote from Thebes.

By a happy chance, a few of Edwin Smith's letters to the British Egyptologist, Charles W. Goodwin, have survived. About as soon as Smith settled in Egypt, he sent to Goodwin copies of Egyptian texts, and an intermittent correspondence followed. It was advantageous for Goodwin to have someone living at Thebes whom he might ask about texts in the monuments there.

The letters clear up allegations in the Egyptological literature that Smith did not own either of the famous medical papyri, the Ebers or the Edwin Smith Surgical. Smith bought them in 1862 and sold the longer papyrus to Ebers in 1872 for $8,000, apparently through a local Egyptian as an intermediary. Smith was quite aware of their value and wrote to Goodwin in 1864: *"I do not wish to sell either Papyrus they are part of my collection and the prices put upon them (as I profess to sell antiquities) are intended to be prohibitive."* In the same letter he refers to a group of papyri which had appeared in 1862—the Ebers, the

1a   The temple of Edfu as Napoleon's expedition saw it

1b   The temple of Edfu after modern clearance

2   Columns of a Christian church standing in temple of Medinet Habu

hermonthis - (Erment) 27 9bre 1828

3*a*   A temple at Armant, destroyed to build a sugar factory

3*b*   Ramses II offering flowers to St. Peter in the temple of Wadi es-Sebua

4 Napoleon examining Egyptian antiquities

5 Napoleon on his expedition to Egypt and Palestine

6a   Frontispiece of the *Description de l'Égypte*

6b   The statue which Napoleon took home for Josephine, now in the Brooklyn Museum

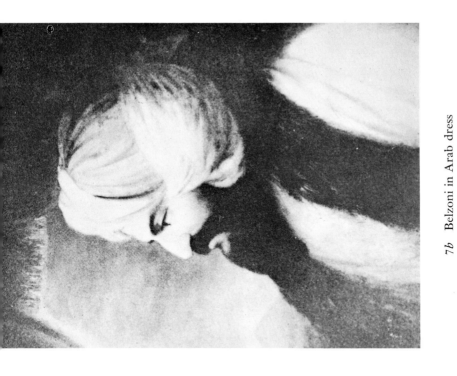

7a Jean François Champollion, decipherer of Egyptian hieroglyphic

7b Belzoni in Arab dress

8   Bernardino Drovetti, arm outstretched, surrounded by some of his agents in the search for antiquities

Edwin Smith, the Rhind Mathematical, the Rhind Leather Roll, and perhaps others—and expresses his high valuation on the text which bears his name. "It may be prejudice on my part but I think my lesser Med. Pap. of more value than the Dorbiney, I am therefore willing to keep it as you know it cost me comparatively little, about 12 £, but since that batch no more have come to light."

Apparently Goodwin wrote some complaints about his financial position in England in 1864, and Smith responded with a very revealing statement on his past life and current interests.

> You say you are in difficulties and expect to leave England, if you can, come here; my expenses do not amount to a pound a month and if you can bring a spare capital of £50 or 100 by disposing of such things as you do not need it will more than support you, as I can assist you and guarantee you to make from 4% to 7% a month on your capital as I am now doing without exertion.
>
> When I was in your case or perhaps worse having a wife & children I parted with what had been the hobby of my leisure in prosperous times, my library & every thing about me; and when after going home to adjust my difficulties with my family and could not, I came out again having only 60£ when I reached here 3 years ago. I have now what has cost me in Antiquities about 150£ and nearly as much more in cash or its representatives—bills against people of abundant means which is [sic] paying interest at between 5 & 6% per month so that it accumulates rapidly.

Put bluntly, Smith was a money-lender, enjoying the lucrative rate of 5 per cent to 6 per cent a month. It is clear why the poor fellahin sold him antiquities very cheaply and why there was hostility to him by his landlord and others. Three years later, after Goodwin had gone to China, Smith did not find his position at Thebes so advantageous.

> Now here though living is not exhorbitant [sic] the opportunities of making a fortune are rare if not absent nevertheless something may be made in good times, as I had begun to accumulate a little something by lending money at 5% per month until the Vice roy came down without notice and as it were confiscated the debts, i.e. he changed the old law by which the Govt. was obliged to collect debts when possible from those who refused to pay, by making payment optional, the govt refusing to interfere, the result of which is that much of my gains are *as they "was" before they "was,"* a very great majority perhaps as much as 9/10 of the people being dishonest and foolish repudiated their debts.

In 1864 Edwin Smith still felt confident and able. He was happily working on the structure of the ancient Egyptian language and sent

Goodwin four rules about the roots of Egyptian words. The most detailed presentation is for the fourth rule. "IV. All words written with the same hieroglyphic signs (particles always excepted) are referable to the same primitive root, no matter what may be its prefix or infix or suffix (called determinative). . . . I consider this 4th. law the most important addition to Egyptology that has been made since Champollion, but I have not the least idea that it will be adopted by any but myself as it will involve changing the *assured* significance of perhaps a quarter of the dictionaries." He then proceeds to illustrate this "law" by examples. Thus the Egyptian words *itn, wstn, wtnw, wtnsw, btnw, mtnw,* etc., must all be based upon a "primitive root" *tn.* Goodwin was proficient in Greek, Hebrew, and Sanskrit; he could hardly have been very cordial to Smith's extraordinary ideas, which were roughly comparable to a claim that the English words "fatten," "distend," and "content" were all derived from a primitive root "ten." Smith was right in his prophecy that no one else would adopt his "law."

The last letter to Goodwin, who was a magistrate in Shanghai in that year, 1870, is tragic. Smith explains why he has not written for six months.

> For a month during March I was blind & suffering terribly from Ophthalmia, I suppose. . . . Last winter I saw a quantity of Egyptologers Lepsius, Brugsch, Lenormant, Neville [*sic*], Dumichen & Eisenlohr. . . . I am expecting a photographic apparatus, when this arrives I shall perhaps be able to send you some texts as I propose to take them small so that they can be conveniently handled, & read by means of a glass, by the way I am obliged to use glasses constantly now age and constant use having impaired my sight.

Poor Smith! He left Egypt six years later and lived on for another thirty years, but we know little of his later life.

The last statement about Edwin Smith comes in the letter of an American tourist written in 1913. This was long after Smith's departure from Luxor and rests upon the memory of Mohareb Todros, who was German consular agent at Luxor for many years. From it we learn that the landlord "Mustapha" in Adams' account of his meeting with Smith was Mustafa Agha, long-time British consular agent at Luxor.

> The German consul remembered Smith perfectly, described his appearance and all about him. Smith was evidently an old man in 1873, as the then consul remembered him from 1869 as having a white beard. The consul stated that Smith was a *money lender,* and said that he had no doubt that he had bought and sold Egyptian relics, as did most of

the people living there. He did not remember having heard of the Ebers papyrus, and he did not recollect Mr. Smith in connection with any papyrus whatever. He thought it quite probable, however, that he might have engaged in the selling of the papyrus as you have described, as he was always on the outlook for "turning an honest penny." He said that Smith lived in a house built for him by the English consul, and it stood on the ground surrounding the fourteen beautiful columns of the Temple of Ramesis II. at Luxor, now excavated, of course. Smith lived there very much alone, and was set upon by thieves one night, who were not successful in robbing his house. A great hubbub arose over this, and the district Didar [sic] personally investigated it. Shortly after this Smith "vanished." No one knew where he went or why, according to the consul.

The Edwin Smith Surgical Papyrus has been described as "an original source of absorbing interest as a unique document in the early history of civilization." Edwin Smith recognized its value, and on this high praise his troubled spirit may rest in peace.

THE UNITED STATES BECOMES INTERESTED

The name "American" may have been practically unknown in Egypt in 1830, but by 1864 so many Americans had visited Luxor that the fellahin were trying to puzzle out the relationship of these speakers of English to the other English speakers. Lady Duff-Gordon writes of a talk with the peasants on the west side of Thebes.

> One of them had droll theories about "Amellica"—as they always pronounce it;—e.g. that the Americans are the Felláheen of the English; "they talk so loud." "Was the king very powerful, that the country was called El Melekeh" (the queens)? I said, "No, all are kings there; you would be a king like the rest." My friend disapproved of that utterly; "If all are kings, they must all be taking away every man the other's money;"—a delightful idea of the king's vocation.

It is likely that the first mass entry of American sightseers, such as those in Mark Twain's Innocents Abroad in 1867, did nothing to dispel the notion that the Americans "talk so loud." Nor did this genial author's humor about the pyramids and the mummies arouse a respect for ancient Egypt in the United States. It did play into the public interest, however, as did other reports of returned tourists. In the year 1870, three hundred American visitors registered at the American Consul-general's office in Cairo, and there must have been many more who did not bother to register.

American academic circles had already accepted ancient Egypt as worthy of intellectual consideration. In 1856 a scholarly group at the University of Pennsylvania received a plaster cast of the Rosetta Stone. It was more than a generation since Champollion's decipherment, but skeptical words were still uttered about man's ability to read these strange picture signs. After solemn consideration, a committee was formed to prepare a new translation of this inscription. Two years later there appeared the *Report of the Committee Appointed by the Philomathean Society of the University of Pennsylvania To Translate the Inscription on the Rosetta Stone*. This was the first book entirely lithographed in the United States. For the attractiveness of the 160 handwritten pages, the authors "ventured to adorn their work of severer science with numerous illustrations," rather stilted engravings of ancient scenes and monuments, set off by brightly colored floral borders.

The Preface modestly states: "This Committee, composed as it is of young men engaged much of their time in collegiate studies, has had neither a superabundance of leisure, opportunity for very extended research, nor a full maturity of judgment. Sensible of their deficiencies, they will only add that they have done what they could and now submit their work to the judgment of their readers."

The library at the University of Pennsylvania must have been comprehensive and up-to-date. The young men pay respectful homage to such European scholars as Champollion, Lepsius, Brugsch, and Birch. Their translation reflects real credit upon students and their professors. For example, we today might translate a brief section of the hieroglyphic text of line 9 as follows: "and the double crown (*pschent*) is in the middle thereof, because his majesty shone forth in it in the House of Ptah." This 1858 version runs: "Also the pschent in the midst above the same, since that it was decorating his divine majesty when he entered Memphis." In an age innocent of strict attention to rules of grammar and syntax, the young men caught the general sense of the text.

They could not refrain from severe moral judgment, however. They ignored the extreme youth of Ptolemy V and the disadvantages he had in competing with the experienced Antiochus the Great of Syria. At the end of their analysis, just above a drawing of an ibis nest resting upon lotus flowers, they wrote: "The character of Ptolemy was not such as to merit the epithet of Epiphanes, the illustrious. It was feeble, effeminate and vicious and his reign will be better remembered as the date of the Rosetta Stone than as the era of any great events."

In that era of spacious munificence which accompanied the opening of the Suez Canal, Khedive Ismail suggested to a visiting American journalist that an obelisk standing at Alexandria might be ceded to the United States. After all, one from Luxor had been removed to Paris in the early 1830's, and a similar suggestion would be acted upon by the British in 1877–78. The obelisk offered was of Assuan granite and had been erected by Thut-mose III at Heliopolis about 1455 B.C. Two centuries later that avid appropriator of fine monuments, Ramses II, added his inscriptions to the column. In the reign of Caesar Augustus, it was removed to Alexandria, together with its mate, which now stands on the Thames Embankment in London. Our obelisk is nearly seventy feet tall, and its estimated weight is 224 tons.

To lower a slender needle of this length and weight, to introduce it into a ship, to transport it in safety for five thousand miles against hazards of weather, and to raise it vertically in a new location—these were formidable problems, as experience in France and England had shown. There were protracted negotiations and varying estimates of cost. While the American authorities were hesitating, Ismail was deposed, and Taufik became Khedive. The project reached the doldrums. Then there entered a determined hero, Lieutenant Commander Henry H. Gorringe of the United States Navy. He proceeded with great skill and perseverance. He would not build a ship around the obelisk, nor could such a weight be carried on deck or towed. He determined to open a hole in the prow of a vessel, thrust the obelisk inside, and then close the hole.

Legal problems vexed the Commander. He was on leave from the navy, acting as a private citizen. When he purchased a ship from the government of Egypt, she could have no recognized registry. "There was no other course than the open defiance of law, which the circumstances fully justified; and I determined to make the voyage from Alexandria to New York without registry or nationality, thereby taking the risk of having my steamer seized by any vessel of war at sea, or by the authorities of any port I might be obliged to touch at," and coaling at some port was necessary.

Gorringe's account of his adventures makes exciting reading. In Alexandria the standing obelisk was incased in wood and was to be lowered by two tackles onto a horizontal stack of timbers. In that process, first one and then the other tackle snapped, bringing the huge weight crashing down upon the wooden emplacement, and there were a few moments of panic. Fortunately, the timbers held, and a first major risk was surmounted.

Rumors of further risk at sea were many and vehement. Under the circumstances, it was difficult to enlist a crew for the SS "Dessoug." "The first and second officers turned out to be confirmed drunkards. . . . The quartermasters would do credit to a pirate's crew. The number of men who solemnly enlisted for the voyage and speedily deserted before it began, was forty-eight." Finally a crew was recruited in Trieste, Italy, where they had had no chance to hear the prophecies of doom, and the steamer set out from Alexandria on June 12, 1880.

Fortunately the weather held good, but in midocean a shaft broke, and for six days the "Dessoug" made little headway under sail. During this period a waterspout formed to windward and moved inexorably toward the helpless ship for five long minutes. At the last moment it changed course, passed just in front of the vessel, and broke up with a loud noise. On July 20 the "Dessoug" moored off Twenty-third Street in New York.

That is by no means the end of the story. It was not until January 22, 1881, that the obelisk was re-erected on a pedestal on Graywacke Knoll, Central Park, behind the Metropolitan Museum of Art. The total cost of the operation was $102,576, and Gorringe is careful to explain that this included bakshish. By bakshish "is meant the various amounts paid to different persons whose good-will was necessary to success, and whose ill-will would have involved delays and lawsuits that would have been ultimately more costly"—a very frank statement.

There she stands in Central Park, a slender shaft covered with hieroglyphic texts. It may not be true that "he who runs may read" such inscriptions, but the obelisk undoubtedly quickened the interest in ancient Egypt in the hearts of thousands of Americans. Two of the bronze crabs which had been under corners of the obelisk and which were inscribed by the Roman Prefect Barbarus in 13–12 B.C. were presented to the Metropolitan Museum. They joined a few small objects acquired in 1874 as the first Egyptian materials in the collection.

The stout-hearted Commander took advantage of his stay in Egypt to acquire a modest collection of antiquities. The most remarkable of these was a brown quartzite model of a portion of the temple of Heliopolis, which the New York obelisk once graced. Seti I had dedicated this model in the temple about 1300 B.C., and it shows the two sockets where the London and New York needles were located. It is now to be seen in the Brooklyn Museum.

ARCHEOLOGY IN OTHER COUNTRIES

While such extravagant glories as Abydos and Karnak were appearing in fuller view, there were sensations in other countries of the Near East.

This is the period of Schliemann's triumph. The poor German boy who had become an American citizen was able to retire as a millionaire at the age of forty-four and devote himself to ancient and linguistic studies. He was a genius with an amazing memory, but completely self-centered and self-assured. Throughout his life, he depended solely upon his own judgment, and he felt that the results fully justified him. Homer's Troy was his objective, despite the warnings of academic scholars that he would be pursuing a legend, and he decided as early as 1868 upon the mound of Hissarlik near the mouth of the Dardanelles. He did not receive a firman from Turkey until 1871, but he soon unearthed a striking hoard of gold and silver, which he promptly labeled "the treasure of Priam." What did it matter that he had misunderstood his levels and located Homeric Troy in the second instead of the sixth or seventh level? What did it matter to the general public that his romantic eagerness to reach something spectacular that must belong to the time of Priam and Hector and Helen ripped away the upper layers beyond later study? Brilliantly he had proved to his own satisfaction that Troy did have historical existence, and his charmingly ingenuous books convinced others. He went on to other triumphs at Mycenae, Tiryns, and Orchomenos in Greece itself. He conquered the academic scholars by his success in producing physical materials, and even though the academics went on to correct his mistakes, they were never the same again. They also went out to dig.

For the general public the story was most capitivating—the self-made man who successfully undertook a new career and confounded the pedants. The name of Heinrich Schliemann symbolizes to the layman the beginnings of field archeology, and his successes in the 1870's did greatly expand public knowledge of, interest in, and support of field work.

On December 3, 1872, a new learned group, formed under the weighty name of the Society of Biblical Archaeology, was meeting in London. A little man named George Smith, who had come to the British Museum a few years earlier to clean and join fragments of cuneiform tablets, rose to read a paper. Without prelude, he began with a sentence which opened up a whole new world: "A short time back I discovered among the Assyrian tablets in the British Museum an account of the Flood." The Flood of the Bible in cuneiform literature? The word flashed across the world like a new comet. It was a London newspaper that picked the new excitement up and financed young Smith to go out and find the one missing fragment of his Flood Tablet. By a miracle he did find it on his fifth day at Kuyunjik. The paper then ceased its support of his searches, but the British Museum sent him back for two more seasons. The poor fellow had never been robust. He did find more tablets, but he collapsed and died on his way home in 1876, only thirty-six years old.

The new world which Smith had opened up was the marvelous cuneiform literature, with long and extraordinary myths and with striking biblical parallels.

The early discoveries in Mesopotamia, such as those of Botta, Layard, and George Smith, were in the north, in Assyrian territory. In 1877 the French Consul at Bosrah, Ernest de Sarzec, began digging at Telloh, toward the south end of the Tigris-Euphrates Delta. His sensational discovery was a new culture, with remarkable statues and sculptures in style which we now know to be Sumerian. Again a new world was exposed for development.

A fourth excitement of this period was of a very different nature. A traveling German scholar by the name of Tischendorf reached St. Catherine's Monastery at the foot of Mt. Sinai in 1844. In the great hall he saw a large basket filled with old parchments, and the librarian informed him that the monks burned such moldered documents. Tischendorf writes that he was allowed to take about a third of these sheets, or forty-three, to Leipzig. The monks later claimed that he had left a receipt, promising to return them. At any rate, when he returned in 1853, the faces of the monks were blank, and he found nothing. In 1859 he returned on a mission for the Tsar, and this august name had more weight with the monks. He was privately shown even more sheets than he had seen fifteen years earlier. The details of devious negotiations were complex, but Tischendorf finally went off in triumph with the manuscript. Then there was a delay, with protests from the monks, until ten years later the Tsar sent them the equivalent of $6,750, together with clocks and imperial decorations. The Codex Sinaiticus, extant in about 390 sheets, was written around A.D. 350 and was one of the oldest biblical manuscripts known. It is critically important for the study of the Old and New Testaments. In 1933 the sheets purchased by the Tsar were sold by the Soviet government to the British Museum for $500,000.

AMERICAN SOLDIERS OF ADVENTURE IN EGYPT

Here we introduce an interlude not connected with archeology. Khedive Ismail, held in check by Great Britain and Turkey, had thought that France was his supporter. When he abolished the *corvée* for the Suez Canal and Napoleon III ruled against him for this, he became disillusioned with France and discharged Frenchmen in Egyptian employ, for example, fifteen who were attached to his army. Then, at the opening of the Suez Canal, Turkey publicly criticized his extravagant festivities. Ismail dreamed of independence from Turkey, but he needed military strength to establish such freedom. Shortly after the Civil War he commissioned an American resident of the Near East to enroll ex-soldiers of that war for service in the Egyptian army. In the United States there were men who had recently held command and were now at loose ends; more than forty ex-Federals and ex-Confederates were enrolled within ten years.

Basically these Americans were after employment, a regime which the army life had given them and which civil life did not, and adventure. They regarded themselves as professional soldiers, and concentration on that objective was enough for most of them. Few of them bothered to learn adequate Arabic, and almost none of them ever understood the Egyptians, the historical situation in the land, or the forces playing upon their local troops. They proved to be successful explorers because the rigors and dangers of opening up new lands appealed to them, but they were bored and haughty under the tedious routine of barracks life. Sporting red *tarbushes* on their heads, they spent a great deal of time gossiping in bars and cafés. Much of their gossip became internal, so there was friction within the group. None of them took active interest in archeology.

The senior officer, who became Chief of Staff of the Egyptian Army, was an admirable person. Brigadier General Charles P. Stone was a West Pointer whose Civil War career had been clouded with accusations which apparently were not deserved but were politically inspired. Now he was offered an opportunity to redeem himself in a new setting. He was devoted to the interests of the Egyptian army, meticulous in the performance of his duty, and always loyal to the Khedive. It does not appear that he was a skillful politician, responsive to the forces of palace intrigue, the beginnings of Egyptian nationalism, or to the pressures of England, France, and Turkey. He stuck to his job.

Stone saw that the Egyptian soldier was a conscripted fellah, illiterate and unskilled, poor material for an army which pretended to be modern; many of the officers and most of the non-commissioned officers were illiterate. Therefore, the paper work and the supplying of the army was in the charge of civilian Copts, who exercised inordinate power and made inordinate profits. Ironically, the American soldiers set up an activity worthy of the Peace Corps. Stone started army schools, teaching soldiers of all grades to read and write, to use arithmetic, and to understand their equipment. Even the children of officers and sergeants were welcomed. Within four years three-quarters of the army could read and write. The result was explosive. The descendants of those printing presses which Napoleon had introduced were grinding out copy in Arabic, seeking betterment and greater power for Egypt. The soldiers began to identify themselves with Egypt. Nationalism took a firm root at the lower levels.

The American explorations were usually for strategic purposes. When Gordon went to the Sudan in 1874, Ismail thought it prudent to send along with him two American officers, Lieutenant Colonel Chaillé-Long and Major Campbell, as an offset to any British ambitions in that region. Gordon did not think highly of Long and was happy to have the dashing young American go off on distant expeditions. For example, Long pushed on south to Uganda, where the king acknowledged himself a vassal of Egypt, much to Ismail's pleasure. We shall return to the young colonel at the end of this section.

An American army engineer, Lieutenant Oscar E. Fechet surveyed the Nile Valley from Assuan to Khartum in 1873–74 and recommended Assuan as the site for a dam to control the flood waters of the Nile. It would be twenty-five years before the recommendation would become effective.

In government circles the American welcome was wearing thin, however. The American officers were not very diplomatic or adaptable, and the army reforms had cut into a lucrative trade in supplying the troops. Further, the Egyptian government was in such financial difficulties that the officers were being paid only in painful arrears. The adventure was nearly over. By June, 1878, all of the Americans except Stone had resigned or been discharged from the army. They returned to the States and enjoyed a brief flurry of popularity, with lectures and books. They had never understood Egypt's difficulties in trying to emerge from the Middle Ages, and they often painted an unfavorable picture of the land or its people.

General Stone later gave his own views on the debacle. For him, in his consistent loyalty to the Khedive, the villains were England, France, and Turkey. The cabinet set up in August, 1878, headed by an Armenian and with two Englishmen and a Frenchman in control of expenditures, destroyed the morale which Stone had so carefully built up. The army schools were abolished; pay was held up, and Egyptian officers were discharged, while Circassian officers were kept on. Since the Egyptian soldier had become proudly nationalistic, these economy measures led to an officers' protest in 1879 and another in 1881. Although Stone sympathized with the officers in their grievances, he was a very correct Chief of Staff, and he had to treat them as mutinous.

After the British had occupied Egypt in 1882, Stone returned to his position as Chief of Staff, but he found every move thwarted, and he resigned and left Egypt in 1883. His last job, in 1886, was to supervise the building of the semipyramidal base for the Statue of Liberty on Bedloe's Island.

In 1874 Colonel Chaillé-Long was exploring in a region of the deep Sudan, and in the Makraka region, several days' march west of modern Juba, he made an interesting purchase. To understand its significance, let us go back to ancient Egypt.

About 2250 B.C. Egypt was ruled by a boy-king. This Pepi II was only in his fourth year of reign, and he still had ninety more years of life. An Egyptian noble, Har-khuf, had gone exploring into the Sudan to bring back "incense, ebony . . . leopard skins . . . ivory, throw-sticks, and every good product." Now he was returning to Egypt, and he sent back word that he was bringing a "pygmy of the dances of the god from the land of the horizon-dwellers." The boy-king wrote back in great excitement, urging Har-khuf to protect the dancing pygmy night and day, because his majesty so eagerly wanted to see this wonder, the like of which was known only in a tradition from a century earlier. Har-khuf was so proud of the royal letter that he had it inscribed on his tomb in Assuan.

In A.D. 1933–34 the Metropolitan Museum of Art in New York was digging near the Faiyum, and Ambrose Lansing found a delightful little toy. Four little pygmies were carved in ivory, naked except for neck-laces and a shawl over the shoulder, the leader beating musical time with his hands, the other three with upraised arms. These three were so carved that they could be set into a pierced ivory base. Then, when a string had been threaded into that base and had been wound around the spools below the little men, a pull at the string would make them jiggle a little dance. Thus Har-khuf's pygmy was illustrated in carved pieces made three centuries after his time.

What Colonel Chaillé-Long bought in the Sudan was a pygmy woman, Ticki-Ticki by name. She was only three feet, nine inches tall, and nearly as broad as she was tall. Colonel Long asked her whether she would come with him, and she answered bravely: "If you don't eat me." Since she was naked, except for beads, he threw her a roll of cloth. This she wrapped around her neck and faithfully trotted after him. When he returned to Cairo, Ismail was very pleased with the results of his explor-ing and gave a reception for the young colonel. At this party, Ticki-Ticki danced before the ruler of Egypt.

In the years between 1880 and 1883, Mariette died, and Maspero took his post; Petrie started his work in Egypt; Wilbour came to spend the first of many winters on the Nile, and Sir Evelyn Baring became British Consul-general and Diplomatic Agent at Cairo. All of these transition points belong to a new age, which we shall treat in the next chapter.

5 CROMER AND MASPERO (1880–1908)

General Stone had introduced something new into the Egyptian army—pride. Officers and soldiers who had been reluctant conscripts, pushed around by Turkish superiors and treated with a patronizing air by Coptic clerks, had become literate, soldierly, and patriotic. When enforced economy cut into this advance and thrust them back into their former inferiority, they resented it. In 1879 and again in 1881, Egyptian officers of the rank of colonel staged demonstrations of protest, with temporarily successful results. One of them, Ahmed Arabi, was the spearhead of these protests, which were very distasteful to the British and French in their efforts to enforce a reduction of Egypt's enormous debt. Arabi Pasha became a national hero because he had been born a fellah and epitomized the hopes and ambitions of the downtrodden Egyptians. In February, 1882, a nationalistic cabinet took office, with Arabi Pasha as Minister of War. Ismail had once encouraged an officers' demonstration, and the new Khedive, Taufik, at first sympathized with these agitators for Egyptian independence.

Egypt's creditors, however, were alarmed. The British invited the French and the Italians to take common action with them. When these two countries were reluctant to join in full force against Egypt, Great Britain decided to do the task alone. On July 11, 1882, a British fleet bombarded Alexandria. Arabi Pasha here made a diplomatic error. Taufik had been offered a chance to leave the country for safety; he courageously elected to stay with his people. Instead of enlisting his support in resistance to the invasion, Arabi kept the Khedive in military captivity near Alexandria, along with General Stone. He thereby alienated the young ruler.

The British occupation was not difficult, and on September 11, Arabi was decisively defeated at Tell el-Kebir in the southeast Delta. British troops thereafter remained on Egyptian soil for seventy-four years, a visible indignity to Egyptian pride. The British, with the support of the

French, took over policy-making for the Egyptian government for two generations.

The effective instrument of British control was an occupying army, but controlling decisions were made by a model of British rectitude and nineteenth-century policy, Sir Evelyn Baring, who was to become Lord Cromer. He had spent a few years in Egypt earlier as the Commissioner for the Public Debt, and a sound economy was his constant goal. In 1883 he became British Agent and Consul-general in Egypt, and from this post he ruled the land for twenty-four years. Although he held plenipotentiary diplomatic rank, he was the junior in the consular corps; he held no formal authority over the Khedive, who was responsible only to the Sultan of Turkey; and he had no legally recognized voice in the government of Egypt. Nevertheless, acting on instructions from London, he was the one effective voice in Cairo.

Cromer fitted his role in every respect. He was a solid, round-faced English gentleman of unobtrusively correct dress and impeccable manners. His moustache was not too small or too flaring. A pince-nez hung, ready for use, across his ample front. He belonged to the Victorian age, with its firm ideals of what is good for other men—ideals which were commonly right, but not always tasteful to the other man. Throughout his regime he instituted heroic economy measures for Egypt which restored financial stability to that unsteady land. In passing we may note that such austerity inevitably pinched the Antiquities Service of Egypt. In 1886 it was noted that the British army was building a fort at the First Cataract and paying local laborers twenty-five cents a day, whereas the Director-general of Antiquities could only pay seven and a half cents a day for workmen on a Luxor dig.

Cromer's first important act was to persuade Egypt to abandon its possession of the Sudan. The desert prophet who called himself the Mahdi had stirred up anti-Western fanaticism in the western Sudan: those fierce warriors whom the British called Mahdists, Dervishes, or Fuzzy-wuzzies. The heroic "Chinese" Gordon was sent to evacuate Egyptian and British forces and bureaus in the Sudan. Then Gordon went his own stubborn way, stayed on at Khartum, and was assassinated by the Mahdists in January, 1885, and Cromer was wrongly blamed for this sacrifice. When a Tory government was in power at home, his firm policies were fully backed; a Liberal government was not so clear on the strong course of empire.

Cromer talked and wrote about his admiration for the oppressed fellahin and his desire to ameliorate their lot. He did induce Egypt to abolish the *corvée* and the *kurbash*, that hated whip of the Egyptian official and policeman. To be sure, forced labor and the lash were still used for some decades after the 1880's, but they had been legally banned. Otherwise, Cromer was too preoccupied with diplomatic work at the top level to get down to the basic problems of the individual fellah, and it may be argued that the unimaginative Kitchener, British Agent and Consul-general in 1911–14, actually pushed through more reforms for the benefit of the fellahin than did Cromer in his twenty-four years.

One example of Cromer's vigorous skill occurred when Khedive Taufik died in 1892. The heir apparent, Abbas Hilmi, was a schoolboy in Vienna. The transition of rule to a minor could have given Turkey the opportunity to intervene and assert its nominal authority over Egypt. Cromer brought young Abbas back from Europe in a hurry, ignored the fact that he was not yet seventeen and a half years old by the Western calendar, calculated his age by the Muslim calendar, found him thereby just past his eighteenth birthday, and proclaimed him of age according to the Turkish law of succession. The slower-moving Turks were unable to find a flaw in this reasoning or procedure.

Khedive Taufik, after some initial show of spirit, had followed Cromer's advice docilely. Taufik was not energetic by nature, and his disillusionment when his own troops besieged his palace in 1882 took away any incentive he might have had toward asserting independence. In his book, *Modern Egypt,* Cromer is able to praise Taufik as amiable, courteous, pious, and strictly monogamous—something new in the ruler of Egypt.

Abbas, succeeding his father in 1892, was a different proposition for the British Agent. Although he collaborated of necessity, there was always an inner resistance. When World War I opened, Abbas was in Istanbul, where he made no secret of his preference for Turkey, Austria, and Germany. He was deposed in December, 1914, and a British protectorate was set up over Egypt.

Cromer introduced British officials into nearly every branch of the Egyptian government, where they had an effective voice in the making of departmental policy. This was increasingly resented across the years, particularly since the representatives of Her Majesty's Government every now and then would announce that they were in Egypt for Egypt's good and would ultimately leave when Egypt's economy was firmly sound and when the Egyptians had been trained for self-rule. The British control was particularly effective in defense, policing, foreign affairs, finance, and public works. To the French they left the influence on education and the arts, including archeology. From 1882 to 1907, the Cromer era, the population of Egypt increased from 6 million to 11 million.

Maspero and Amelia B. Edwards

Gaston Maspero, the Director-general of the Service of Antiquities, was a stout little man with a short beard. He was a jolly companion to his many friends. As a scholar, he had many aspects of genius. His work over the years was prodigious, and it was illumined with a rare insight. Maspero's uncanny ability to arrive, on the basis of relatively inadequate evidence, at conclusions which later proved to be correct was brilliant, but it was dangerous for his disciples. They lacked the esthetic sensitivity which permitted his graceful and successful flights of fancy. With them the intuitive approach was highly insecure, and it led to a famous scholarly feud between members of the "French school" of Egyptology and those of the "Berlin school," who practiced a pedestrian cataloguing and analysis. The French felt for truth and then were deductive; the Germans refused to recognize truth until they had arrived at it inductively. At the height of his powers, Maspero's brilliance made him "the acknowledged greatest living brain on Egyptology," in the words of one admirer. His personal charm everyone enjoyed.

In administration Maspero followed the principles of Mariette in holding a check on excavation, but his was a looser rein. The Copt who was American consular agent at Girgeh in Middle Egypt and who was also an antiquity dealer received a concession to dig, and he kept no records, published nothing, was merely looking for salable objects. There was a steady, but moderately controlled, flow of materials to European and American museums. When circumstances forced Maspero to give an excavator a poor division of his finds or no division at all, he saw to it that the man received other pieces from the Egyptian storerooms as a "don gracieux."

There were flaws in this genius. Petrie, visiting a pyramid which Maspero had excavated five years earlier, wrote in his journal that the monument "has been barbarously mangled, to open it, all one side torn out in a great gash from top to base, just as Maspero wrecked the brick pyramids at Dahshur." The ever-questing Charles Wilbour was puzzled at Maspero's lack of scientific curiosity and observed that the great Frenchman "does not seem to care much for what he does not intend to write about; he watches diggings while there are most important texts within a stone's throw, which he has studied in bad copies, but has not the curiosity to examine." Wilbour concluded that those who make their living by scholarship must confine themselves to those things upon which they can write an article, thus winning and holding a reputation.

Maspero's influence upon fellow scholars was tremendous. His writings were marked by a light and lucid style, so he became well known to the general public.

Working in friendly co-operation with Maspero was a remarkable volunteer publicist, Amelia B. Edwards. This British spinster had an assured career as a novelist and essayist. On a trip to Egypt in 1873–74, she fell in love with the ancient land and for nearly twenty years was the chief promoter of interest in Egyptian archeology. A spirited woman, with large, dreaming eyes, she commanded a pen and a tongue in round, romantic Victorian style. Here are passages from her famous trip, *A Thousand Miles up the Nile.* The first is as the party comes to the island temples of Philae at the First Cataract.

> The approach by water is quite the most beautiful. Seen from the level of a small boat, the island, with its palms, its colonnades, its pylons, seems to rise out of the river like a mirage. Piled rocks frame it in on either side, and purple mountains close up the distance. As the boat glides nearer between glistening boulders, those sculptured towers rise higher and ever higher against the sky. They show no sign of ruin or of age. All looks solid, stately, perfect. One forgets for the moment that anything is changed. If a sound of antique chanting were to be borne along the quiet air—if a procession of white-robed priests bearing aloft the veiled ark of the God, were to come sweeping round between the palms and the pylons—we should not think it strange.

Her most famous descriptions deal with the sunrise upon the great rock-cliff temple of Abu Simbel.

> Every morning I waked in time to witness that daily miracle. Every morning I saw those awful brethren pass from death to life, from life to sculptured stone. I brought myself almost to believe that there must sooner or later come some one sunrise when the ancient charm would snap asunder, and the giants must arise and speak.
>
> It is fine to see the sunrise on the front of the Great Temple; but something still finer takes place on certain mornings of the year, in the very heart of the mountain. As the sun comes up above the eastern hill-tops, one long, level beam strikes through the doorway, pierces the inner darkness like an arrow, penetrates to the sanctuary, and falls like fire from heaven upon the altar at the feet of the Gods.
>
> No one who has watched for the coming of that shaft of sunlight can doubt that it was a calculated effect, and that the excavation was directed at one especial angle in order to produce it. In this way Ra, to whom the the temple was dedicated, may be said to have entered in daily, and by a direct manifestation of his presence to have approved the sacrifices of his worshippers.

Even though this may be florid to the taste of today, it is writing which still can move one, and there are few letdowns in Miss Edwards' books. There was a curious adventure just south of the First Cataract, as her boat returned northward. These were Victorian travelers, and they had clear ideas on the maintenance of national dignity in a foreign land. One member of the boat's party went off hunting, and as the quail swept over a field of barley, he fired, spraying with shot an unseen child who was crouching in the grain. The hunter was immediately beset by villagers, who wrested his gun from him, and he received a blow on the back of his head from a flying stone. With slow dignity, he walked back to the boat, followed by the shouting and angry rabble. The gang-plank was hauled in to prevent an invasion of the boat, and a council of war was held. It was decided that since the child was, "if hurt at all, hurt very slightly, we felt justified in assuming an injured tone, calling the village to account for a case of cowardly assault, and demanding instant restitution of the gun." A parley was held; the child was brought aboard and given medication; the father was given a napoleon, and the gun was restored to the hunter.

This might have closed a suddenly dangerous affair, but the passengers "agreed that it was expedient, for the protection of future travelers, to lodge a complaint against the village; and this mainly on account of the treacherous blow from behind." Accordingly, a formal accusation was lodged with the Governor at Assuan, who, "charming as ever, promised that justice would be done." Fifteen of the villagers were arrested and taken to prison in Assuan. The hunter was invited to sit with the Governor and the Mudir. After a formal sipping of coffee, he was told that the man who had struck the blow had been identified. The Governor proposed that the other fourteen villagers receive one month's imprisonment each and that the culprit receive one hundred and fifty blows of the bastinado and two months' imprisonment. The hunter was shocked to find himself in the seat of sentencing and asked that the fourteen be set free and that the culprit receive only a few strokes of the bastinado. The fifteen prisoners were brought in, "chained from neck to neck in single file." The fourteen "could hardly believe their ears" at the word of clemency; the condemned man "was overjoyed to be let off so easily." He was thrown upon the ground and beaten on the soles of his feet. After the sixth stroke, the hunter formally requested that the remainder of the sentence be remitted, and the Governor assented. "The prisoners, weeping for joy, were set at liberty." When the hunter thanked the Governor, that official protested "that his only wish was to be agreeable to the English, and that the whole village should have been bastinadoed, had His Excellency desired it."

Thirty years later, the British were hunting in a very different Egypt. In 1906 British officers were shooting over village lands near Dinshawai in the Delta, and they killed some of the treasured pigeons of the fellahin. There was excited protest, and in the turmoil an Englishman was killed. Britain lodged a formal demand that the village be punished, there was a trial, floggings, and public execution of the fellahin. Now nationalism had advanced so far that no Egyptian felt that justice had been served. There was even protest in England, and the Dinshawai affair became a famous source of bitterness in Egypt, known to the lowest villager. The Consul-general who succeeded Cromer started his career with an amnesty for the imprisoned fellahin, but the name Dinshawai was kept alive by the Arabic press as an example of overriding British domination.

In 1882 Miss Edwards and others formed the Egypt Exploration Fund (EEF) in England "to organize expeditions in Egypt, with a view to the elucidation of the History and Arts of Ancient Egypt and the illustration of the Old Testament narrative, so far as it has to do with Egypt and the Egyptians." The concern with the biblical narrative was typical of the time. The Egypt Exploration Society, as it is now called, is still vigorous and productive after eighty years. During a lecture tour of the United States in 1889–90, Miss Edwards enrolled Americans in support of the work of the EEF.

These were not the only forces exciting interest in ancient Egypt. A younger brother of Sir Henry Rawlinson, Rev. George Rawlinson, was turning out a series of widely read histories of ancient Near Eastern countries. Then there were the novels of Georg Ebers and H. Rider Haggard. In a letter which Maspero wrote to Miss Edwards in 1879, he suggested that Ebers' stories had done more for Egyptology than all the scientific studies of the great Lepsius. He may have been right.

A WINTER IN EGYPT

In the last two decades of the nineteenth century a trip to Egypt was "the thing to do." Europeans could spend the earlier winter months in southern France or Italy, cross over to Alexandria, have a time of vigorous pleasure in and around Cairo, then hire a houseboat or join a party for a leisurely trip up the Nile. The more adventurous might then go to the Holy Land for Easter, but Palestine under the Turks was not as luxurious as the Egyptian sojourn.

In Cairo, Shepheard's Hotel was the focal point, a rambling building with a vivid décor in pseudo-pharaonic style, founded in the 1840's. From Shepheard's famous terrace, over a coffee or a lemon squash, one could sit idly and watch the teeming throng sweep past: Egyptians in from the villages returning one's stare openly, barefooted Nubians of great dignity, two-wheeled donkey carts, and then shouts and a rumble as an open landau carrying some fat Turkish dignitary in a red *tarbush* careened past, preceded by running *saises*, who cleared the way with sticks. Veiled ladies rode by, fiercely guarded by eunuchs. A diplomatic carriage would have a fiercely moustached *kavass* mounted beside the driver and clothed in brilliant costume and carrying a curved saber and staff as insignia of his master's sublimity. It was an easy and fascinating way to see the East.

He who plunged into the "native city," as it was then styled, had need of a stout stick to keep off the beggars, peddlers, importunists of various pleasures and bargains, and dogs. The market place would be endlessly fascinating with its variety of goods not simply from Egypt but also from farther east. One needed a good bath on return to the hotel.

On specified days of the week, a smart and speedy coach would drive from Shepheard's the ten miles out to the Mena House Hotel, at the foot of the pyramids of Gizeh, for the arduous climb to the top of the Great Pyramid, lunch at the hotel, and the spooky penetration of the pyramid in the afternoon. Everything conceivable was provided for the tourist, attired in his light but hot serge, with a pith helmet on his head and a heavy veil hanging down the back of his neck. No one could control the dust or flies or heat; for the rest, one was assured that every effort had been made for his comfort and pleasure. Legally, one was not completely away from home; under the Turkish Capitulations, foreigners had extraterritorial rights, so any offenses they might commit would not be tried by Egyptian courts, but by the Mixed Courts, benched with Europeans and utimately also Americans.

When the tourist was ready to go up the river, to visit Assiut, Abydos, Luxor, Assuan, Philae, and Abu Simbel, there was the dahabiyeh, "the thing of gold," a commodious sailing houseboat. Most tourists signed up with Thos. Cook & Son for one of his dahabiyehs or for a tour on one of his steamers; the more leisurely and well-to-do might rent or buy their own vessel. In 1881 the Cook boats carried eight hundred tourists to Luxor; in 1882, the year of the Arabi uprising, the number had fallen off drastically, and as late as 1884 there were only twenty by mid-season. Charles Wilbour noted at Luxor in 1882 that "there are only three dahabeeyehs here now and all are American; it would seem that the English are very much scared this year." Wilbour is here referring to the privately rented boats.

The dahabiyeh was not a particularly safe vessel, and it often had to tie up in a strong gale. It had a shallow draft, to escape the sandbanks, and abruptly rising high sides. Cabins, a dining salon, bathrooms, and the observation lounge were aft; the kitchen and quarters for the servants and sailors forward. A huge triangular sail was toward the prow and a lesser sail mounted astern. It was a thrilling sight to see one of these "golden things" sweeping up the river with a favorable wind. A dahabiyeh could be bought for £600 to £1500; £60 a month was a high rental cost. Any amount of money could be spent on equipping it with a library, fine foods, and wines. A very small dahabiyeh, with accommodations for two persons, might require a crew of only four; a large private boat, carrying six persons, had a crew running up to twenty. A good rais, or captain, was a supreme treasure.

When the dahabiyeh hove into sight of Luxor, there would be a great excitement. If it were flying an American flag, the American consular agent at Luxor would come hurrying out of his house and have his men fire off a twenty-one-gun salute with their muskets, while the consular agents of other countries might honor a known visitor with five or ten guns. These consular agents usually lived in houses inside the Luxor temple, and as they claimed diplomatic immunity, it proved to be very difficult to dislodge them when the Service of Antiquities proposed to clear the temple in the late 1880's. They were Egyptians, Muslims or Copts, and were as engaging a series of rascals as any tourist might hope to enjoy.

The senior of them we have already met in connection with Edwin Smith. Mustafa Agha was a Muslim who served as consular agent for Britain, Russia, and Belgium. His house lay between the great processional columns in the Luxor temple, and it could not be cleared away until after his death. He used his diplomatic status to deal in antiquities—as all of them did—and after the uproar over the discovery of the royal mummies, Belgium thought it prudent to deprive him of his agency. His entertainment for visitors, particularly British visitors, was famous. There would regularly be a feast and a *fantasiyeh*, an entertainment with music and dancing of a kind that Victorian women may not have seen elsewhere. On request, he could produce a skillful snake-charmer for his guests.

A Copt, Todros Boulos, served at Luxor as Prussian, then German consular agent, succeeded in that post by his son, Mohareb Todros. Todros Boulos had been trained as a silversmith, and he used his skill in forging antiquities of metal. As late as the 1950's this family used to show visitors their guest book, which had signatures of very high distinction. Actually, it was not originally theirs. When Lepsius came to Luxor in 1844, he used the old Wilkinson house on the west side. He initiated a guest book, beautifully decorated by one of the artists of his expedition, and left the book with his caretaker. Todros thereupon assumed possession of the book, pretending to act for Prussian interests, but this useful historical record thereafter became "my family's visitors book," jealously held as a memento of proud and active days.

The consular agent for the United States at Luxor did not have the same showmanship as Mustafa Agha or Todros or Bishâra, who served the French, but his activities were much the same. This Muslim, Ali Murad, faithfully went through the noisy salutes for the arrival or departure of a boat of Americans; he gave *fantasiyehs* for parties of visitors, and he exchanged invitations for meals with regular visitors, such as Charles Wilbour. He rented out a boat to the Service of Antiquities, and this favor and his quasi-diplomatic status secured for him a license to conduct excavations. As in the case of the American consular agent at Girgeh, these authorized digs were mere plundering for salable antiquities, without control or recording.

On his first visit, Wilbour was incredulous that Ali Murad dealt in antiquities and recorded a rumor that an American visitor was taken by Ali "to his brother in Goornah, who makes false antiquities, Aly supplying the capital, and they showed him a very fine mummy for one hundred pounds. . . . I doubt the whole story for it seems to me that if Aly had any interest in anybody's selling antiquities, true or false, he would not have concealed it from me." On that first trip Wilbour was accompanying Maspero, and it is probable that Ali Murad was reticent about his trade in the presence of a companion of the Director-general of Antiquities. Later Wilbour was shown the antiquities for sale at Ali Murad's house, and his notebooks have extensive descriptions of the genuine and false pieces there. Nearly seventy-five years later some of the forgeries were on sale in New York.

The somewhat equivocal position of being an Egyptian national but serving a foreign country might have its penalties. In 1884 the American Consul-general at Cairo sent Ali Murad an official letter bearing the consular stamp, asking for thirty scarabs of assorted colors, guaranteed to be ancient. Poor Ali did not know whether such a formal document implied that his consular duties forced him to pay for this assortment or not, because such scarabs were no longer common and cheap. The old man would occasionally run into financial difficulties and borrow money from Wilbour, and he was not reluctant to take advantage of the gratitude of American visitors for his services. One woman acceded to his request to send him a watch and chain, whereat he followed up with a second request. "What do you think the old fellow wants Mrs. Moulton to send him now? Encouraged by the watch and the watch chain he wants a half dozen pair of woolen stockings, the Paris stockings that are so much softer than those they make here and he must wear woolen in the summer because it is better for the eyes. The dark but romantic admirer!"

Ali Murad had a relative in Luxor who became the most famous antiquity dealer in that town. Mohammed Mohassib had been a donkey boy, and Lady Duff-Gordon had taught him English. For a dealer, his character was exceptionally fine, and for nearly half a century he operated the most reliable shop in Luxor. Of course, if tourists, ignorant of the genuine or false, were stupid about the use of their money, the law was always *caveat emptor!*

THE COUNTERFEITERS

Amelia B. Edwards writes of blundering into a shop in Luxor thinking that she was visiting a consulate. By mistake, she was admitted to a room with a workbench strewn with tools, scarabs, amulets, and little statues in the process of manufacture. A large wooden mummy case provided the wood for the figurines so that the seller could swear that the manufactured piece was old. When the owner of the establishment appeared, he hastily bowed Miss Edwards out of the place.

In the 1890's Wallis Budge found great skill in forgery. Black basalt bowls and statues were carved with short funerary inscriptions skillfully enough to fool experienced collectors, "but whenever they attempted to reproduce a long inscription they *always* made some silly mistake in the form or direction of some character and so betrayed themselves." Funerary statues were carved from ancient wood in Upper Egypt, and they were often peddled furtively at night so that their imperfections could not be clearly examined. In Alexandria jewelers used ancient clay molds to cast amulets and figurines of gods in gold, silver, and bronze. Both Europeans and Egyptians made scarabs. A native of Luxor used genuine steatite, which he covered with a beautiful blue-green glaze, manufactured by pounding up old mummy beads. An English Egyptologist had supplied him with a long list of the principal Egyptian kings written in hieroglyphs, and another had sent him a small crucible and furnace. This careful craftsman would sometimes discard dozens of pieces before he made one which satisfied him. When he died, one of his friends asked Budge to help the widow. In the house Budge found several hundred scarabs, with a few genuine pieces to serve as models, and he persuaded Maspero to buy them for the Cairo Museum as instructive examples of the best forgeries.

Wilbour used to chat with the old woman of western Thebes who baked bricks bearing the name of Ramses III for the benefit of tourists. A favorite device at Thebes and elsewhere was to steal a genuine piece from an excavation and then to use it as a model for forgeries. The forgery would then be planted so that some well-to-do visitor might himself discover it—with some suggestions from the planter—and thus give a generous bakshish. The bakshish which excavators gave to their workmen for good finds even led to fakes being planted in the dig for the puzzlement of the digger.

A capable French Egyptologist, Urbain Bouriant, died in 1903, and five years later his son began to circulate impressions of two exciting scarabs. They were identical, large, and carved with an inscription relating the circumnavigation of Africa by Pharaoh Necho's fleet about 600 B.C., just as Herodotus had claimed. This would have been of the greatest historical importance. Jean Capart, the Director of the museum in Brussels, bought the two scarabs for twenty thousand francs and presented his sensational discovery to a learned congress in Geneva. Meantime Schaefer and Erman at the Berlin Museum had entertained doubts about the genuineness of the text and had gone about analyzing it in methodical German fashion. Capart, Naville, and Petrie vehemently attacked the "Berlin school" for unimaginative grammatical rigidity. But Erman went on pulling cards out of the files of the Berlin hieroglyphic dictionary cabinet and matching words and phrases. He proved conclusively that whenever the text was grammatically correct, it had been copied from a variety of ancient sources, but whenever it contained new material, it was grammatically incorrect. Seven different sources could be established for various parts of the text. Obviously someone had had a knowledge of Egyptian, but the knowledge was imperfect.

When Capart was convinced by Erman's demonstration, he wanted to sue young Bouriant. In court a sculptor of Paris appeared and testified that he had made the two scarabs for Bouriant, who was then sentenced to imprisonment. The next time Capart went to Cairo, the French language newspaper wrote haughtily that it was unheard-of presumption for a man who had sent a French "scholar" to jail to come to Egypt and work in the French-directed museum. Sensitive nationalism has always been a strong factor in this narrow field of study.

AMERICAN MISSIONARIES, STUDENTS, AND COLLECTORS

Well before our Civil War, the United Presbyterian Church had established vigorous mission stations in Egypt. The American evangelists worked under the two difficulties of inadequate means and local hostility. That hostility was not so much Muslim as it was Christian. The Egyptian government and the Muslim leaders were dogmatically opposed to anyone who might attempt to convert people from Islam to Christianity, but they set few legal difficulties in the way of the missionaries. Islam was the dominant religion in Egypt, and those of high position and power were normally Muslims. Further, defection to Christianity might bring death. There were practically no converts from Islam. It was the Egyptian Christians, the Copts, who regarded the proselytizers with hatred and fear, because Copts did defect and become "Brotestants," often for the advantages of alliance with Westerners. The Copts were a minority group and might gain foreign protection if they became Protestants. The Coptic leaders responded to this threat with a vigor which can rightly be called persecution of the missionaries.

Living this lonely and even dangerous life, the American missionaries were always glad to entertain visiting compatriots. Three of them had relation to the present picture. Dr. Alexander was head of the American College at Assiut, for many years the junction point between the railroad line from Cairo and the boats which went farther south. He was able to steer many visitors toward promising antiquities in this area, notably some fine Greek papyri. Dr. Gulian Lansing was the scholar and school administrator of the group, a good student of Hebrew with some knowledge of hieroglyphic, and he had thirty-five years' service in Egypt. Wilbour read proof on an article by Lansing which sought to find Egyptian words in the first five books of the Old Testament and commented: "As he knows Egyptian speech remarkably well and Hebrew well, his contributions are important." He was the intermediary for the British Museum's purchase of a fine hieratic papyrus, which was named Papyrus Lansing in his honor. He was credited with establishing high quality in the mission schools, which were then clearly superior to government schools. After his death this standard unfortunately was not maintained.

The lowliest and most interesting of the group was Rev. Chauncey Murch, posted at Luxor. This portly man had to maintain his family on a miserable salary, so he followed a bent of interest and became a dealer in antiquities. Budge praises him as a sound businessman who had a good collection, particularly of scarabs. Murch helped Budge to make useful connections with local dealers and later received and cashed the treasury warrants sent out by the Trustees of the British Museum to pay the locals for what Budge had purchased. Wilbour's picture of him is not always so flattering: the "fat parson," who "preaches in Arabic and shows a fine collection of anteekeh which he will sell from, as a favor to a friend." In 1890 Wilbour noted with regret that the fine Middle Kingdom tombs at Beni Hassan and el-Bersheh had been brutally cut up to secure fragments of text for sale. He was shocked to find some of these plundered pieces exhibited in Murch's house. The missionary had purchased them from a dealer in Middle Egypt who was indignant because the Service of Antiquities had seized his merchandise and therefore had taken his revenge by mutilating famous tombs. Murch must have been enough of a student of Egyptian things to know where these fragments had come from. Chauncey Murch's materials were sold to the British Museum and to the Art Institute of Chicago. The bulk of his collection—3,370 pieces—was presented to the Metropolitan Museum of New York in 1910.

The most interesting Murch piece has a curious history. When the cuneiform tablets were found at Tell el-Amarna in the late 1880's, Murch bought a fragment of one of these new texts. Two scholars made independent copies, but when they did not agree and the piece dropped out of sight, the editor of the Amarna Letters had to omit the fragment, with the remark that it must be "somewhere in the United States." In 1916 T. George Allen, of the University of Chicago, was studying the Egyptian materials at the Art Institute in Chicago. The Institute had purchased from Murch scarabs and other small pieces in 1894, along with this scrap of a clay tablet, which was certainly no *objet d'art*. Dr. Allen recognized it, and it has now been published as the completion of a tablet in the British Museum which carries a letter from King Tusratta of Mitanni to the famous Tiy, widow of Amen-hotep III. It is one of those few Amarna Tablets with a hieratic docket on the margin. The Trustees of the Art Institute generously presented it to the University of Chicago.

Americans who were attracted to the study of ancient Egypt had no place to study in this country, and some of them began to drift to Europe. William Groff and William Berend, a New York banker, went to sit at the feet of the great Maspero in Paris, while William Goodyear studied in Heidelberg and Berlin. Despite earnest writing of articles for the learned journals, they could not dispel the impression of being dilettantes.

No one will ever know how many Americans brought home antiquities from Egypt which ended up in attics or the storerooms of local museums.

Some collectors are known. A California engineer by the name of Sutro came to Egypt in 1884 and "astonished Luxor by buying yesterday a room of antiquities for twenty-five hundred francs of Mohammed Mohassib, much good, more bad. To-day everybody is agog to sell him. He took three mummies yesterday in addition, on which I find the price high"—thus from the letters of Wilbour. Cesnola was collecting for New York about the same time. He had been dealing with the slippery Emil Brugsch; Wilbour advised him to go straight to Maspero, who "is now making up five thousand dollars worth for him." Charles Freer of Detroit, a collector of great taste, acquired some fine Coptic manuscripts while he was building up that great art collection which he presented to our government. In 1886 the Metropolitan Museum of Art purchased from the Egyptian government twenty-nine objects from the Nineteenth Dynasty tomb of Sen-nedjem at Thebes. These, added to a few small pieces and the bronze crabs which had come with the New York obelisk, started the Metropolitan toward its ultimate status as one of the great Egyptian collections in the world.

A graduate of Columbia University, Charles E. Moldenke, had gone to Germany to study and returned eager to start the teaching of Egyptology at his alma mater. He was not successful in that desire, but he built up a modest collection of antiquities and published a number of studies. In 1887 he wrote an appraisal of American collections: those in New York were exceptional; there were good collections elsewhere; and there must be thousands of pieces in private hands. At the time he was too flattering in his estimate, but it does show the advance which had been made in one generation.

We must not omit one bizarre figure, Frederic Cope Whitehouse, son of an Episcopal bishop and once a resident of Chicago. Out in the desert south of the Faiyum, this American had studied a great basin, the Wadi Rayyân, one hundred and fifty square miles in area, with some parts as much as one hundred thirty feet below river level. This he identified with ancient Lake Moeris. Sayce writes:

> "Cope," as he was familiarly known, was brilliantly clever in certain directions, but the brilliancy was dangerously close to insanity. Besides his Wadi Rayyân scheme, he had two other topics which he introduced in season and out of season. Staffa [an island off Scotland], he maintained, had been artificially excavated by the Phoenicians in order to house their fleet during the winter months, and the great pyramid was built from the top downward. When I first knew him these two latter paradoxes were mere *jeux d'esprit*, which he defended in the spirit of an ancient sophist, but eventually they became the obsessions and beliefs

of insanity. In 1888, however, he was still an amusing and brilliant conversationalist, and I have heard him pass, without a moment's hesitation, from fluent French to fluent Italian.

Whitehouse proposed that the Wadi Rayyân be connected by a canal with the Nile and used as a great reservoir for the season of low inundation. The irrigation engineer, Sir William Willcocks, studied the plan with approval. Ultimately, however, this American suggestion for the husbanding of Egypt's water was abandoned in favor of the 1873–74 recommendation of the American army engineer Fechet that a dam be constructed at Assuan.

ROYAL MUMMIES

The desert hillside of western Thebes is honeycombed with the tombs of nobles; more than four hundred of them have been deemed worthy of modern listing and guarding; another fifty were described in the past but have now been lost. For centuries the local inhabitants have lived in these tombs. Only government authority can thrust them out into mud-brick structures in front of the tombs. A venture by the Egyptian government in the present generation to move them into a model village out in the plain failed because of their unwillingness to move. They clung to the homes they knew; they claimed that the air was better on the hillside than on the watered plain; and they resisted the surrender of their ancient privilege of burrowing through the hillside and finding new tombs and salable antiquities.

Up to the 1870's investigation of the royal tombs back in the Valley of the Kings had uncovered only burials plundered in antiquity. Until that time no mummy of a pharaoh was known. Then, in that decade, evidence began to appear on the market that royal burials had been found somewhere by somebody. The story is told by so many people with different emphases that the truth is difficult to establish. I shall have to pick and choose out of the varying accounts.

About 1871 an inhabitant of Gurneh in western Thebes, Abd er-Rasul Ahmed, went after his goats and found that a kid was missing. He climbed up a steep desert shoulder south of the temple of Deir el-Bahri and discovered that the kid had fallen down a steep shaft. The shaft was about six feet square and forty feet deep. Investigation at the foot of this pit quickly showed him that he had stumbled upon materials of tremendous value. He later stated that he took only two brothers and his son into his confidence about the discovery and that he was very cautious in his exploitation of the treasure: in ten years they went into the burial cache just three times and took out only objects easy to conceal—two or three *shawabti* boxes, Canopic jars, half a dozen papyri, scarabs, and so on. At any rate antiquities bearing royal names gradually began to appear on the market.

Maspero claimed credit for the effective detective work of locating the place of discovery and the criminal family. In 1874, *shawabtis* of a Twenty-first Dynasty pharaoh appeared on the Paris market; in 1876 a British general named Campbell bought a papyrus; in 1877 another papyrus appeared in Syria, and Mariette bought others at Suez; in 1878 a wooden tablet was purchased. All seemed to be of the Twenty-first Dynasty, royal, and from Thebes.

Emil Brugsch told a slightly different story. In the middle 1870's an Austrian collector sent him photographs of a necklace with the name of a pharaoh, and shortly thereafter, a letter came from England describing another part of the same necklace. The police of Cairo and Alexandria were warned to look for a man from Gurneh who might be spending more money than would be normal for a fellah, and the Alexandria police came up with the name of an Abd er-Rasul. Meantime, the brothers had had a quarrel over the distribution of the sudden wealth, and this squabble became known to the Luxor police.

It is difficult to weigh the other rumors. The statements that in the 1870's an American visitor purchased a head and a hand from the Abd er-Rasul brothers and that another American was offered the mummy of Ramses II, but turned it down as an incredible opportunity, do not accord with Abd er-Rasul Ahmed's claim that they took out of the cache only easily portable pieces. Nor would this illiterate man know that he had found Ramses II. Abd er-Rasul Ahmed later, in an outburst of confidence, told Wilbour that he had sold two papyri from the cache to a British general named Stanton and that a young American, unnamed, had bought another. Did he confuse General Stanton with General Campbell? Is there a royal papyrus in storage somewhere in the United States? Wilbour's other testimony is more direct. Two months before the case broke open, an Abd er-Rasul, described as "Mustafa Agha's man for Gurneh," offered Wilbour for £350 a funerary papyrus which the American judged to be of the Twentieth Dynasty. On the very day that orders went out from Cairo to arrest the Abd er-Rasuls, Ibrahim Mohassib privately told Wilbour that an Abd er-Rasul "found some years ago a tomb in which were £40,000 worth of antiquities; he himself saw 'with these eyes' thirty-six papyri from it." Two years later in Cairo an Egyptian pasha showed Wilbour a Book of the Dead papyrus from the cache, which may still be in private hands somewhere. How many others disappeared from view?

Suspicion had focused on Abd er-Rasul Ahmed and his patron, Mustafa Agha. The latter was protected by diplomatic immunity. On April 4, 1881, Maspero telegraphed the police at Luxor to arrest Abd er-Rasul and telegraphed the Mudir of Qeneh, Daûd Pasha, a request to conduct an inquiry. Emil Brugsch and the Marquis de Rochemonteix, on behalf of the Service of Antiquities, queried Abd er-Rasul and searched his house, with negative results. Wilbour was incredulous that his friend had done any major wrong; he thought that it was a mistake, that Maspero was aiming at Mustafa Agha, who could not be touched, and that he was using Abd er-Rasul as a lever against the British consular agent; Wilbour wrote that he would try to get the poor man out of prison.

On April 6, Abd er-Rasul Mohammed and his brother, Hussein Ahmed, were sent in chains to Qeneh to be examined. The delicacy of official reports draws a veil over the inquisition, and Maspero reports laconically that Daûd Pasha examined them "with his habitual severity." As I remember a secondhand description made many years later, the scene was a medieval tragicomedy. Daûd Pasha was suffering from a skin ailment, so he sat in court inside a huge pottery jar filled with water up to his neck. The accused were flung upon the ground and beaten with the bastinado on the soles of their feet, just as Theban tomb robbers had been "examined" three thousand years earlier. Six years later the brothers told Budge a story, which their hatred and resentment may have touched up somewhat. According to this version, all members of the family were tortured in the inquisition, first tied to posts and beaten, then thrown to the ground and beaten with palm rods on the soles of their feet, then tied to chairs, with heated iron pots placed upon their heads. One of the brothers showed Budge the scars he still carried from the heated pots. They claimed that one of the brothers died under the torture, and it is true that Hussein Ahmed drops out of the story after he had been taken to the inquisition.

This severe examination produced no confession. Abd er-Rasul Ahmed protested his innocence and tried to invoke the protection of his patron, the British consular agent. A host of witnesses appeared to swear that their friends, the Abd er-Rasuls, were men of sterling character, had never been interested in antiquities, and were incapable of finding and plundering ancient tombs. Abd er-Rasul Ahmed had to be released, and he returned to Thebes.

The tortured man now quarreled with his brothers; he felt that his suffering entitled him to a half share of the loot instead of a fifth. Various neighbors told Maspero about the quarrel, among them our old friend Ali

Murad, who wanted to seek the favor of the Service of Antiquities. The case broke wide open when the eldest brother, Mohammed Abd er-Rasul, went secretly to Qeneh and confessed to Daûd Pasha. By that time Maspero was in Europe, and the investigation on the spot devolved upon Emil Brugsch.

In the heat of July, Brugsch was led by Mohammed to the royal cache. All the other residents of Gurneh were bitterly hostile. Brugsch was heavily armed, but he and his assistant, Ahmed Kamal, were understandably nervous. At the end of a rope Brugsch was lowered down the deep shaft, groped his way along an extended corridor, and stood in the presence of buried royalty—Thut-mose III, Seti I, Ramses II, Ramses III, and about thirty others. No Westerner had ever seen such a tumble of majesty.

Under the circumstances one can understand the haste to clear the burial. They hauled kings and queens away without ceremony. In only eight days the boat started north with the mummied majesties and their treasures. For twenty-five miles northward a formal funeral ceremonial lined the banks of the Nile—men firing their shotguns into the air and women wailing and tearing their hair. They were not mourning the pharaohs; they were mourning the defeat of one of their men by the government.

The reason for the hiding place of the pharaohs goes back into ancient history. With elaborate ceremony and with elaborate security precautions, the pharaohs and their families had been buried in the Valley of the Kings behind Thebes. The wealth of burial equipment was always a matter of knowledge or speculation, so some of the tombs were robbed immediately after burial. But essentially they were intact until the evil financial days around 1130 B.C. Then, to relieve the pinch of inflation and the government's arrears in salaries, there began a wholesale pillaging of the Theban tombs, royal and private. This went on so long that it must have enjoyed official connivance. Finally, some time after 1100 B.C., the Theban priests felt obliged to protect the buried royalties. Secretly they rewrapped the plundered bodies and conveyed them, with what was left of their equipment, to the tomb of an obscure queen near Deir el-Bahri. There, stacked up in jumbled indignity, they rested for nearly three thousand years.

Mohammed Abd er-Rasul was rewarded for his confession with £500 and was appointed rais of the excavations at Thebes. He was hated by his brothers and their neighbors. The men of Gurneh told Wilbour that they all liked Abd er-Rasul Ahmed. "They say he is a man and Mohammed is not." In the long run the family did not suffer; to this day they exercise an effective control on the employment of the men of Gurneh as guards of the monuments of Thebes or as workmen on excavations.

Maspero was not happy about some of the activities of Emil Brugsch, for example the unwrapping of the mummy of Thut-mose III, "without order and in my absence." Maspero himself did not inspect the burial cache until January, 1882, when the pit was reopened for examination by himself, Emil Brugsch, Mohammed Abd er-Rasul, and an American photographer, Edward L. Wilson, who happened to be in Egypt and available. They picked up the scraps which had been passed over in the previous frantic haste, and they established that the cache had no connection with any other tomb. In Cairo the first formal inquest was held in the presence of the Khedive on June 1, 1886, with the unwrapping of the mummy of Ramses II.

One final story I have on verbal memory. One of the mummies was that of Mer-ne-Ptah, who is the traditional Pharaoh of the Exodus. It puzzled pious people that Mer-ne-Ptah could have been buried at Thebes, because they believed that he should have been drowned in the Red Sea, when Pharaoh's host was pursuing Moses. A delegation of clergymen waited upon Maspero in Cairo and stated their unhappiness about this find. The Director-general smoothly informed them that the examination of the body of Mer-ne-Ptah had disclosed extensive traces of salt on the skin. They went off in grateful relief. M. Maspero did not bother to tell them that the normal process of mummification involved a pickle in salt for many days.

THE AMARNA TABLETS

By the 1880's Orientalists were very familiar with cuneiform clay tablets. They had been found in profusion in Assyria and were now being found in Babylonia. That was a long distance from Egypt. The mind set into this new pattern and became rigid. They would be found only in Mesopotamia.

About 1370 B.C. the heretic Pharaoh Akh-en-Aton moved his capital from Thebes more than two hundred miles north to a place which we now call Tell el-Amarna. The garden city which he built at this point lasted only a generation and then was deserted. Such ancient settlements have chemicals in the soil, produced by the refuse thrown out by man, and the fellahin use this *sebakh* as a mild fertilizer for their fields. In 1887 a fellahah was loading her donkey with some of this soil and unearthed a pile of consolidated mud patties with curious impressions on them. No one knows how many she found—at least four hundred—but she sold them to a man for ten cents. They then passed to a dealer for fifty dollars, but thereafter the difficulties began. The hard feelings engendered by the government's activity in taking over the royal mummies had made people wary. These objects were strange and did not look very significant. They jounced around on donkey-back and camel-back, and we shall never know how many of them were ground to powder at the bottom of a bag.

M. Frénay, the Frenchman who managed flour mills at Akhmim, served as agent for the Louvre. He bought a few of the tablets and sent one of them to Paris. There Professor Jules Oppert, who was sixty-one and going blind, firmly pronounced it a forgery. It certainly did not look, in color or texture, like tablets of any known kind, and there was nothing then of a textual nature with which to compare it. The lot was divided up and jounced around Egypt, with further destruction.

In London Wallis Budge received a letter from an Egyptian telling about these cakes of clay with "nail writing," similar to objects brought to Cairo from Baghdad a few years earlier. The writer of the letter wanted Budge to come and buy the tablets before the Service of Antiquities seized them and threw into jail those who had them. Maspero's ill health had forced him to return to Paris, and the new Director-general, Eugène Grébaut, was initiating a firmer policy. Indeed, when Budge reached Egypt in December, 1887, the British Consul warned that official duty forced him to prevent Budge from exporting any antiquities. Grébaut called upon Budge at a Cairo hotel and threatened him with arrest and prosecution if he tried to negotiate with any antiquity dealers. Budge went on to Luxor, where he acquired some excellent finds, including the famous Book of the Dead of the scribe named Ani. Wilbour wrote that he paid $1,200 for this papyrus.

Budge was talking shop in the house of Mohammed Mohassib when the police arrived, ordered by Grébaut to take over every Luxor house having antiquities and to arrest their owners and Budge, if he were dealing with them. Since the police had no warrants for arrest, they simply surrounded the house, awaiting Grébaut's arrival. The rais of the Director-general's boat had succeeded in running it firmly onto a sandbank twenty miles north of Luxor, near a place where the rais's daughter was to be married the next day. Very strangely, not a donkey could be found in this village to bring Grébaut's party to Luxor.

Despite the police guard, a man arrived from the neighborhood of Tell el-Amarna with six cuneiform tablets. Budge was able to examine them and to decide that they must be genuine. Whereat another man from the same place slipped through the guard with seventy-six more! This sounds like legerdemain on the part of Mohammed Mohassib. Budge made arrangements to buy the whole eighty-two, but when he asked for more,

9   Belzoni removing the colossal head from the Ramesseum at Thebes

10   Maxime du Camp's 1850 picture of a colossus at Abu Simbel was
one of the first photographs taken in Egypt.

11   Commander Gorringe lowering an obelisk at the port of Alexandria

12*a* One of the first private collections in the United States, now in The Johns Hopkins University

12*b* Objects in the first museum collection of Egyptian items, at the East India Marine Society in Salem

13a Egyptian architecture as employed in a cemetery in Cambridge, Massachusetts

13b Egyptian architecture as employed in the New York City prison, the "Tombs"

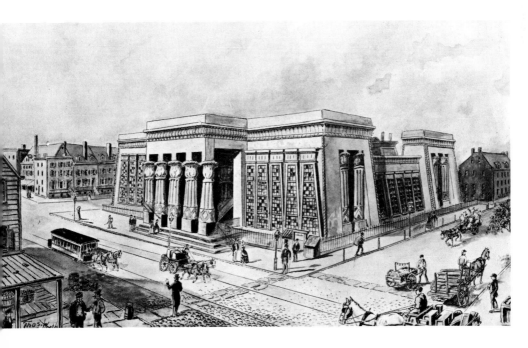

14   The hillside of western Thebes, honeycombed with tombs of nobles. The remaining tower of Gardner Wilkinson's house is here marked with an ✕.

15   The temple of Luxor as seen from the Nile, still encumbered with modern houses

16a   Auguste Mariette examining some of his finds

16b   A sailing dahabiyeh of a size to accommodate a single
family

he was told that they were in the possession of Cairo dealers who were committed to the Berlin Museum as agents.

Now comes the comedy element, with poor M. Grébaut cast in the role of the dupe. Budge had stored his other Luxor purchases in the basement of a small house which backed up against the wall of the garden of the Luxor Hotel. The police had sealed this house and were guarding it. The manager of the Luxor Hotel offered the police a fine meal of mutton and rice. While these guards were busy about the heaped tray, gorging themselves, the hotel gardeners tunneled through the wall into the basement of the guarded house and removed the antiquities stored there—leaving only two pieces to reward Grébaut's zeal. Since these two pieces had been purchased at the request of the Commander of the Egyptian Army, Grébaut might experience some difficulty in seizing and holding them. When the Director-general arrived, Budge refused to accept arrest and boarded the steamer to Assiut, where he took the train to Cairo, accompanied always by police. The train was very late in reaching Cairo, and there were no carriages or donkeys at the station. Budge was encumbered with heavy luggage, the tablets, papyrus, and other objects, so he persuaded Grébaut's police to carry all this to the British barracks at Qasr en-Nil. Since Budge was an official of the British Museum, an officer at the barracks felt that it was his duty to take over the property of the British government and convey it to London. Wallis Budge could leave Egypt with empty hands and an innocent face.

Meantime, Charles Wilbour had come to Egypt on his annual visit, and a Cairo dealer, Nicolas Tano, told him about the new find. Tano's information was that he had sold a Greek collector forty tablets, that the Cairo Museum had succeeded in getting possession of twenty, and that Mohammed Mohassib had about fifty. Wilbour came to the conclusion then, and repeated it five months later, that Tano had planted these tablets at Tell el-Amarna: "He has for years been buying such tablets from Baghdad. He made the most fuss about them and his ways are devious." Wilbour learned from Grébaut that he proposed to confiscate Mohammed Mohassib's fifty tablets and pay him $200 for them; rumor said that Mohassib had already refused $600. As we have seen, the tablets slipped out of Grébaut's grasp. He was able to send Mohassib and another dealer to Qeneh in chains, but formal charges were difficult, and they did not stay under arrest very long.

Now we go to the testimony of Rev. A. H. Sayce, a scholar working in cuneiform, who did not happen to spend the winter of 1887–88 in Egypt, as he usually did. "The whole collection of tablets would have passed into my hands intact; as it was there was no one in Egypt who was acquainted with cuneiform, and the antika-dealers regarded the tablets as so many worthless bricks." As it happened, Sayce did not come off so well. He received copies of tablets from Bouriant in Cairo, pronounced them genuine, but dated them eight hundred years too late. When Wilbour was on his way home in May, he learned in Italy that a Cairo dealer had sold a hundred and sixty of the tablets to the Berlin Museum, where they had been read and dated to the reigns of Amenhotep III and Akh-en-Aton.

The Tell el-Amarna Tablets, carrying international correspondence of the fourteenth century B.C., form a body of material of supreme importance. It is tragic that so many of them were destroyed before they reached a good market and that they are now so widely scattered— Cairo, Berlin, Paris, and London, with lesser numbers of fragments in Oxford, Brussels, New York, Chicago, and in private hands.

When Sayce returned to Egypt the following winter, he found that Grébaut had seized every tablet he could find, without compensation. In revenge, the Egyptians living near Tell el-Amarna began wrecking monuments, including famous tombs at el-Bersheh and Beni Hassan. It was this vandalism which provided Rev. Chauncey Murch in Luxor with some of his pieces.

BUDGE BRINGS HOME TREASURES

Budge wrote with bland satisfaction about the clever way in which he slipped the Amarna Tablets, the Papyrus of Ani, and other pieces out of Luxor under the nose of the Director-general of Antiquities and then out of Egypt. In an earlier chapter we saw how the zodiac in the temple of Dendereh had been "preserved" by being carried off to Europe. Was the rescue of antiquities by taking them out of Egypt preservation or smuggling? How widespread was it? I cannot answer the second question, although I am sure it must have been a common practice in those days when the Egyptian Service of Antiquities was so poorly paid and poorly staffed and when European visitors felt assured that their culture was safer and more appreciative of works of art and antiquity. It is only Budge who has given us any detail on the methods of taking pieces out against local law.

Wallis Budge might have posed for a portrait of John Bull. Indeed, rumor said that he was related to the highest British families. He had a sturdy and portly frame, and his round face carried just the raising of the eyebrows which denotes a haughty and independent character. He always went his own way, which fortunately coincided with the desires of the Trustees of the British Museum. He was, in trying circumstances, a vigorously successful agent in procuring Egyptian and Mesopotamian antiquities. His publication of texts was astonishingly abundant, not all good. An admirer said: "He was in too great a hurry to finish. Definite in all his ways, he grudged the time spent in 'rounding off the corners,' and this impatience was frequently to stand in his way." Both the manner in which he tossed off defective publications and the blandness with which he carried off antiquities under hostile eyes earned him many enemies. Another admirer wrote of him: "Probably no Egyptologist of his stature—which none could deny him—enjoyed a worse reputation among his colleagues than did Budge at the height of his power and productivity." Then, recognizing the wide use of Budge's textbooks, the same British critic said: "I think that it is beyond question that Wallis Budge did more than any other man to rouse in the ordinary reader of this country an interest in the language and writings of ancient Egypt." A similar statement might be made about American readers. The poet Vachel Lindsay once told me that he knew the Book of the Dead better than I could ever know it. It turned out that Lindsay, on his poetry-reading trips around the United States, used to carry with him Budge's 1901 translation, in the belief that it was an exact rendering of the ancient Egyptian.

We have already seen how he whisked the Amarna Tablets and the Papyrus of Ani out of Egypt. In the same year he was in Baghdad and found himself under restrictive surveillance by the Turkish police. There was no hotel in Baghdad in 1888, so Budge accepted the invitation of the captain of the British gunboat "Comet" to reside on board that vessel, anchored in the Tigris River. Under the nose of the customs boat, his antiquities were loaded onto the "Comet" and were thus officially on British territory, so they might start their journey to England.

A most successful exploit in 1896 was the acquisition of a valuable Greek manuscript in Egypt. A man came from Meir in Middle Egypt to Cairo and showed Budge a roll of papyrus written in a particular type of Greek script called "uncials." Budge was unable to identify the text, but he copied off a few lines to send back to London and paid a deposit on the papyrus. He then departed for Upper Egypt. The owner of the papyrus showed it around Cairo, and an Englishman copied off a single line. When Sayce's boat moored off Cairo, he saw this line and from one word in it recognized that it must be the Odes of Bacchylides, a lyric poet of the fifth century B.C. whose works were unknown except in quotation. Sayce tried to acquire the papyrus for the Bodleian Library at Oxford. When Budge returned to Cairo, he found that he had active competition and that the Service of Antiquities had learned of his interest and intended to seize the manuscript. Cromer himself was obliged to warn Budge not to acquire the papyrus. Yet the Librarian of the British Museum had written him, instructing him to secure the manuscript, which was of great importance.

> To avoid all complications and the possible loss of the papyrus, I determined to buy it for myself. . . . The Trustees' regulations do not permit any of their servants to make a private collection of antiquities with which his department deals, but as Greek papyri went to the Department of Manuscripts, and not to the Department of Egyptian and Assyrian Antiquities, I broke no official rule in buying the manuscript for myself.

Thereupon the Service of Antiquities instructed the Egyptian customs authorities to take possession of the papyrus when Budge left the country.

> As it was hopeless to attempt to send the papyrus out of Egypt packed in a box, I cut it up into sections and laid them between layers of photographs, bought for the purpose, and paper, and packed all between two thin deal boards, about 20 inches long and 12 inches wide, and these I tied up in the gaudy coloured paper which the Cairo shopkeepers used for wrapping up the purchases of customers.

Budge then gave instructions to a trusted helper named Ahmad, who bought tickets from Cairo to Suez and a crate of two hundred tangerine oranges. Budge and Ahmad took the train at Cairo, and their luggage was searched by government officials, who neglected to examine Budge's ulster and the papyrus wrapped in boards, which he was carrying by hand. At Ismailiyeh, where the line branched to Port Said or to Suez, Budge first boarded the cars for Port Said. At the last minute he told the porter on the car that he wanted to buy some food, purchased some eggs, dates, and cakes, and boarded the fourth-class coach on the train to Suez, where he sat on the floor and invited the other passengers to share his meal. The station guards were running up and down the platform, looking for him, but they never thought to look in fourth-class. About dark the train reached Suez, and Ahmad joined him. They went into the customs house, Budge carrying the crate of oranges, and Ahmad the ulster and the papyrus.

> When I reached the door of the office the officials looked at the crate of oranges, and two of them tried to snatch it away from me to carry it to the counter in the office, where parcels were unpacked for examination. I held on to the crate and protested loudly, but they tugged and pulled, and I did the same, and the mob on the platform crowded

into the office, and took sides, and some of them encouraged the officials and some encouraged me. Among those who crowded into the office was Ahmad, who, when the noise and confusion over the oranges was at its height, took the opportunity of slipping through the other door into the street, carrying the papyrus wrapped up in the ulster with him. I had given him the name and address of an official who was a good friend of mine, and he took the papyrus to his house and told him what was happening, whilst the octroi officials and myself were still quarrelling over the oranges. At length the crate was opened and the oranges turned out and counted, and the officials called upon me to pay 15 piastres (3 s.) octroi, but I refused. . . . I resisted until I saw Ahmad coming towards the office, and then I paid.

His friend explained that Budge was a warm-hearted person who had bought the oranges for the sick in a little hospital run by French sisters in Suez, and there were bows and apologies on both sides. "Thus I got my papyrus into safe keeping, the Sisters got the oranges, the clerks got the 15 piastres, and my friend much amusement over the incident, and so everybody was pleased."

The next day his friend helped him board a P. & O. steamer by private launch, thus avoiding further contact with customs officials. Two weeks later he turned the papyrus over to the British Museum and was repaid for his personal outlay of money.

> The papyrus contained nearly forty columns of the text of the Odes of Bacchylides, a great lyric poet who flourished in the first half of the fifth century B.C., and the experts thought that it was written about the middle of the first century B.C. Sir Richard Jebb told me that he thought it was worth more than all the other things I had acquired for the Museum put together!

When Budge returned from Baghdad in 1888 with tablets and the British public learned of his methods, there was an outcry from the "archaeological Pecksniffs," who felt that he had disgraced the country and should resign.

> But I had a perfectly clear conscience about this bit of smuggling, and besides this, I felt that I had only done what anyone would have done who had the welfare of Babylonian and Assyrian Archaeology and his employers' interests at heart. . . . I saw for myself and was firmly convinced that more than nine-tenths of the tablets came from the sites which the Trustees had spent some thousands of pounds in excavating. . . . Had the supervision of the sites been better, and had the proper precautions been taken, these tablets would have left Baghdâd five or six years before. . . . In buying these tablets and smuggling

them out of Turkey in Asia, I felt that I was merely recovering for my employers, the Trustees, property which had been stolen from them. . . .

If the Turkish authorities could not enforce their own laws and take possession of the tablets, and make the Ministry of Instruction send them to their own museum in Constantinople, I could not see that it was my business to help them. I had to decide whether the tablets should go to Berlin, or France, or America, or to the British Museum. . . . It was exactly the same in Egypt, although the Trustees had no claim at all on the Tall al-ʿAmârnah Tablets. Had I not come to a decision at once, and taken the eighty-two tablets when I had the chance of getting them, they would certainly have gone to the Berlin Museum, or into the possession of some private collector, or anywhere except to the Government Museum of Egyptian Antiquities, Cairo. When the Directors of Museums in the East make it worth the while of natives to bring their "finds" to them, nothing of importance will find its way to Europe or America.

Nearly a century had passed between the pious words justifying the rape of the Denderah zodiac and the writing of these sanctimonius words, yet the claim of a higher law is still the same. Would we write today an apology for the higher claim of the West? It is unfortunate that the exploits of Budge and others were so widely known that it was assumed that many archeologists engaged in such practices, and this assumption tightened nationalistic control against Western "exploitation." Even law-abiding Westerners were tarred with Budge's brush.

PETRIE PLAYS THE ROLE OF MOSES

In 1886 Charles E. Wilbour was already an inveterate visitor to Egypt. That winter he landed in Alexandria, and a British judge urged that he stop off in the western Delta and see the work of a young British excavator, Flinders Petrie, "But it rained in the night and when I passed the nearest station, Tell el Barood, in the morning, the roads looked greasy and discouraging. So instead of donkeying six miles . . . I came straight to Cairo." Thus the patrician reacted to the work of the grubber. Yet Petrie was destined to change not only Egyptology but excavation everywhere by his insistence that every artifact which is dug up must be considered as evidence and that archeology is conditioned by the "unconsidered trifles" and not solely by gold, coins, inscriptions, and works of art.

Wilbour's published letters contain a spare half-dozen references to Petrie, not all of them disapproving. The most extensive statement is based on a visit to his camp at Meidum.

He has a cot bed in the tomb of Nefer-maat, whither he retires at dusk to write and read, for he has a few miscellaneous books, "a pinch of books," he said, and two tents, one a kitchen with a petroleum stove. He lives mainly on London food, sent out to him from Civil Services Stores in boxes, each holding three weeks' rations, does his own cooking, lives with Arabs only and pays the men who dig for him by the cubic metre, they trusting to his fairness both for the measurement and the rate. My Quakerish patient to whom I introduced him in Cairo said that he had the eyes of an animal. . . . [The ladies on my boat] call them eagle's eyes.

Others found Petrie's Spartan life extreme. "He ignored physical comforts for himself and, therefore, neglected to provide the ordinary amenites for his staff." His table for working and eating "stood in the dining room, lighted by a few very small apertures in the wall just below the ceiling. In a trough down the center of the table stood a double row of tins containing various kinds of food, and near by a can opener. His idea of satisfying the pangs of hunger, when they became intense, was to eat from several tins at random until they were empty. He took for granted that his staff would do the same, and this in a hot climate! Prior to their marriage, Annie and Edward Quibell, as fellow members of one of Petrie's expeditions, became engaged while nursing each other through ptomaine poisoning." Thus wrote an American observer about the Petrie camp. An Englishman who had spent several seasons working with Petrie recalled that under this regime, "One lives in a bare little hut constructed of mud, and roofed with cornstalks or corrugated iron; and if by chance there happens to be a rain storm . . . one may watch the frail building gently subside in a liquid stream upon one's bed and books."

An American woman wrote in the 1890's: "He must have lost many of the niceties of feeling by so continuously 'roughing it.' I was sitting talking to him, when off came his shoe, right before me, while he shook out the stones. He wore no stockings and his dusty foot was exposed."

Yet this man did have the look of eagles in his eyes. Rather, with his patriarchal beard, his high brow, and his searching eyes, he looked like Michelangelo's "Moses." His feet were dusty because his work was in dusty places. Ultimately the patricians on their private dahabiyehs, with elegant cuisines and baths and proper beds, faded from the scene, and Petrie and his disciples took over. Those disciples might still shudder at the memory of his rigorous camp, with its flies and questionable food, but they could never lose a reverence for the strict methodology which they learned under him. The parsimony with which he lived in order to save every penny for the dig, the inexpensive gadgets with which he produced excellent results, and his indifference to any conclusions other than his own produced an irreverent oral saga about him which does scant justice to the tremendous volume of his achievements.

Petrie had been a solitary child, making his own collections of stones and coins as a boy does, but studying them. In 1880, at the age of twenty-seven, he was encouraged by his father to visit Egypt, and by measuring the Great Pyramid, support the remarkable notions of Piazzi Smyth about the construction of that monument. The young man had already written a book on the science of measurement. At Gizeh Petrie completely discarded Smyth's fancies and made painstakingly accurate measures of the pyramid with instruments which we today should consider inadequate. He was always a distinct individual, and his devotion to step-by-step methodology was exceptional in an age that looked for the showy and sensational.

As Mariette had done before him, he moved on to a new site nearly every year, but Petrie's choice for a dig was not based on the need to produce impressive monuments which would please a ruler. He picked a place with promise of information. In forty-five years of excavation in Egypt, he skimmed the cream of the best locations. No one has ever provided a similar year-by-year progress. Further, he insisted on prompt annual publications of his results so that they might be immediately available to the scholarly world.

From the beginning, he was shocked at the pillage which passed for excavation. He saw how archeology destroys forever the meaningful context of materials. Egypt had so great a wealth of monuments that the first excavators could be very prodigal of what they found: they cheerfully ignored stone or mud walls, undecorated or broken pottery, wooden timbers, uninscribed weights, tools, and weapons. Petrie made these "unconsidered trifles" important. As only Rhind had done before him, he recorded groupings of materials and associations. Although Egyptian archeology does not normally provide stratification of cultural levels, with older material lying under more recent, he recognized that possibility, and in a brief visit to Palestine in 1890, laid down the essentials of attacking a stratified mound.

One of the prize locations in Egypt was Abydos, a center of the Osiris cult and a place of ancient pilgrimage. The cemeteries of Abydos had a range of thousands of years. A French *abbé* in 1894 received the concession to excavate the cemetery of the earliest kings of Egypt at Abydos. Since he was looking for decorated or inscribed pieces, he scorned the run-of-the-mill drab or broken objects. In fact, he not only discarded the bulk of what he found, but he directed his rais to break it to pieces so that it would not excite the desire of the locals or of other archeologists. Petrie wanted Abydos, but he was denied a concession there as long as Abbé Amèlineau held the fort. Then at last he was told that the place was exhausted; but he persisted, and finally in 1900 he was permitted to investigate the cemetery. Not only did he map and record and photograph what had previously been studied in a superficial way; he picked up the broken materials discarded by Amèlineau, published them, and made sense of them. For nearly thirty years thereafter our chief knowledge of the material culture of the first two dynasties came from Petrie's work at Abydos.

In 1898, working in Upper Egypt, Petrie excavated graves having material of a strange and primitive nature. At first he argued that these artifacts had been left by a "new race," outsiders who had intruded into the Nile Valley in historic times. This idea was opposed by a Frenchman, de Morgan, who insisted that the material was prehistoric. This was a French flash of insight, for little was known about predynastic material at that time. Characteristically, Petrie had to satisfy himself and work out the relation of these objects to dynastic materials. Since the pieces came from an age before writing, there were no inscriptions to form the basis of dating. What index do you then use for finding your sequence of materials?

To simplify the method, imagine a very long table. On the floor beside the table lie the groupings of excavated objects as they were found: these pots go with these beads, this ivory comb, these arrowheads, and this macehead. In broad general terms, the materials were all pots, tools, weapons, jewelry, and toilet articles, but each grouping of associated objects was different from every other assemblage. Some had beautifully made pottery but were scanty in other objects and had no metal at all. Others consisted of a larger number of pieces, with an appreciable amount of copper, while the pottery was large and coarse. These latter groups had strong affinities with the materials which were being found at the tombs of the first two dynasties. Very well, they might be the latest, since they tied in with historic times. They may be put at the near end of the table. What about the assemblages with no metal and fine pottery?

There was one class of pottery which was present in some quantity and which came down to the beginning of history. In the relatively simple assemblages this was carefully made and was functional. It was a gritty buff ware, with a rounded body and high shoulder, and its chief characteristic was a wavy ledge handle just below the shoulder. This must have been a jar for storing heavy stuff, such as oil, and the wavy handle was to accommodate four fingers to lift the weight. In other examples the handle had lost the precision of its wave, and the jar was less rounded out. Finally, in the assemblages which came into historic times, the wave had become a mere decorative scroll; the pot was not so well made and had become a cylindrical jar, sometimes even a little concave in profile.

Thus it was possible to put the truly functional wavy-handled jars well down toward the middle of the table and to fill in with the progressive degeneration of form and function, down to the vestigial types at the near end of the table. Here was a sequence which was convincing.

Then, made of the same gritty buff ware, there were certain pots which overlapped with the earlier wavy-handled jars but never came down into historic times. They had a decoration painted in red on a well-rounded surface. Here again there proved to be a degeneration of ware, form, and decoration from the excellence of material at the far end of the table to merely traditional forms in the middle.

Finally, in the three chief categories, there was a very different pottery, a dark, clean ware which fired into a beautiful red, sometimes highly polished, sometimes with a black mouth. This overlapped with the ware having a painted red decoration, but not with the wavy-handled jars. It came in rather simple assemblages, rarely with any metal present. It should be the earliest, to be placed at the extreme far end of the table, away from the end which tied into the dynasties. Thus we have polished red ware the oldest, decorated buff pots next, and the wavy-handled jars the most recent.

Not only the pottery but also ivories and figurines, slate palettes, combs, stone vessels, tools, and weapons could be lined up in this sequential way. Petrie arbitrarily assigned fifty numbers to the sequence of progressing materials. He left thirty numbers open for future discovery and called his earliest material Sequence Date 31 and his latest Sequence Date 80. To be sure, "Date" does not mean "date" in chronological years, and when we say that certain prehistoric materials fall into the range of S.D. 63–68, we have no idea of the date B.C. The Sequence Date system has been freely criticized and, in at least one respect, radically modified. Yet it is still a critical analysis which speaks of genius, a genius with a patriarchal beard and the eyes of eagles.

In the early 1890's Petrie excavated at Coptos, or Quft, in Upper Egypt and started a service which is still a chief reliance of archeologists. The men of Quft could learn and carry on what they had learned. He gave them special training, and the next season he summoned them elsewhere to be his foremen. From that time on Quftis have been the Egyptian trained and experienced diggers. Now in their fourth generation, they are the excavator's right hand.

Petrie was always confident of his own revelation of the truth and contemptuous of the analytical methods of others, particularly of the Berlin group of Egyptologists. Some of his books contain a chronological table along these lines:

APPROXIMATE DATES

Dynasty	By Egyptians	By Berlin
I Mena	5500 B.C.	3400 B.C.
IV Khufu	4700 B.C.	2900 B.C.
XII Amenemhat I	3500 B.C.	2000 B.C.
XVIII Tehutmes III	1500 B.C.	1500 B.C.

Needless to say, Petrie identified himself in this analysis with the Egyptians, or, should we say, the Egyptians with himself.

The American archeologist, Herbert Winlock, wrote a penetrating portrait of Petrie. "He was entirely self-taught in everything, including his knowledge of Arabic, and with his Arabic he was not always correct." Early in his career, he confused the two words "push" and "pull" and thereafter, "every young Egyptian was told never to forget to 'pull' when the Khawagah yelled to 'push.'" When he first went to Egypt,

> Mariette, director of the Service des Antiquités, and Emil Brugsch, keeper of the Cairo Museum, were his particular hates at this time. Maspero, who came out to succeed Mariette in 1881, he seems to have barely tolerated. For Amelia Edwards of the Egypt Exploration Fund, Edouard Naville, its excavator, and the officials of the British Museum, he had anathemas of various strengths. The Arabs who worked for him he seems to have thought of as one might of rather pleasant but hardly trustworthy children. . . . His great complaint seems to have been that no one could tell him more than his own natural gifts already made clear. . . . No one ever questioned Petrie's cleverness. He was in many ways the most remarkable genius it could ever be any one's fortune to meet. . . . He took an old camera, put a bit of rubber hose in the front-board with a good-sized lens in it, and had a wire fixed so that he could hold the lens wherever he wanted it and, as he needed, crooked or not in regard to the plate

and he took superb pictures with it. Winlock records the ultimate tragedy of Petrie, that he burst like a great light on the scene but then never changed his methods or attitudes. Other men were to take up Petrie's attitudes and improve his methods—particularly the American, Reisner.

The catalog of those who worked under Petrie is long and honorable—

Griffith, Newberry, Howard Carter, Quibell, Mace, Davies, Engelbach, and Brunton—to mention only a few of them; and while they character-istically rebelled against unsanitary living conditions and poor food, their scientific careers were shaped by him. He made Egyptology a science instead of a pastime. The "unconsidered trifles" of excavation, particularly pottery, became controlling tools. Whether one had been trained by Petrie or not, his influence shaped all responsible excavation in the Nile Valley down to the present day.

6 THE HOUSEBOAT ON THE NILE
(1880–1908)

There was great excitement at the river port of el-Baliana when the two great sailing dahabiyehs, the "Istar" and the "Seven Hathors," came to a mooring. The Reverend Mr. Sayce and Mr. Wilbour were back for a look at Abydos and el-Mashâikh. The antiquity dealers would check over their available wares and rehearse their stories of government injustices. The guard at the temple of Seti I at Abydos would explain carefully what had happened to the £30 allotted to him to put a protective wall around the monument—an intermediary agent had absorbed it before it could be applied to the work. The Cook's tourists, a chattering party which arrived in the morning and left in the afternoon, could be taken in stride by the people of el-Baliana, but Mr. Sayce and Mr. Wilbour were *khawagat*, gentlemen, who came twice a year and whose friendly interest was worth cultivating.

Rev. Archibald H. Sayce had become an institution in Egypt. A British bachelor and Oxford professor, he had the means to gratify his purposes in life, which were winters in Egypt on his own boat, with his own library, in the company of relaxed scholars and friends. His health was never robust; yet he was always able to scramble up hillsides and down into newly found tombs. He even survived the bite of a horned viper and went on working within a few weeks. His spare frame, sunken eyes, little goatee, and steel-rimmed spectacles looked even further out of place when he was visiting a dusty dig, because he wore a long-tailed ecclesiastical black coat, a reversed high collar, and a flat black hat. He was most hospitable to scholars of every country and to casual visitors and had an endless fund of stories for tourists and children.

He could be caustic on occasion, as he was about Chicago in 1916 when, at the age of seventy-one, he visited that city.

> At Chicago my nephew met me and put me up at the University Club. Chicago is the ugliest and noisiest city I have ever seen, and my

> first experience in it impressed me with a sense of its size. . . . In spite
> of Chicago and its climate the University flourishes, and forms an oasis
> of intellectual and artistic tranquillity in the midst of noise and mechan-
> ical ugliness. Naturally I saw a good deal of the Professors, more espe-
> cially Professor Breasted. . . . Even more incongruous with its setting
> is the Newberry Library [with its fine collections of early books and
> incunabula]. It was the last institution I should have expected to see
> in "Porcopolis."

This prissy but kindly man had been a great scholar. He had been a
pioneer in some of the lesser-known cuneiform writings, and his great
delight was the reading of a new text or the decipherment of an unknown
language, as in his forays on Elamite and Vannic. To his work in 1876–79
we owe the recognition that the Hittites of Anatolia had been a powerful
empire in antiquity. Yet he felt no compulsion to follow up his flights of
bold insight and would drop a study after a few magisterial generalizations. A kindly critic said of him: "His width of knowledge and interests
was amazing, and he had little liking for the laboriousness of a specialist.
. . . His attitude to life was that of a fastidious ascetic, almost one might
say of an austere sybarite. . . . He was impatient of the claims, the pride,
and the reticence of exact scholarship. He himself was quite accustomed to
making mistakes." Around his head raged a controversy which shook Old
Testament scholars and clergymen, the debate over the Higher Criticism.
He blandly brushed aside the arguments of the "German" theological critics, using that national term as though it were condemnatory in itself, proclaimed himself a "champion of orthodoxy," and then did little to defend
the orthodox view against attack. A distaste for continuous hard work
and for the rough-and-tumble of controversy made him supple enough
to escape hard and fast conclusions.

Sayce first visited Egypt in 1879. His ambition became the ownership
of his own houseboat on the Nile, with a working library and an adequate
cuisine. Ideally, he might travel in the company of a like-minded amateur
scholar, such as Charles Wilbour, and these two sailed together in their
separate dahabiyehs from 1889 to 1896. At first Sayce rented a boat, but
he wanted his own. "In Egypt I enjoyed what I enjoyed nowhere else—
life for life's own sake; there my literary labours were unhampered by
illness or the effort to live, and I had on all sides of me the inspiration
of a cultured past and the means of satisfying to the fullest my archaeological tastes. In those days, moreover, the Nile was as yet untrammelled
by the railway bridge or barrage; the sailing dahabia could go or stop
where it would, and there were still many spots where those who chose
could escape from the European world." So in 1890 he bought one of the

largest sailing dahabiyehs on the river and named it the "Istar," after a Babylonian goddess.

The purchase had its Oriental element. An Egyptian official had built the boat, laying out £1,800 on its construction. This bey was in disgrace, however, because he had been implicated in the Arabi revolt of 1882. Sayce therefore was able to buy the dahabiyeh for £800 and the promise to intercede on behalf of the bey with Cromer. That proved to be easy. Additional work was necessary on the boat to accommodate Sayce's books. "My dahabia was an ideal home for a 'literary man.' My library at the end of the boat contained about two thousand volumes and included all the books I required." So large a vessel required a crew of nineteen, in addition to Sayce's two servants. On the "Istar" he had seventeen idyllic winters.

"THE FATHER OF A BEARD"

The Arabs delight in descriptive names, so Charles E. Wilbour was named by the Egyptians *Abu-Dign*, "the Father of a Beard," as Western children might call someone "Old Whiskers." It was not disrespectful: they honestly admired the patriarchal dignity of a full beard. Wilbour was a fine figure of a man, large, broad-shouldered, with a fine brow, a well-sculptured nose, and that wonderful white bib of a beard reaching down to the second button of his waistcoat. A fellah could have respectful confidence in such a man.

Charles E. Wilbour was described by Maspero as "*le plus aimablement yankee que je connais,*" and Sayce told a British jurist that Wilbour was "the best Egyptologist living." Yet he remains a shadowy figure as a scholar, deliberately seeking the background to give more room to Maspero, Sayce, and others. Some aspects of his career will always lie hidden behind the defenses of that beard and those brooding eyes.

Wilbour was a Rhode Islander and became a New York journalist. Work as a court reporter gave him entree into journalism, and he published a daily legal newspaper in New York and was also associated with Dana and Greeley of the *Tribune*. Suddenly, in the early 1870's, when he was only thirty-eight, he left New York and went to live in France. He shook the dust of New York from his feet. Although, after the first few years, he did make summer trips back to the United States, his career was chiefly that of a self-exile. In 1881 he wrote his family: "I had a bad dream last night of being back in New York." He had acquired sufficient means to satisfy his interests, which were literary. He became a friend of Victor Hugo and translated *Les Misérables*. When he was attracted to the study of Egyptology, he studied with Maspero in Paris and with Eisenlohr in Heidelberg. He was a patrician expatriate.

Newspaper records give the reason why Charles E. Wilbour accepted complete exile from 1874 to 1881 and never again resided the full year in America. Shortly after the Civil War, William Marcy Tweed—Boss Tweed—established his corrupt and lucrative plundering of New York City. The Tweed Ring needed a complacent press, took over the *New York Transcript*, and brought Wilbour over from the *Tribune* to manage it. Even more profitable was Wilbour's presidency of the New York Printing Company, to which the Tweed Ring steered the city's printing work. He was able to start his European exile as a wealthy man. His ability to return to the States after seven years and his friendly relations with American consuls abroad show that he had not been an inner member of the Tweed Ring. Yet he must have served their purposes, since he abruptly left New York and stayed abroad until the initial fury had died down.

In 1880 he made the first of his annual visits to Egypt. To begin with, he traveled the Nile in the company of others, for example, enjoying the hospitality of Maspero on a government boat. In the fall of 1886 he bought his own sailing dahabiyeh for £650. He named her the "Seven Hathors," after ancient Egyptian goddesses of fortune. "It lends itself to hieroglyphic decoration and Egyptians will call her 'Seven,' *Seba*. We find the Seven Hathors on most of the more perfect temples. When the Doomed Prince was born, the Seven Hathors came to make him a destiny. In the sky they are the Pleiades." He put on board his library and $400 worth of provisions. Sometimes he was accompanied by the ladies of his family and his son-in-law, the successful American artist, Edwin H. Blashfield. This was the life Wilbour wanted.

Wilbour had a willing agent to help him on the oversight of repairs on the boat, provisioning, and so on. *Abu-Dign* was helped by Insinger, called *Abu-Shenab*, "the Father of a Moustache," in honor of his prominent facial adornment. Insinger was a Hollander whom tuberculosis had sent to a warm and dry climate. His health was never good, and his purse was as thin as he was. He eked out a living by taking photographs for Maspero, dealing in antiquities, lending money, and doing errands for people like Wilbour. His meager life was summarized by Wilbour in 1888: "Insinger's health was poor; I think that he suffered more than I have ever seen him before. He has begun his house at Luxor, hoping to finish three rooms so that he could sleep in it cold nights next winter; this winter there were few. He would be willing that M. Mohassib should use it as an antiquarian shop, inviolable under the Dutch flag." That was about the time that Mohammed Mohassib was having his troubles with Grébaut over the Amarna Tablets, and he and Insinger must have been seeking mutual advantage.

There is a curious combination of detachment and involvement in Wilbour. Despite his exile, he subscribed to American newspapers and gloried in every victory of the Republican party. In Cairo he sought out American visitors for talk, and when word came that an Egypt Exploration Fund would be instituted in England, he went with the American Consul to talk with Maspero. After that conference, Wilbour said, the Consul "is going to try to get the Smithsonian Institution—he is a Washington man—to make a similar appropriation for diggings. So that America may not be behind England." Nothing came of this patriotic initiative, since Miss Edwards persuaded the Americans to support the work of the EEF.

His fellow countrymen sometimes amused him, like the American who wanted to do Egypt in a week: "He cannot hope to rival the young American who asked Mr. Faber if he thought he could do Cairo in a day." He could still be a New England provincial, when he wrote of a young woman on a visiting dahabiyeh: "She is a sweet woman if she does come from Chicago." Chiefly his friendly but reserved soul came out to meet the fellahin whom he saw year after year. When he returned to Luxor one year, he noted that he did not see the old woman Bemba; that Libiad had become a barber, with different prices for Egyptians and tourists; that little Yussuf still cracked his knuckles; and that Ali Murad's son Ahmed had sent back his last summer's bride and gone into the antiquities trade. A few years later he wrote sadly: "My old friend Aboo Gamb, who had taken me into scores of tombs and who always saved for me the things he thought unique, walking to Keneh with some anteekeh and some guineas was waylaid three months ago and his body found in the river near Dishneh. He lived near old Kamoory, also gone. Even here my friends are going." Yet this kindly interest was still reserved, as it would be in his day, and there was a disapproving withdrawal when he saw Insinger's "little folks yesterday playing with their Rais Ahmed's five-year-old boy just as if he was not a nigger."

When the fellahin established that Wilbour was *Amerikani* and not *Inglizi*, they would sometimes open up to him with their grievances against British control. At the time of the Mahdist uprising, he records their satisfaction at the defeats of the British-Egyptian forces by the Dervishes: "The people were glad that Baker was beaten, though their own friends were killed. . . . They would welcome the Mahdi, though they would fight for nobody." One day Abd er-Rasul Ahmed, he who was tortured in the inquisition at Qeneh, took him to copy tombs at Thebes.

> In one of them where there was no danger of being overheard, he told me that the Mahdi was really coming and a man from him had come to Gurnah and told him that it would make no difference what soldiers were opposed to him because he did not fight as men do. His army was all dervishes, a million and a half, already. And his sword is not of steel but of wood, and he himself does nothing but say *Allah, Allah,* day and night and he uses no cannon as men do, nor any powder, but in the battle he takes dust up in his fingers, so (and Abd er-Rasul took up some dust and blew it smartly away) and they are all dead. And as he said this and did this his eyes flashed so that I felt he believed it.

This American was learning a very different side of the British occupation of Egypt from that heard by the English or by the American visitors in the hotel. Sayce could write that in 1885–86 British firmness in Egypt was all to the good: "The Egyptians accepted the situation with Oriental placidity; we had not yet taught their school-boys to go on strike, or encouraged newspaper writers and hungry beys and pashas to stir up the passions of a Mohammedan mob." Years later Sayce could look back and state that the Egyptians had known and liked the officers and men of the British army in Egypt. An American could write of the Cromer era that the fellahin would add to their swearing upon the Koran the words *kalam Inglizi,* "the word of an Englishman." Wilbour heard differently. "Mustafa Agha's son, although his position entailed all politeness and attention to English travellers . . . really hates the English."

> I forgot to tell you a good story which Dr. Lansing told us at Keneh. He overheard a man abusing his boy roundly and instead of calling him as usual *ibn el kelb,* son of a dog, or *ibn esh shaytan,* son of Satan, or *ibn el Khanzeer,* son of a hog, he called him *ibn el Ingheleez,* son of an Englishman. The glee with which all the people, even those in office, recount the victories of the Mahdi . . . indicate(s) which side their sympathies are on even against their own soldiers. How, said the Mudeer of Keneh to Maspero, can I work with any heart? An Englishman may come tomorrow to take my place.

Wilbour's donkey boy at Luxor "explained to me how the fallaheen hate the English who came and beat them and were taking all their money away, and I relieved his mind somewhat by telling him how we had beaten them in two wars so that they dared not fight us." This is the only time that Wilbour encouraged the anti-British feeling; for the most part he was a passive reporter on what he saw and heard.

He loved the land of Egypt. From a high hill at Gebel Abu Foda, he wrote: "The view was magnificent over the island, the west branch, the railway, the Ibraheemeeyeh Canal and the boats sailing on it, the broad miles of green to the desert with the *deyrs* and the western mountain horizon." Then at Luxor:

> Aly Moorad came to see us and I returned his visit and saw the sunset from his balcony, you do not know how much that means, but when you have seen it, you will never forget it. It is the river and the mountain of Bridgman's picture glowing with the transforming glory of the Sacred Sunset, over the grand tombs of the Mighty Dead. More than a million times has this transforming miracle been wrought and of the millions of times it has yet to be before the sun fires shall fail and our system cease to be habitable I hope that you may enjoy not a few.

"The Best Egyptologist Living"

Wilbour's friend Sayce called him "the best Egyptologist living," and when someone asked about Maspero, Sayce responded, "Maspero was less inclusive." Heinrich Brugsch praised him as "a man of scholarship in the best sense of the word." Maspero turned out over two hundred books and articles on every phase of ancient Egyptian life; Brugsch's publications must number about one hundred and fifty. Only one article, about a page in length, appears over Wilbour's name, and the publication of that was inadvertent. For the benefit of other scholars, he lithographed his discovery of an important text at the First Cataract. Maspero thought it worthy of a larger reading public and published this little note, "Canalizing the Cataract," in the *Recueil des Travaux* in 1890. We shall see how Wilbour was puzzled by the eagerness of the employed scholars to publish, publish, publish. He went to the other extreme. He never published.

He enjoyed visiting excavations and taking notes; he collected some very fine antiquities; he liked to make sketch plans of tombs and temples; but his great passion was to copy inscriptions. He wrote frequently, with satisfaction, of "correcting" the published copy of Champollion or Lepsius by collating a text on the spot. His cup was full when he had the chance to read and copy a text which no other modern had seen. "It is a great pleasure to be the first after twenty-five hundred years to read what has been a sealed book so long. I go to study it tomorrow." At Cairo, "I made no effort to go to the Khédive's reception last night; why should I seek his acquaintance? He has no papyrus." When the boat was tied up at the temple of Kom Ombo, he copied until dark, but there was still one text he wanted to finish. The other Egyptologists were busy with chess and books. The servants were in terror of the ghost that haunted the temple, but he finally persuaded two of them to accompany him. "And so with fear and trembling, a lantern and a chair, they went to the temple. It was much better than the cigars in the salon; the air was soft and warm, and I did not need my old cloak which I had carried." And so he copied on and on in happiness.

Wilbour's fame among Egyptologists rests chiefly upon his discovery of the Famine Stela on the island of Siheil in the First Cataract. In February, 1889, he was checking some of the hundreds of stelas and graffiti carved on that island. "The best inscription I found was of thirty-two long lines, and very hard to make out, of a King Kharser, whose name I have never before seen." A year later he went back for three days to check his copies, and his comment accurately spots a prime difficulty in the stela: "The unknown King of my stele bothers us greatly. The character of the inscription puts it in Ptolemaic or Roman times and how a King not a Ptolemy or an Emperor could have reached the eighteenth year of his reign, passeth understanding." That statement shows Wilbour's high competence in the language and history.

The puzzling factor about the Famine Stela is that it was a pious fraud, carved in the second century B.C., but pretending to be of the twenty-seventh century B.C. It purports to justify the claim of the god Khnum to ownership of a stretch of land in Nubia by relating how, under King Djoser of the Third Dynasty, there were seven years of famine in Egypt, the result of low Niles, and how the god relieved the famine after the King gave him his land. Of course the "seven lean years" greatly excited those who knew their Bible. Wilbour misread the name Djoser as Kharser; otherwise his rendering of the text was admirable. The text was so unusual that malicious gossip in Cairo held that Wilbour must have forged it for fame.

Wilbour circulated his copies of this inscription to the scholars of several countries. The Russian Golenischeff thanked him for the photographs and urged him to publish. Ultimately the text appeared from the pen of Heinrich Brugsch, who was scrupulous to give Wilbour credit for the discovery and for the accuracy of his work.

Wilbour's sometime companion on Nile boats, Édouard Naville, would hardly have thanked him for sending the material to Brugsch. These scholarly feuds puzzled the gentle American. At first he tried to understand them on a scholarly basis. Naville arrived at Luxor and immediately went to copy a text. "Brugsch has lately given on it a translation which of course differs widely from Naville's. Naville wants to get some help from the next text so that he may in turn find fault with Brugsch and this is the way translations grow better." A month later he decided that personal emotion was a strong factor: "Naville is happy. He has found a text which, he thinks, will upset one of Brugsch's discoveries. Everybody seems to think this is a great thing to do." After another month, he was still striving to understand the feud, this time as internecine politics: "It is not pure love of gossip in Naville which leads him to seek something against Brugsch; the Egyptian magnates in Berlin like it and he wishes to find favor with them."

Wilbour's scholarly associates were frequently French, and he was sometimes affected by their prejudices, as when he wrote: "Erman of the Berlin Museum finds the Cataract Canal inscriptions I sent him, equal in interest even to the Famine Stele; he wants me to alter them a little to suit his grammar." This is like the gleeful sarcasm of Maspero, when a German scholar applied for permission to open a pyramid and to check inscriptions which Maspero himself had copied. When this collation showed Maspero's copies to have been accurate, he chuckled and said: "Of course the ancient Egyptians did not have the benefit of using M. Erman's Grammar."

Yet Wilbour was not above enjoying a victory over the great Maspero. At el-Mashâikh the party found a seated statue of the lioness-headed goddess Sekhmet. Since it was like those found at Karnak, "I said Ramses brought it thence to ornament his temple and it is of Amenophis III. No, said Maspero, it is the lion-headed Menheet of this eighth Nome. Khaleel cleared away the dust beside her knees and Maspero lowered himself into the hole, large enough for only one. He lighted a match and was silent. Then I knew that it was not Menheet. It was indeed a Sekhmet and of Amenophis III."

Wherever Wilbour went, they came to him with antiquities, and he sent out his trusted servant Said to scout for more. He purchased carefully and would not pay high prices. Today we read with envy about his acquisitions. A delicate stone plaque with the heads of Akh-en-Aton and Nefert-iti for a little over a dollar and for thirty cents more two faïence rings, one carrying the name of Akh-en-Aton and the other the name of his son-in-law Smenkh-ka-Re. In 1890 he bought a lovely torso of an Amarna princess, for which "the Louvre would pay any price," but which now graces the Brooklyn Museum. A fair esthetic sense, a knowledge of historical value, and an unwillingness to be taken in conditioned all his purchases. He was taken in once, in 1887, when he bought a perfectly good Nineteenth Dynasty statue to which a modern head had been affixed. But anyone can take a chance on a piece with a long inscription when it can be acquired for only fifteen dollars.

For a dozen years Wilbour enjoyed his meetings with the women on the island of Elephantine near the First Cataract. "I went over to Elephantine, was assailed by a crowd of women and children and soon loaded Saïd with inscribed potsherds. Quite free out of doors, the women were in hysterics when I crossed their thresholds; indeed it seems contrary to Elephantine etiquette to call on the ladies when their lord is away. One offered to show me where they dug fragments of papyrus out of the ground; she said there had been some in a little room. I went and in a little while she and others picked out from the rubbish some small fragments, scarce large enough to tell their language." Two years later Said went "over to see my lady friends of Elephantine, and brought back a few tax receipts and some fragments of papyrus." Ultimately these regular visits were to pay off handsomely.

In January and February, 1893, Wilbour purchased nine papyrus rolls at Elephantine. His notebook has the laconic statement: "All these pap. from Kôm, shown me by 3 separate women at different times." He examined only one of them—brittle papyrus is not easy to unroll—and an envelope carrying a few small fragments has a note in his handwriting: "Is not this authentic Phenician?" Another handwriting, surely that of Sayce, answered the question: "It is Aramaic passing into Palmyrene and Hebrew like the Carpentras text. It should all be carefully copied."

Very strangely, neither of these gentlemen did anything more with the papyri. Seven years later Sayce was to aquire an Aramaic papyrus at Elephantine and to recognize its importance, but apparently he did not remember Wilbour's purchase, for Wilbour left the nine papyri rolled up, tied with their original cords with clay sealings which could be dated to Persian times. They were packed away in biscuit boxes in the bottom of a trunk until 1947, when they came to the Brooklyn Museum by legacy from Wilbour's daughter Theodora. They were records of a Jewish colony on Elephantine in Persian times, documents of extraordinary interest and importance.

Somehow these untouched papyri crystallize our impressions of Charles Wilbour. This gifted man, despite his friendliness to others, despite his generosity in distributing copies of his discoveries, was withdrawn into himself, a collector, not a scholar whose chief desire was to organize knowledge. He was happiest when he was copying a newly discovered text or checking someone else's copy against the original. Hieroglyphic and hieratic were his joy, and the possible presence of Aramaic writers near the Egyptian First Cataract did not excite him enough to follow up by unrolling his purchases. There was tragedy here. The former protégé of Boss Tweed was a man who could not any longer find a full and assured life. His inner fires were banked low; they did not inflame him to generate a heat of scholarship.

Sayce wrote somberly that the winter of 1895–96 "was the last I spent on the Nile in the company of Wilbour, who died the following autumn."

THE "GERMAN SCHOOL" AND THE "FRENCH SCHOOL"

Certainly the scholars who did generate heat generated friction also, to the puzzlement of such detached observers as Wilbour. It is an oversimplification of the problem to insist that there was merely a difference in working attitudes between the "German school's" reduction of observations to classified cards, which could then be analyzed and inductively lead to systematized conclusions, and the "French school's" esthetic rationalism, which sought to establish a general pattern from which specific observations could be treated deductively. There was also pride of national traditions, the successors of Champollion against the successors of Lepsius. Even that was complicated by personality factors, since Naville had studied under Lepsius but would have nothing to do with Heinrich Brugsch. Britons like Birch and Renouf were more inclined to "understand" a text as a whole and work out a translation than to parse it out piece by piece and then put the pieces together. It goes even beyond that, since an individual like Petrie could attack the careless excavations of Mariette, Maspero, and Naville of the "French school" and also attack members of the "German school" for sitting at home and analyzing material according to their own armchair methods, instead of coming out to Egypt and accepting what the ancients offered by excavation.

In Berlin Adolf Erman, using the analytical method, was busy with a grammatical revolution, which meant a philological revolution, which meant a historical revolution. In 1880, when he was twenty-six years old, he published a grammar of Late Egyptian, chiefly the hieratic material between 1400 and 700 B.C., and followed this in 1894 with a grammar which presented the older stages of the language. Around the turn of the century his student, Kurt Sethe, came out with a massive study of Egyptian verbs. Now for the first time the would-be translator was caught in a one-way street of grammatical rules based on case studies. The "pseudo-participle" form of the verb should be rendered in such and such ways and no others. Of course there was resistance to this: the free-and-easy attitude that the ancient Egyptians had written no grammars and could therefore be understood by reading individual words instead of syntactical constructions could be surrendered only at the price of hard work. Scholars do not enjoy changing ideas and work habits.

Erman was a gifted soul, and he did not confine himself to grammar. In 1885 he brought out a brilliant book on life in ancient Egypt. The old Wilkinson *Manners and Customs* had taken the classical and biblical accounts of Egypt and added to them a wonderful series of illustrations from Egyptian monuments. Erman had so much Egyptian material that he could treat non-Egyptian accounts as secondary and thus tell his story of ancient life essentially from Egyptian texts and scenes. For a German, he had a writing style which was simple and straightforward. The book had a tremendous influence.

Eduard Meyer, a German historian of encyclopedic competence, began in 1884 to publish his *Geschichte des Alterthums,* a series of five volumes on ancient history, with repeated new editions. Written without the brilliance which characterized Maspero's historical style, Meyer's book was solid, comprehensive, and delivered with a magisterial air. It was German, and it did not please the Francophiles.

Joseph Lindon Smith tells an amusing story about an incident in western Thebes early in the twentieth century.

> That season Professor Sethe of the University of Berlin was among the scholars at the "German" house. . . . He was a small, thin man with a birdlike look accentuated by pinched features. And in great physical contrast to the solemn-faced Sethe was Edouard Naville of Geneva, Switzerland, a large, heavy-set man with an engaging manner and a pleasant smile. Naville was excavating the temple of Deir-el-Bahari for the Egypt Exploration Society. These two men, for some months on end near neighbors in a lonely desert area, were not on speaking terms because of a disagreement between them, carried on in print, concerned with events in the reign of Queen Hatshepsut, the builder of Deir-el-Bahari, and dead almost thirty-five hundred years. . . . The feud was awkward in a small archeological community, when carried to such an extent that Sethe would not remain in the same room with Naville.
>
> During Naville's excavations a great stone was suddenly loosened, and in falling brought down with it a mass of debris . . . causing the undermining of Naville's simple camp house, built near his excavations. In any case, Naville's kitchen collapsed into a tomb pit, with cook, utensils, and stove.
>
> The rumor reached Sethe that Madame Naville was utterly discouraged at this housekeeping calamity, and insisted that her husband's excavations should be discontinued immediately and he return with her to Switzerland, whereupon Sethe invited the Navilles to stay with

him—on condition that Hatshepsut's name was not to be mentioned. The invitation was accepted, and the German and Swiss scholars had a delightful time together exchanging ideas on learned subjects. After several weeks, when the kitchen had been rebuilt, the cook had recovered, and the utensils had been reclaimed or replaced, the Navilles returned to their camp house—and the feud over Hatshepsut was resumed.

Feuds of this kind—perhaps not so intense—were to engage the American Egyptologists when they came upon the scene.

ARCHEOLOGY IN OTHER COUNTRIES

In the generation following 1880, Wilhelm Dörpfeld brought Schliemann's excavation of Troy under control, reassigned the levels in the mound to other cultural periods, and—perhaps regrettably—made that site an archeological reference point instead of a romantic fancy.

Americans entered the scene in two other countries. In southern Mesopotamia an expedition from the University of Pennsylvania worked at the mound of Nippur, a city which proved to be the religious and intellectual capital of Babylonia. The expedition had an ill-fated start in 1887, due to the inexperience of the field director, who relied upon a hated Turkish commissar and resorted to fireworks and magic tricks to try to impress the locals. A later result of this mismanagement was a controversy between Pennsylvania scholars, which shows that feuding is by no means limited to the Egyptologists. The expedition did solid work from 1890 to 1900, however, with splendid results. About thirty thousand cuneiform tablets were found, and well over two thousand of them were Sumerian literary texts. After sixty years scholars are still enjoying this rich harvest.

In Palestine Petrie made a brief visit and laid down a methodology of digging a stratified mound. On this basis an American, Frederic J. Bliss, excavated Tell el-Hesi, about fifteen miles northeast of Gaza. This was the first sober, orderly, and scientific excavation in Palestine, setting a pattern for all future work.

There were storms in the learned societies of Europe and the United States during those years. Darwinism had had its first debates twenty years earlier, but bitterness still lay between the orthodox and the evolutionists. In the period we are considering Herbert Spencer brought out his *Principles of Sociology*, presenting a theoretical framework for the evolutionary development of social communities. Inevitably this played its role in the understanding of ancient civilizations, a role of controversy between those who wanted to understand an old culture as fully formed at birth and thereafter static and those who overeagerly sought to find constant evolutionary process forming and reforming cultures. In the social optimism of the day some liberals confused evolution with progress and happily sought indications of man's continuing betterment.

In biblical circles there arose a violent storm over Higher Criticism. There had been previous attempts to see the Bible as a stratified document of various overlays during Hebrew history, but the faithful cherished it as the revealed word of God, with the first five books of the Old Testament written down by one man, Moses. Then in 1882 Julius Wellhausen published his *Prolegomena*, which was promptly translated into English. Here was an analysis of the first books of the Bible as a composite of several sources coming from different historical times and situations. Again liberalism and orthodoxy engaged in a heated debate, during which each side was driven by its own argument into a more extreme position. The controversies over evolutionary theory and over biblical criticism had much in common and tended to gather the same types into the conservative or the liberal camp. It was a period which changed the face of Oriental scholarship.

Since Egypt was one of the "biblical lands," these wars might have penetrated scholarship there. But Egyptology, without willful purpose, was in the process of divorcing itself from a primary concern with the Bible. We have seen that when the Egypt Exploration Fund was established in 1882, one of its fundamental purposes was to illustrate the Old Testament with evidence from Egypt. Yet by the time that Erman was writing his first book on life in ancient Egypt and Meyer's history was appearing, that culture could be studied in and for itself, with the biblical narrative serving only as a passing familiar illustration. There was so much physical and literary material from ancient Egypt that it could consume the entire attention of the scholar. Further, Egypt had contributed very little in fuller illustration of the biblical narrative: no record of Joseph at Pharaoh's court, no record of Moses, no record of the Children of Israel in bondage in the land of Goshen, no record of a daughter of Pharaoh who married Solomon, and so on. There would always be an interest in any bit of evidence which might illuminate the stories in the Bible, but the expectation that excavation and the study of texts would produce dramatic new confirmation of biblical stories was slowly dying out. Ancient Egypt was now a phenomenon which was to be studied for itself, although the Book of Genesis or the history of Herodotus might be occasionally helpful.

SIGNS AND WONDERS

We may immediately illustrate and qualify what we have just said by a discovery in Egypt in 1895. Flinders Petrie, excavating at Thebes, found a stela of Mer-ne-Ptah, the traditional Pharaoh of the Exodus, upon which the name "Israel" appeared. This is still its only appearance in hieroglyphic, but the proud statement by the King: "Israel is laid waste; his seed is not" raised a storm of excitement. Even today we do not know how literally we can take this claim: did Mer-ne-Ptah actually fight and decimate the Children of Israel, or is this one of those vainglorious boasts which had become an empty tradition with the pharaohs of Egypt? The very question shows how little the passage has helped us in understanding the biblical Sojourn, Exodus, and Wandering.

We have seen that Wilbour purchased Aramaic papyri at Elephantine in 1893 but did not know what he had. The first scholarly recognition of a Jewish colony on that island in Persian times was made by Sayce in 1900.

> While moored at Elephantinê opposite Assuan I obtained from one of the villagers an Aramaic papyrus which he had just found among the *sebakh* or nitrogenous earth of the ancient city on the island. It was the first memorial in the shape of papyrus of the early settlement of the Jews on the island which had come to light, and indirectly led to the discovery a few years later of the long rolls of Aramaic papyri which have thrown such an unexpected illumination on the history of the Jews shortly after the exile, and revealed the existence of a Jewish temple in the extreme south of Egypt.

The really significant finds of these documents were made in the years 1902–6, and their publication gave a fascinating glimpse of a garrison group of Jews, with their families, who served Egypt as frontier soldiers and attempted to live an orthodox Jewish life in this distant exile.

Meanwhile, another wide vista was opening up in Egypt through the discovery of papyri of Greco-Roman date, written in Greek. We have seen how Budge spirited the Odes of Bacchylides away from Sayce. Let us now give Sayce a moment of triumph. In the 1890's he asked Dr. Alexander, head of the American College at Assiut, whether any interesting antiquities were being offered. The American missionary said that a man had just come in from Meir with a Greek papyrus, but the price was too high, and the man had gone away. Sayce asked whether the manuscript was written in cursive Greek or in uncials. When he heard that it was written in uncials and was therefore literary, he asked Alexander to send a servant to find the man. The servant caught him just in time.

He had been unable to sell because the professional dealers were then interested only in papyri written in hieratic or Coptic. He was afraid that informers would tell the authorities that he had been engaged in illicit digging and that he might be arrested. He was now on his way to the Nile to throw the incriminating manuscript into the river. Since he had been riding for two or three days with the papyrus in his pocket, it was badly frayed and broken at the edges. All the fragments were present, however, and he was happy to deliver it up for a price. It contained a text of the *Politics* of Aristotle, the humorous *Mimes* of Herondas, and other valuable works.

The treasures began appearing in quantity. In 1889–90 Petrie, digging at Gurob in the Faiyum, found very crude late mummy cases. They had been made of cartonage, formed of used papyri, which had been dampened, pressed together, and molded into shape. Here were parts of Euripides' *Antiope* and Plato's *Phaedo*. These were the literary prizes, but there were other papyri of a great volume of interest: family letters and accounts. The Egypt Exploration Society formed a papyrological branch, and in 1897 Grenfell and Hunt began excavating at Behnesa (Oxyrhynchus) in the Faiyum. Among the wealth of documents they found were the *Sayings of Jesus*, and passages from the poems of Sappho and Alcman. Nine years later, at the same place, they discovered parts of Plato's *Symposium*, Pindar's *Paeans*, Euripides' *Hypsipyle*, the *Hellenica* (a historical work by an unknown author), and other treasures. Papyrology became a field of major interest to the classical scholars.

Another strange source for papyri was the crocodile. From 1898 to 1902 the University of California excavated at Tebtunis in the Faiyum. Their continuously rewarding finds came from the bodies of mummified crocodiles: these had been filled out in contour by being stuffed with the crumpled-up documents from family wastebaskets two thousand years ago, official documents of the Ptolemaic period.

The Egyptian government in the 1890's had recognized that there were destructive forces working against the ancient monuments and had started repair and reconsolidation, but funds were too limited to provide much activity. Over the centuries, as the bed of the Nile has risen through the deposit of alluvial soil, the water table in Egypt has become higher. Further, excavation took away the protective bed of debris at the bottoms of the walls of the monuments. Thus the subsurface water came very close to the foundations and pavements of temples, particularly in the time of inundation. This water would rise to the surface by capillary action, evaporate as it lay upon the bottom of a wall or column, and leave a scale of corrosive salt. Excavation had thus exposed the monuments to an erosion at the base of huge weights of masonry. The great Hypostyle Hall in the temple of Karnak is one of the majestic sights of the world, with its soaring forest of one hundred and thirty-four columns. On October 3, 1899, eleven of these columns crashed down, with a roar which could be heard in Luxor, two miles away. Their foundations had been progressively weakened, and when one toppled over, it brought down a line of its mates, like a row of dominoes. From that time forward the repair and consolidation of the Egyptian monuments has been a regular concern of the Service of Antiquities. It is a constant battle against an implacable enemy.

The Patron on the Dahabiyeh

In that elegant age of Egyptology, what could be more gratifying than to have one's own dahabiyeh on the Nile as a base from which to watch one's own excavations? To be sure, the Egyptian government was now insisting that the work had to be carried out under the immediate direction of an experienced archeologist, but that was also in order: the monotony of watching a dig from dawn to dusk, keeping up a payroll, discussing the progress of the work with the Qufti rais, and handling the newly found materials were matters for the digger, rather than the patron. It was still a hobby of great personal satisfaction.

Thus in the late 1890's the Marquis of Northampton financed excavations in the Theban necropolis. Slightly later, a British chemical industrialist, Sir Robert Mond, began nearly thirty years' support of diggings and clearances in the same cemetery. Mond was a generous and enthusiastic amateur of Egyptology, who loved to show visitors "his tombs."

An American copper magnate, Theodore M. Davis of Newport, Rhode Island, became the best-known patron of this era. About the turn of the century, Sayce and Newberry won him to an interest in Egyptology, and he applied for a concession in the Valley of the Kings at Thebes. Davis was a nervous little man with marked mannerisms, self-centered but generous in supporting the work and ideas of his assistants. His concession stipulated that he was to have a digging monopoly in the Valley of the Kings but that all of his finds were to remain in Egypt. To direct the work, he engaged the services of a series of Englishmen who had learned their first archeology under Petrie: Howard Carter, Arthur Weigall, and E. R. Ayrton.

From the first the expedition was crowned with spectacular success. In 1903 Carter found the tomb of Thut-mose IV, still containing some fine furniture, especially a decorated chariot of state. In further years, up to the termination of his work in 1912, the Davis expedition would discover the tombs of the kings Hor-em-hab and Si-Ptah, Queen Hat-shepsut, and Prince Montu-her-khepeshef—in addition to those which we shall examine in closer detail. Davis also published promptly and well; scholarship owes him a debt of warm gratitude.

On February 5, 1905, Weigall, Davis' director of work at the time, found the top step of one of the most exciting tombs of the royal cemetery, that of Yuya and Tuya, the parents of Queen Tiy and parents-in-law of Amen-hotep III, the magnificent pharaoh who reigned about 1400 B.C. When they dug down to the sealed doorway, they found that the seals had been broken, showing that the tomb had been robbed in antiquity, but that the door had been resealed, so there was promise that something might still be lying in there. A small hole was broken in the top of the doorway and the workmen were dismissed, with only Davis, Weigall, the rais, and the rais's small son remaining. They tied the boy's turban under his arms and lowered him through the hole. He was crying with fright, because he felt there must be a guardian spirit in that pit. From the passageway near the door the boy handed up things discarded by the ancient robbers: a wooden staff, a gold-handled cane, a large scarab, a pair of sandals, and the gilded yoke of a chariot. It was then the end of the day. The doorway was blocked up again and guarded overnight. Davis tied the discoveries to his saddle, draped his overcoat over them to hide them, and rode his donkey out of the valley and across the plain to his dahabiyeh. None of these security measures were as strong as the local grapevine, and the villagers of Gurneh congratulated him on the way and told him just what he had under the coat.

In the morning Weigall and Joseph Lindon Smith, the American artist, who had volunteered his assistance, opened up the doorway, and then awaited the arrival of Davis and Maspero, who had gone off into another part of the valley. It happened that the Duke of Connaught was in the neighborhood and had asked to be informed if a good find were made. Was this find good or not? The two waiting men finally decided that in justice to the Duke they should make sure that it was worth his visit and then get a message to him. "We lit two candles and started down those tantalizing steps." Today we shudder at that statement: two open flames carried into the long sterile air of a tomb cluttered with dried-out wood would now be considered a terrible peril. At the bottom they found a second sealed doorway pierced by a hole made by robbers. "Thrusting our arms and candles through this opening into the darkness behind, we peered at an extraordinary sight. Directly in front of us was a great wooden box or case. . . . Within were three coffins. . . . In the innermost coffin, which was of wood richly carved and gilded, lay a mummy. The wrappings had been torn away from the face and hands of an old man of striking appearance and dignity." Near by was a second box. "In it lay exposed the mummy of a woman, also in a rich gold coffin. The face was serene and interesting, a low brow and eyes wide apart, and a curiously expressive, sensitive mouth." And there was a welter of interesting furniture, including a perfectly preserved chariot.

Until the discovery of the tomb of Tut-ankh-Amon, seventeen years later, the tomb of Yuya and Tuya was the finest "royal burial" discovered fairly intact. The noble furnishings, cleared from the jumble which the robbers had made, gave the Cairo Museum a unified display.

The tomb was cleared in three weeks—that also gives the modern a slight shock—under the supervision of the Inspector for Upper Egypt, James Quibell, with Smith assisting. On the last day everything was packed and padded, ready for transport to the river the next morning, except for one of the finest pieces, a chair which had been a gift from Sit-Amon, the granddaughter of Yuya and Tuya. This was handsomely carved in wood, with paneled scenes and a seat of woven reeds. Quibell and Smith were now ready to wrap and pack this charming piece. They heard voices outside, speaking in French. A woman insisted that she would go down into this tomb, and a man, addressing her as "Your Highness," begged her not to tire herself. Soon there appeared inside the tomb an old woman, walking with a cane. Quibell took his cue from the title he had overheard and apologized that the tomb was now practically cleared and that he could not offer her Highness a chair. She replied: "Why, there is a chair which will do for me nicely" and seated herself in the thirty-three-hundred-year-old chair. By a miracle it held up nobly. She remarked to her companion on the Empire style of the carved heads on the chair, and suddenly they recognized her. It was the former empress, Eugénie, revisiting Egypt thirty-five years after her regal journey to the opening of the Suez Canal.

WHERE WAS QUEEN TIY?

Of all the triumphs by Theodore M. Davis there is one which still stirs Egyptologists to take up the cudgels and fight a battle of words. That is the question of the occupant—or successive occupants—of a royal tomb which Davis found in 1907 in the Valley of the Kings. In January the workmen came upon a sealed doorway. After this had been photographed, it was breached, and it was seen that there was rubbish in the corridor almost up to the roof. A plank was thrust into the hole in the doorway so that it lay on top of the debris. Maspero looked at Davis and Weigall: they were nearly as portly as he. So Joseph Lindon Smith, the slender American artist, was instructed to crawl through the hole and report what he saw. The air in a newly opened tomb is not safe for a long stay. He had time to sketch a scene showing a queen worshiping a sun disk and crawl back. Maspero immediately identified the queen as Tiy, the famous wife of Amen-hotep III. Davis was exultant: he had set his heart upon finding her tomb.

Arthur Weigall, on the other hand, was a devoted admirer of Tiy's son, the heretic pharaoh, Akh-en-Aton, and he had been hoping that someone might find the burial of that king. When the corridor had been cleared enough for the party to enter the tomb, the name of Queen Tiy was still prominent, but the evidence rapidly became confusing. Although Davis kept murmuring: "We've got Queen Tiy!" Maspero soon saw that there had been a reburial and refused to commit himself to a positive identification. What did it mean that the name of the fallen heretic, Akh-en-Aton, had been hacked out of the inscriptions, whereas a prayer to the god of heresy, the Aton, had been left intact? The truly orthodox, who had wanted to blot out every memory of the sacrilegious interlude, should have hacked out both names. Maspero felt that the tomb inscriptions and furnishings pointed to two persons, rather than one.

The next day the mummy was examined. Unfortunately, water had seeped into the tomb, so the skin on the body disintegrated upon touch. It is a grisly story of a once-royal personage going to pieces before their eyes. When the jewels had been removed from the body, only a pile of disarticulated bones remained. The Canopic jars, which carried the entrails of the deceased person, were fashioned with heads, and Maspero felt that the wigs on these, as well as the wig on the coffin lid, resembled the headdress worn by men rather than by women. Davis' spirits went down; Weigall's went up.

The body was small, with delicate bones. Someone suggested that there might be a physician among the tourists visiting the Valley that day, and sure enough, an obstetrican was found. No one seems to have asked him his name or anatomical experience. After an examination of the pelvic bones, he expressed his conviction that the skeleton was that of a woman. Davis' hopes went up again. When the publication of the discovery appeared in 1910, it was proudly titled "The Tomb of Queen Tîyi." Maspero allowed Davis to have one of the Canopic jars, and it is now in the Metropolitan Museum in New York.

Unfortunately, the confusion of evidence was not ended. Between the Valley of the Kings and formal registry at the Cairo Museum, some of the material disappeared, a sheet of gold with an erased name, probably

17*a* Shepheard's Hotel in Cairo, a picture of Victorian elegance

17*b* Barracks of the British army in Cairo

18 Egyptologists in the Karnak temple. *Left to right:* Rochemonteix, Gayet, Insinger, Wilbour, and Maspero

19*a* Limestone plaque depicting Akh-en-Aton and Nefert-
iti, now in the Brooklyn Museum

19*b* Charles E. Wilbour's dahabiyeh, the "Seven Hathors"

20 The desert bay at Deir el-Bahri, Thebes. The cache of royal mummies lay on the distant side of the bay. In the foreground is the temple of Queen Hat-shepsut; beyond it, the temple of Mentuhotep.

21b Sir Flinders and Lady Petrie in Jerusalem in his
eighty-sixth year

21a Petrie watching his workmen on an excavation

22*a*   Chair of a princess from the tomb of Yuya and Tuya, admired by the empress Eugénie

22*b*   Mummy case of unidentified royalty, as found in the so-called tomb of Queen Tiy

23a The Valley of the Kings in western Thebes. In the lower center is the entrance to the tomb of Ramses VI. The tomb of Tut-ankh-Amon was discovered under and slightly to the right of this.

23b Sir Robert Mond, in the center, entertains his workmen and guests with a *fantasiyeh* in the Ramesseum. Walter B. Emery is behind the table; Dr. and Mrs. Breasted, at the right.

24 The Breasted Nubian expedition of 1906, before the temple of Abu Simbel. Dr. and Mrs. Breasted and their son Charles are in the center.

therefore the name of Akh-en-Aton. Some months after the tomb had been cleared, the experienced Professor of Anatomy at the School of Medicine in Cairo, G. Elliot Smith, examined the bones, without knowing from which tomb they had come. He announced firmly that this was the skeleton of a man about twenty-five or twenty-six years old—with an allowable range of a few years either way—and that the skull showed "the distortion characteristic of hydrocephalus." The peculiar appearance of Akh-en-Aton's body had long been a source of pathological speculation. Here are Smith's severe words written a few years later (his "Khouniatonou" is what I write "Akh-en-Aton"):

> The mummy under consideration . . . was found in its original wrappings, upon which were gold bands bearing the name of Khounia-tonou. It is hardly credible that the embalmers of the Pharaoh's mummy could have put some other body in place of it.
>
> Thus we have the most positive evidence that these bones are the remains of Khouniatonou.
>
> I do not suppose that any unprejudiced scholar who studies the archaeological evidence alone would harbour any doubt of the identity of this mummy, if it were not for the fact that it is difficult from the anatomical evidence to assign an age to this skeleton sufficiently great to satisfy the demands of most historians, who want at least 30 years into which to crowd the events of Khouniatonou's eventful reign.

The rub was that there were no unprejudiced scholars with regard to the enigmatic person Akh-en-Aton. Theories ran wild. Maspero first advanced the idea that the adherents of Akh-en-Aton had buried their king at Thebes, but wishing to conceal from his enemies the fact that the heretic king was being laid away in hallowed ground, had used the furniture of Queen Tiy, on the pretense that the burial was hers. Maspero immediately felt that this was farfetched and proposed an alternative: Akh-en-Aton had first been buried at Tell el-Amarna, then there had been a furtive reburial at Thebes, and in the secret haste the furniture had been mixed up. Others suggested that a tomb had been prepared for Queen Tiy and that Akh-en-Aton had later been reburied there, with the necessity of cadging some furniture belonging to others. None of the partisans of Akh-en-Aton seemed to be daunted by the certainty that he must have been more than thirty years old at death or by the observation that he should never have been buried with furnishings from which his own name had been erased.

Some years passed before Elliot Smith's successor as Professor of Anatomy in Cairo, Douglas Derry, was asked to examine the bones again. By that time the tomb of Tut-ankh-Amon had been discovered, and we knew something more about the heretic family. Derry concluded that the young man had been no more than twenty-three years old, did not have a skull distorted by hydrocephalus, but did have a skull very wide and flattened in a way known in only one other skull from ancient Egypt—that of Tut-ankh-Amon. Both the coffin and the Canopic jars had originally been made for a person who was not royal and had then been altered to carry the indication of royalty. Who was he, and what had happened?

Every Egyptologist will give his own answer to those questions. Akh-en-Aton had been succeeded by two young sons-in-law, first Smenkh-ka-Re and then Tut-ankh-Amon. One reconstruction of the story would be that these two were full brothers, on the basis of their exceptional skulls. Akh-en-Aton, while still alive, had conferred upon Smenkh-ka-Re a coffin and Canopic jars with no symbols of kingship on them. The inscriptions on the coffin had carried prayers to the Aton and Akh-en-Aton's name. After the death of the older king, Smenkh-ka-Re had had a very brief reign—too brief to have his own tomb excavated and equipped. By the time of his death, the worship of the Aton had been proclaimed a heresy, and the family position was shaky. When Smenkh-ka-Re suddenly died, his brother Tut-ankh-Amon gave him a hasty and furtive burial in a tomb which had been prepared for Queen Tiy but later plundered. The proscribed name of Akh-en-Aton had to be hacked out of the inscriptions, but the coffin and Canopic jars were altered to carry the symbols of kingship. Under the political atmosphere, the burial was a quick makeshift, and the tomb then suffered almost immediately from robbers, who snatched away much of the gold.

With such a confusion, it is no wonder that scholars are still writing conflicting reconstructions of the episode of that burial more than thirty-three hundred years ago. What Theodore M. Davis found was a mare's nest. One's sympathy goes out to that obstetrician tourist, called in from the blinding sunlight of the Valley to fumble the pelvic bones of an ancient body, with Davis, Maspero, and Weigall breathing heavily over his shoulder. He might be forgiven for offering a hasty opinion: after all, the great Elliot Smith looked at the same bones and fell into error.

One's heart also goes out to Mr. Davis: he never did get his Queen Tiy.

WHERE WAS TUT-ANKH-AMON?

Theodore M. Davis did not enjoy a triumphant discovery every season. The indications of a royal burial were known to his predecessors and to the locals. The tombs of the kings and queens had been quarried back into the hillside in the Valley of the Kings, so there was a tell-tale pile of stone chips near the mouth of a buried tomb which pointed to its location. Thus the search had its rules and limits. Others had made their finds before him. Writing in 1912, Davis summarized the work of his later years.

> In the winter of 1906, while digging near the foot of a high cliff in the Valley of the Tombs of the Kings, my attention was attracted to a large rock tilted to one side, and for some mysterious reason I felt interested in it, and on being carefully examined and dug about by my assistant, Mr. Ayrton, with the hands, the beautiful cup described [below] was found. This bore the cartouche of Touatânkhamanou. The following year, in digging to the north of Harmhabi's tomb, we came upon signs of another, and my assistant, Mr. E. Harold Jones, put his men to work, and at the depth of 25 feet we found a room filled almost to the top with dried mud, showing that the water had entered it. . . .
>
> We found a broken box containing several pieces of gold leaf stamped with the names of Touatânkhamanou and his wife Ankhous-namanou—also the names Divine Father Aîya and his wife Tîyi, without title or prenomen. We also found under the mud, lying on the floor in one corner, the beautiful alabaster statuette described [below]. A few days after this we came upon a pit, some distance from the tomb, filled with large earthen pots containing what would seem to be the débris from a tomb, such as dried wreaths of leaves and flowers, and small bags containing a powdered substance. The cover of one of these jars had been broken, and wrapped around it was a cloth on which was inscribed the name of Touatânkhamanou.
>
> The finding of the blue cup with the cartouche of Touatânkhamanou, and not far from it the quite undecorated tomb containing the gold leaf . . . and the pit containing the jars . . . lead me to conclude that Touatânkhamanou was originally buried in the tomb described above, and that it was afterward robbed, leaving the few things that I have described.
>
> I fear that the Valley of the Tombs is now exhausted.

Davis' involved sentences fall short of clarity, but there were three separate finds. The first was the hiding place for a cup carrying the name of Tut-ankh-Amon. The second was a mud-filled room, within which was a box containing gold leaf stamped with the names of Tut-ankh-Amon, his wife Ankhes-en-Amon, and his parents(?). The third was a pit containing jars, and Tut-ankh-Amon's name was written on linen wrapped around one of those jars. Davis assumed that the mud-filled room was the plundered tomb of Tut-ankh-Amon and that the other two finds were caches made by robbers who had plundered that tomb. If the burial of Tut-ankh-Amon were thus accounted for, the Valley of the Kings had yielded up its secrets.

With the wisdom of fifty subsequent years, we know that the tomb of

Tut-ankh-Amon was discovered by Carnarvon and Carter in 1922. Then what did Davis find? Part of that question can be answered.

Writing in 1941, Herbert E. Winlock of the Metropolitan Museum gave his memories of Davis' time. His testimony relates to that third find, the pit containing jars, flowers, and small bags holding some powdered substances.

In January, 1908, Winlock was about twenty-four, just beginning his successful career for the Metropolitan Museum. One morning he visited the Davis dig and found a state of excited anticipation. Cromer's successor as British Consul-general, Sir Eldon Gorst, had written a letter saying that he wanted to watch an archeological find being discovered. There is implicit in such a request a belief that the work of the archeologist has some kind of legerdemain and that he can know in advance when a sensation is to be uncovered. Sir Eldon "had heard that [Davis'] men found a royal tomb every winter and [he asked], as he intended to be in the Valley of the Kings in a few days, that all discoveries be postponed until his arrival." Now in the materials from the pit, along with those ten or twelve large white jars, there was an attractive miniature mummy mask, and of course the name Tut-ankh-Amon had been read on the linen. It was proposed to entertain Sir Eldon by opening the jars in his presence, in the anticipation that they contained a king's treasures.

Winlock was then too junior a person to attend such a high ritual. He went away and came back in the evening. He found a lot of scattered pots, jar lids woven out of strips of papyrus, linen bags containing natron, and floral collars. The expected sensation had collapsed. Ayrton, Davis' archeologist, "was a very sick and tired person after the undeserved tongue-lashing he had had all that afternoon. Sir Eldon complimented Mr. Davis on his cook, and that is the last of him as far as this story is concerned."

The unwanted finds remained around the Davis headquarters for a year. Mr. Davis used to entertain his guests by demonstrating the strength of thirty-three-hundred-year-old papyrus. The visitors were encouraged to strip it off the jar lids and try to tear it apart. Otherwise, the materials were simply a storage problem. In the spring of 1909, Maspero was persuaded to let the Metropolitan Museum take anything it might want from the find, and the little collection was shipped off to New York.

At that time no one saw any reason why the ancients might dig out a pit for the deposit of floral wreaths and bags of natron. The little assemblage was a puzzle. By the 1920's there was some comparable material. The little pit proved to be about 350 feet southeast of the actual burial of Tut-ankh-Amon. Hieratic labels on small pottery cups identified their ancient contents as food—loaves, cakes, grapes, and a drink of some kind.

Then there were those bags of natron and the floral wreaths. Winlock realized that this pit was not a robbers' cache, but the purposeful burial of the materials which had been used in embalming Tut-ankh-Amon, together with remains from his funeral meal. Whatever had been part of the solemn ritual of laying a god-king to his eternal rest was sacred and had to be given a separate and dignified burial.

With our later knowledge, we can now see that this pit might have indicated to Davis' archeologist that the Valley of the Kings was not exhausted but that the burial of Tut-ankh-Amon must be somewhere in the vicinity. In fact, the three separate clues which Davis found were taken by Howard Carter as leads toward his 1922 discovery.

J. L. Smith gives a sad final picture of Davis, a sick old man, on his dahabiyeh in 1912. "He seemed to want me to be near him, but most of the time he just sat with a lack of animation in his face and in a silence I could not break down by attempts to arouse his interest in his own notable record as an excavator. . . . His interest in archaeology was that of a hobbyist; therefore, at the first test, it was quick to go."

Sayce wrote the epitaph on the Cromer age.

> The winter of 1907–08 was my last winter in my floating home. Life on the Nile had ceased to be the ideal existence it once was. Modern conditions had made the sailing dahabia an impossibility. For some years I had been obliged to use a steam-launch, and therewith most of the charm of life on the Nile had disappeared. Instead of sailing beside the banks and watching the ever-changing scenes on the shore it was now necessary to remain always in the middle of the stream and to substitute the smoke of the steamer for the sights and scents of the fields. The excitement of watching the winds and the evolutions of the sailors was gone; even the great sail was folded up. The race of dahabia sailors was becoming extinct; they found it more profitable to serve on board the steamers, where wages were higher and work less. Moreover, the quietude of Upper Egypt was also gone. The population had multiplied and the waste-places of the desert were waste-places no more. The railway was now running to Assuan, the river was full of steam-craft, and it was difficult to escape from the postman or telegraph boy. Prices had risen accordingly: where I had bought twenty fresh eggs for a piastre (five cents) or a turkey for fourteen piastres, I now had to give ten or fifteen piastres for the one and sixty or eighty piastres for the other. In my earlier voyages the sheep with which I presented my men at Girga cost a dollar or four shillings, in 1907 I had to pay 137 piastres (nearly $7.00) for an inferior animal.

With these words we clearly have left the days of the lotus-eaters and advanced into a grimmer era.

7 JAMES HENRY BREASTED AND THE RESCUE OF TEXTS

NATIONALISTS AND DERVISHES

The struggle for territorial control is a contest for power, but it must find justifying terms for itself. England was striving for a *Pax Britannica* under which trade might proceed in orderly fashion, debts might be collected, and a "civilizing mission" might be extended throughout the world, to sanctify and justify those ends. It was intolerable that the British arms should suffer defeat, even though the Mahdists in the Sudan lay off the beaten path. Other peoples must be taught the lesson that England might lose a battle, but never a war. The long-range control of India and Egypt was felt to be at stake.

On their part, the Arabs and Muslims had now seen that the British might be discomfited and forced to retreat from territory once held by arms, as in the Sudan. The more advanced Muslim thinkers, however, did not place their hope of ultimate independent power in religious fanaticism like that of the Mahdists. They saw that the Western nations had techniques of power—military, industrial, sociological—so the centuries of the Crusades, when Islam held the upper hand, could not be revived simply by calling for a holy war. Islam had to rethink and regroup its resources, if it was to face the West successfully. No Arab and few Muslims thought that the answer lay with Turkey, which was justifying its title of "the sick man of Europe." There emerged two overlapping concepts: Pan-Islam and Pan-Arabism.

Cairo was a center of this argument about the future of Near Eastern peoples. Two successive forces in the argument were the fiery al-Afghani and the moralizing Mohammed Abduh. Al-Afghani, as his name shows, came from the east to Istanbul and then to Cairo in 1871. He preached a fervent revival of Islam and was a factor in the forces leading to the Arabi uprising. Unfortunately for him, not only did the British and French find him a revolutionary, but the sages at the al-Azhar University were too tenacious of tradition to accept his ideas about the reform of Islam. He left Egypt in 1879.

His successor as a spiritual-political force, Mohammed Abduh, was a different man, a gradualist who carefully sought the sanction of religion for reform. He had been born a fellah in Egypt, was the editor of a religious journal in Cairo in 1880, was banished after the Arabi rebellion, returned to Cairo in 1889, and won an increasing following for his teachings. Mohammed Abduh sought a return of Islam to some of its original simplicity. That, in his view, would have included some degree of participation in government by the people. The fanatical Mahdi had stirred up his followers to die gloriously for the faith; Mohammed Abduh gave them something to live for. From the British standpoint, he was ultimately more dangerous. There were other patriotic agitators: Lutfi es-Sayyid; Qasim Amin, the advocate of women's rights; and Mustafa Kamel, who was much more of a secular nationalist. A few years after the death of Mohammed Abduh, the Wafd party was founded by Saad Zaghlul and started a long career of agitation for Egyptian independence, using Abduh's philosophy to justify al-Afghani's activism.

Meanwhile, the British had their own nationalistic necessity, that of recapturing the Sudan from the Mahdists. Kitchener methodically mounted a campaign to move up the Nile. From May to November, 1896, the army moved south to the recapture of Dongola. In 1897, a railroad was boldly thrust across the desert from Wadi Halfa to Abu Hamed. An index of the fierceness of the fighting is the record that of the fifteen hundred in the Dervish garrison at Abu Hamed, thirteen hundred were killed or wounded. On September 2, 1898, came the climactic Battle of Omdurman, which had one of the last crucial cavalry charges in history. Participating in that knightly assault was the young Winston Churchill. Although the Dervishes outnumbered the British by two to one, the Mahdist casualties were estimated at 60 per cent, the British-Egyptian at 2 per cent. British rule had been re-established.

Kitchener barely had time to reoccupy Khartum and hold a memorial service for Gordon, now dead more than thirteen years, before he was called south by a crisis. The French had looked with envious eyes at the Nile River. A heroic little force, under Major Marchand, had marched across Africa from the French Congo and raised the French flag at Fashoda on the Nile, less than five hundred miles south of Khartum. Kitchener moved up rapidly with superior force, and the French had to give in. A year later France formally abandoned claims to the Nile Basin, and in 1904, under the Entente Cordiale, France agreed not to interfere with the British prior interests in Egypt.

At the turn of the century, the Cromer administration undertook a serious step for the welfare of Egypt, the construction of a dam at the First Cataract. In the fifteen years between 1882 and 1897, the population of Egypt had increased by nearly 50 per cent. Uncontrolled high Niles were destructive, uncontrolled low Niles brought famine; much of the inundation swept rapidly out into the Mediterranean, with only a hasty profit to agriculture. From 1899 to 1902 the Assuan Dam was built to a height of 100 feet, or about 348 feet above mean sea level. It was subsequently heightened in 1912 and again in 1933 to nearly 400 feet above sea level, backing up a lake 225 miles long.

Immediately above the proposed location of this dam lay the splendid temples on the island of Philae. Archeologists raised a great outcry when they heard that "the Pearl of Egypt" was going to be under water most of the year. The great French literary figure, Pierre Loti, wrote a book, *La Mort de Philae,* and other opponents of the "damnable dam" made things so uncomfortable for the Egyptian and British governments that the original dam was built twenty-five feet lower than had been planned. Since no one could gainsay the need of the modern Egyptians for water control and since the archeologists found themselves both unorganized and outmaneuvered, this concession had to be accepted. The dam was built; Philae was not moved to another site. It was simply "surveyed" by Colonel Lyons and Ludwig Borchardt. Later the two increases in the height of the dam negated the governmental promises to the archeologists. On the whole, the temples on Philae have stood up better than had been predicted. Yet the situation sixty years ago presents a contrast to the present program to save the Nubian monuments threatened by the new High Dam, since there is now a massive and co-ordinated international program which has attracted sympathy and support. Back in 1900 there was no UNESCO to which appeal could be directed.

The rising tide of nationalism in Egypt, the questions raised in a Liberal government in England by the Dinshawai incident, and the consciousness of Lord Cromer's long service and decreasing popularity forced his retirement in 1907. His successors, Sir Eldon Gorst and Lord Kitchener, faced a very different situation, and the Liberal government in London did not give them the firm instructions that had emanated from the Conservatives. The new conciliatory attitude in Egypt pleased no one— to the British it was too precipitate a surrender of strong position; to the Egyptians it was too slow. Though Maspero, a Frenchman, continued to run the Service of Antiquities as a one-man show, even he had to be responsive to new demands for the integrity of Egyptian things. The Italian archeologist, Ernesto Schiaparelli, discovered the intact burial chamber of a Theban noble in 1906 and was permitted to take it all to Turin. Within a few years such a ceding of unified treasures became impossible. The standards of Egyptology were tightening.

World War I struck Egypt with the same cataclysmic force that it had elsewhere. The presence of Turkey as an enemy forced the British to use Egypt as a base, with the British fleet lying in the harbor of Alexandria. Even though the Egyptians had long been restive against Turkish claims, they now saw their fellow coreligionists fighting the hated British. Martial law was immediately proclaimed, and within a few months, Khedive Abbas Hilmi was deposed and Egypt was declared a British protectorate. For some time it was touch-and-go whether the British could hold out, but then finally Allenby rolled back the Turks in Palestine. Two days after the armistice, Zaghloul Pasha requested permission to lead a delegation (*wafd*) to London, in order to negotiate toward Egyptian independence.

It was a very different world from the assured days of Cromer.

ARCHEOLOGY TIGHTENS ITS STANDARDS

Flinders Petrie alone did not invent scientific archeology. After nearly a century of plundering, conscience was asserting itself not only in Egypt, but in Mesopotamia, Palestine, and the classical world. There would continue to be pillage and smuggling until the 1920's, but the brutal rape of monuments for their showpieces was increasingly condemned as a work of destruction, rather than one of rescue.

Nevertheless, Petrie was the insistent exponent of controlled method. Whether other persons were attracted by his method—and highly successful results—or were shamed into following him is immaterial. In an atmosphere of mature responsibility, his example was effective. Digging, the recognition of levels and associations, recording, preservation, and publication were all improved and steadily approached professional standards.

There were other factors in this new maturity. An increasing body of inscriptions could now be controlled by a firmer grasp of the ancient language, thanks chiefly to Adolf Erman and his school. One could no longer make sweeping generalizations about the ancient Egyptians, since their own words spoke for them. (Perhaps, even as late as the 1960's, I should write, "One *should* no longer make sweeping generalizations," since the field still attracts some crackpots.)

Many of those who had survived the rigors of an apprenticeship under Petrie were off on independent careers: Griffith, Newberry, Carter,

Quibell, Mace, Davies, and later Brunton and Engelbach. In some cases they outstripped the master in the firmness of their results because they felt that adequate control could be improved by a greater expenditure of money for workers and equipment, but they did not deviate from his essential lessons.

The finest of them was Francis Llewellyn Griffith, a gentle and absent-minded genius. Amelia Edwards had "discovered" this self-taught master of language and had encouraged him to go out and work with Petrie. When Petrie left the Egypt Exploration Fund in 1886, he and Griffith journeyed up to Assuan, much of the distance on foot, copying inscriptions. As a result of this experience, Griffith wrote in 1889:

> If a small portion of the sums of money that . . . have been spent in Egypt on treasure-hunting for antiquities, on uncovering monuments and exposing them to destruction . . . had been utilized in securing . . . accurate and exhaustive copies of the inscriptions above ground and in danger, the most important part of all the evidence of her past that Egypt has handed down to our day would have been gathered intact, instead of being mutilated beyond recovery.

Vigorous words from so shy a man, and words as true today as they were seventy-five years ago. A result of this conviction that monuments must be saved by careful copying was that the Egypt Exploration Fund set up the Archaeological Survey under Griffith's editorship. In the notable series of volumes that followed—the tombs of Beni Hassan, el-Bersheh, Deir el-Gebrawi, Tell el-Amarna, Meir, etc.—the name of a little giant appeared, N. de Garis Davies. This gifted copyist was known in the trade as "poor Davies," to distinguish him from "rich Davis," whom we visited in our previous chapter. With his talented wife, Nina, Davies produced an astonishing quantity of exquisitely careful copies. No one in Egypt ever set down records of such permanent quality until the finer equipment and integrated teamwork of the University of Chicago took over in the late 1920's. Even so, the personal quality sensible in the copies by Mr. and Mrs. Davies makes their work more attractive.

There were others in the field. The great, genial Georg Steindorff of Leipzig worked frequently in Egypt and edited superb editions for Baedeker. Ludwig Borchardt of Berlin, a round, opinionated little man of great ability, conducted a number of excellent excavations and gave us a far firmer understanding of Egyptian architecture. At the Berlin Museum Heinrich Schaefer was laying down the basic principles behind Egyptian art in an elaborately detailed and documented way. He had to invent new language to do it. At Göttingen Kurt Sethe was carrying the grammatical studies of Erman to new refinements. In 1897 the German government sanctioned a most important forward step for Egyptology, a historical dictionary of the ancient Egyptian language, to be based on all the available copies in Egypt and in the museums of the world. Erman was to be the editor-in-chief. Sethe, Schaefer, Borchardt, Steindorff, and other Germans were enlisted to make better copies, as were the Austrian Hermann Junker, the Englishman Alan H. Gardiner, and the American James H. Breasted. It was a magnificent and nearly backbreaking plan.

The French were not idle. At Karnak, Georges Legrain carried on the honorable work of strengthening that threatened monument. Pierre Lacau began a distinguished career as a copyist and analyzer of texts. The Russian Vladimir Golenischeff was at the height of his distinguished success as explorer, collector, and translator. These were all mature scholars; suddenly it seemed as though the field had come of age.

The interest was increasing in America. It was always an uphill struggle for the Egypt Exploration Society or the British School of Archaeology (BSA) to finance a season's excavation. They eagerly welcomed contributions. Any American museum which contributed $50 or $100 would be rewarded with a share of the next season's finds. Around the turn of the century such interest was confined to a few of the larger collections. When the EES excavated at Dendereh in Upper Egypt, materials were sent to the Universities of Chicago and Pennsylvania and to the Boston, Detroit, and Metropolitan museums. The BSA dug at el-Arabah near Abydos and sent objects to Chicago and Pennsylvania.

Within a dozen years the interest had broadened. From the 1912–13 dig of the EES at Abydos, antiquities went, in recognition of contributions, to Chicago, Pennsylvania, Wellesley College, the Smithsonian Institution, the Brooklyn Museum, the Cincinnati Museum, the Art Institute of Chicago, the Jefferson Institute at Louisville, Kentucky, the Public Library at Brattleboro, Vermont, and the Masonic Library at Cedar Rapids, Iowa. From the 1914 excavation of the BSA at Harageh, near the Faiyum, objects went to the University of Pennsylvania and to museums in Brooklyn, Cleveland, and St. Louis. A larger number and wider variety of institutions were able and willing to invest a little money and express an interest in ancient Egypt. The United States had become increasingly aware of the old culture on the Nile.

A LAST BOW BY BUDGE

To be sure, the nineteenth century lingered on into the twentieth, as is illustrated by the case history of a fine four-thousand-year-old stela. In 1903, an American visitor to Egypt, Mr. Pier, saw the stela of Tjetji in the possession of a Luxor antiquities dealer and made a hasty and inaccurate copy of it, which he later published in an American journal. This was an affront to Wallis Budge, who wrote:

> We dug out the stele in the year 1902, when I was on my way to the Sûdân, and I left it at Luxor in charge of a native who was to take care of it for me until I returned. During my absence this man allowed an American tourist to see it, and though—so I was assured by the native—he was told that the stele was the property of the British Museum, he made a faulty copy of the text and published it. Others hearing of the stele wished to buy it, and tried to bribe the native to deliver it into their hands for examination, but without success. One enterprising German Professor went so far as to spread a rumour to the effect that I had died in the Sûdân, and renewed his efforts to bribe the native. Having failed to obtain the stele, they raised an outcry and said that I was stealing antiquities out of the tombs and carrying them off to London.

It is typical of Budge that he ignored any implication of smuggling and branded the charge of stealing as "absurd" because he always paid "fair prices." Maspero tacitly supported Budge, so Budge's aggrieved rivals attacked Howard Carter, who was then Inspector of Antiquities for Upper Egypt. "The Father of a Moustache," Insinger, wrote a letter to an Alexandria newspaper, charging that Carter's lack of supervision permitted Budge to smuggle out of Egypt antiquities coming from badly guarded excavations. The Egyptian press gleefully engaged in a flurry of charges and countercharges. For example, the *Egyptian Gazette*, while acknowledging that Budge was a "somewhat unscrupulous collector of antiquities for his Museum," suggested that Insinger himself might be a good authority on how antiquities left Egypt without export licenses. In fact, hinted the *Gazette*, Insinger was probably objecting that Carter was too active and vigilant for the financial profit of rival collectors.

While the storm of words was whirling, the stela of Tjetji arrived in London and was registered as number 614 in the Egyptian collections of the British Museum.

A HONEYMOON WITH A NOTEBOOK

Now we approach a mystery. With the gradual growth of the American interest in ancient Egypt, it might have been predicted that the retrospective atmosphere of New England or the cloistered halls of Harvard or of Pennsylvania would have produced the first professional American Egyptologists. In point of fact, both Breasted and Reisner came from Middle West homes of modest means. That the Corn Belt brought forth such exotic flowering was a historical accident which cannot be explained. In the case of each man there was a logical progression of career toward a goal which could not be foreseen in advance.

James Henry Breasted was the son of parents whose means had been reduced by the Chicago Fire of 1871. The generosity of a friendly "aunt" helped in his education. For a time he moved toward a career as a prescription druggist but suddenly felt a call to the ministry and enrolled at the Chicago Theological Seminary. Here he developed an unexpected gift for language. When he won a prize for Hebrew without a mistake in written and oral examinations, his career took a new and decisive bent. He went to Yale in 1890 to study under the brilliant and dynamic William Rainey Harper. At that time much of American education stood in vast awe of a Ph.D. degree from a German university. That was felt to be a crowning certification of scholarly ability. Toward the end of the year at Yale, Breasted confided to Harper that he wanted to study Egyptology in Germany, since there was no chair in that subject in the United States. Harper, who was then planning the shape of a new university, responded with vigor: "Breasted, if you will go to Germany and get the best possible scientific equipment, no matter if it takes you five years, I will give you the professorship of Egyptian in the new University of Chicago!"

Breasted's devoted parents and "aunt" found the means, and in the autumn of 1891 Breasted went to study hieroglyphic and Coptic under Adolf Erman at Berlin, with Hebrew and Arabic under other professors. He proposed to live on $40 a month. Despite deep concentration on his studies, he was not unaware of the outside world. In the autumn of 1893 he became engaged to the stately Miss Frances Hart of San Francisco, a young woman who was studying at the Home School for American Girls in Berlin.

Breasted won his Ph.D. in Egyptology *cum laude* in July, 1894, married Frances in October, and the young couple set off immediately for a honeymoon in Egypt. The kindly Erman had seen how nervously exhausted the young American was and suggested the trip to Egypt, both for Breasted's scholarly future and his health. Erman added that Breasted could help the new Berlin Dictionary by collating some inscriptions in Egypt. The proud "aunt" once more came forward with expense money. And a letter from President Harper advised the young Ph.D. that he had been appointed Instructor in Egyptology at a salary of $800 a year. The sum was disappointing. Married life and the responsibilities of a career at that rate of pay were rather alarming, but after all, this was the first teaching position in Egyptology in the United States. Surely the Lord would continue to provide.

This was nearly the first chair of Egyptology in the English-speaking world. France and Germany had long maintained the teaching of Egyptian, but in England it was only in 1894 that Miss Edwards founded the professorship for Petrie at the University of London. Griffith did not receive the first professorship of Egyptology at Oxford until he was sixty-two years old. In the United States, Reisner was appointed to the Harvard staff in the middle 1900's, and a German scholar, W. Max Müller, served the University of Pennsylvania from the end of the 1890's. Universities were slow to recognize Egyptology as a proper academic subject.

Cook's tourists might accept a packaged trip, but a scholar who knew what he wanted to see in Egypt had to control his itinerary. He had to have his own dahabiyeh. This was a formidable expense for a young couple of limited means. He wrote his family: "Our boat, with bedding, linen, kitchen equipment, a crew of four sailors, captain and second captain, dragoman, cook and boy, and including all table and household expenses and hire of donkeys at all stops, will cost us $4.84 each per day. Some unavoidable purchases of equipment will bring the daily expense up to $5.00 a person." This $10 a day for a floating home, food, nine servants, and all shore expenses seems absurdly cheap in these days, but in the 1890's it was a heavy drain on a thin purse.

Besides a dahabiyeh, all that was needed for a young enthusiast on his first visit to the land of his chosen scholarship was a notebook, a bride, and two donkeys. He visited monument after monument; he copied inscriptions; he bought antiquities for the University of Chicago with funds supplied by Harper. He quickly came to the realization that the hieroglyphic copies in the books he had used were often defective: nothing could substitute for one's own painstaking copy. In personal relations, he was a kindly soul, but for careless scholarship he quickly developed a caustic contempt, which appears often in his early writings. He set himself the personal task of copying every Egyptian inscription of historical interest—a staggering assignment.

As the leaky little dahabiyeh pushed its way southward along the Nile, Breasted reveled in monuments he had never seen. Like Wilbour, he copied, copied, copied, even by moonlight. Unlike Wilbour, he was copying not for himself, but for scholarship: he proposed to publish translations of all these inscriptions. He was a part of the spirit of the time—Griffith starting an epigraphic survey, Erman demanding that all extant copies be collated again for the Dictionary—but he saw his own place in the process. Like Griffith, he had the vision of preservation rather than exploitation.

On this scholarly honeymoon he was seeing for the first time the actual state of temples and tombs; these monuments were published in the books in apparent clarity, but in stark actuality they showed the effects of thousands of years of decay. He saw further that as soon as a temple or tomb was freed by excavation from a protecting blanket of sand and debris and was thus exposed to the forces of destruction, it began to decay at an alarmingly accelerated speed. Not only was the monument now naked to the forces of wind and weather, but it was a victim of human predators, who attacked it for some gain of their own.

North of Luxor, at a placed called Negadeh, the dahabiyeh put into shore. In boyish contrast to Charles Wilbour's indifference about meeting Flinders Petrie at the first opportunity, Breasted did not wait for a gangplank or a donkey but sprang ashore and hurried off on foot to see Petrie at work.

They were a strange contrast, Petrie and Breasted. Petrie was the bearded, solitary, eagle-eyed genius who loved to figure out simple ways to do hard things, who loved to sort out material objects. Breasted was an ardent, flamboyantly moustached youngster, compact and dextrous, whose real love was translation of languages. For some reason, probably the flaming determination within each of them, the two men took to each other at first meeting. For some days Petrie explained every procedure and principle of the excavation. Petrie's camp and table were characteristically Spartan: he and his assistant needed only $1.20 a week for provisions. The work, using seventy laborers, cost $140 a week. Further, the Western excavator had to compete at a disadvantage with Egyptian antiquity dealers, who collaborated with Emil Brugsch of the Service of Antiquities to pillage the richer sites.

Before the two parted, Petrie offered Breasted a share in future excavations, with joint financing between the University of Chicago and the Egyptian Research Account in England and with an equal division of their allotted share of the finds. This was high flattery and temptation for a young man, but Breasted did not commit himself. Perhaps he knew that one might work under Petrie but not with him. More likely the study of an excavation emphasized for Breasted the different role which he was shaping for himself. He was first and foremost a text man, not a digger. The excavator who wanted fresh results and financial support spent each season at a new place and then moved on to another opportunity. Breasted saw that Egyptology had a continuing obligation to the monuments which were cleared by excavation. Since the evidence was visibly perishing, it must be fully recorded before it disappeared. To him "inscription salvage," the systematic copying of visible material, became far more important than digging for new material. By neglecting to accept Petrie's offer he set his sails on a less sensational but highly responsible tack.

One has compassion for the bride, Frances, sitting under her parasol in dusty and incomprehensible temples, while her man scrambled excitedly up some wall in pursuit of a historical text. A honeymoon in competition with hieroglyphs must have had the bitter taste of rue. Surely she saw the signs of greatness in him. Surely she had a responsive pride when he wrote his father: "I want to read to my fellow men the *oldest* chapter in the story of human progress. I would rather do this than gain countless wealth."

Eighteen-Hundred Miles up the Nile

We shall reserve the ten years after 1895 for the next section and pick up Breasted's career in November, 1905, when he returned to Egypt to begin that formidable task to which he had set himself: the copying of all the historical texts of Egypt. After repeated disappointments in trying to secure funds and leave of absence from the University of Chicago, he was now assured by President Harper that the time and means were available. Breasted had picked upon the stretch between the First and Second Cataracts, Lower Nubia, as a territory which might promise the freshest results for the epigrapher.

At the time Breasted's health was such that his doctor had forbidden him to make the journey unless accompanied by a physician or his wife. The expedition consisted of Breasted, his wife and eight-year-old son Charles, a draftsman, who had several weeks of fever before they left Cairo, and a photographer, who also developed a fever at the very outset. Rarely had so shaky a company undertaken so rigorous an expedition. In Nubia they were to encounter temperatures up to 135° F., biting cold winds, blinding sandstorms that shook the scaffolding or camera tripod and obliterated the walls of temples, and dead calms which produced swarms of gnats. The photographer produced superb pictures on glass plates, which had to be developed in the warm water of the Nile. The water was so full of sand and silt that it had to be filtered before washing the glass negatives. After a sandstorm the gelatin surface of these plates was pitted with roughness. It was a heroic enterprise.

Heretofore copyists had made freehand copies in their notebooks, draftsmen had facsimiled scenes by measurement, and photographs had been taken as separate controls. Breasted introduced a new technique. The photographer took a picture and made a blueprint from it. Breasted took this blueprint to the temple wall and made his collation directly upon it. "The method, not heretofore employed, is proving very success-ful, and saves an immense amount of time, besides producing a palaeo-graphically correct copy." This was the seed of the Chicago method, applied twenty years later at the temple of Medinet Habu.

The ardent copyist was very critical of inaccurate recording in the past. At Abu Simbel he felt that "those familiar with Champollion's plates will hardly recognize the Sardinians as they actually appear on the wall." This was both exaggerated and unfair to the work in Egyptology's innocence seventy-five years earlier. It does illustrate the high standards which Breasted was setting for himself and others.

On Washington's Birthday, 1906, Breasted had one of those experiences which delight the philologist. On the so-called Marriage Stela at Abu Simbel, he read that Ramses II had prayed that when the Hittite princess and her party passed through the northern hills there might be no "rain or *srq*." He recognized the hieroglyphic word which we here have given in transliteration. "This is, of course, the Egyptian transliteration for [Arabic *theleg*, Hebrew *sheleg*], 'snow,' which is the earliest occur-rence of the word as applied to Syria. It is curious to come to snowless Nubia to find such a word for the first time."

While he was at Abu Simbel, Breasted had another experience worth recounting. The desert west of the Nile has long cherished the legend of a lost oasis, Zarzura, "the place of little birds." No one you talk to has seen it himself, but he has heard about it from others. A fifteenth-century Arab author wrote of a white city out in the desert, whose king and queen were fast asleep, into which you might enter and take great treasure. Sir Gardner Wilkinson in 1835 had written that the oasis Wadi Zarzura was five days west of the road from el-Hez to Farafra, with many palms, springs, and ruins of uncertain date. The inhabitants were blacks who had been carried off by the western Muslims as slaves. It is typical of this fabled city that its location varied in different accounts: in the Sand Sea west of the oases of Dakhleh and Farafra; to the south in the area circumscribed by Dakhleh, Selimeh, and Mergeh; or some-where between Dakhleh and Uweinat. It was a lodestone to the imagina-tion.

The locals at Abu Simbel urged Breasted to visit an ancient temple in the desert to the west. After three hours' ride by camel to the north-northwest, Breasted came upon a natural crag of rock, pierced by two holes, one of which looked like a doorway from a distance. The alleged temple writings proved to be prehistoric carvings of animals, which are fairly common on the rocks of Nubia. It was no lost temple.

At the end of a three-months' season the expedition had copied ten temples, five chapels, a tomb, and several stelas in the stretch between the First and Second Cataracts.

In January, 1906, Breasted learned of the death of President Harper. With the passing of his energetic patron, the young Egyptologist was most uncertain about the future.

There was a second expedition the next year, after which the available funds were to run out. This time the objective was the Egyptian evidence from the Sixth Cataract north to the Second. A new photographer joined the party, and the able Davies was the draftsman. Mrs. Breasted and the boy Charles were to join the party at Kareima, at the lower end of the Fourth Cataract. In Khartum, Sir Reginald Wingate, Governor-general of the Sudan, was most co-operative and alerted all the British agents down the river to help the expedition.

They started in the pyramid fields of Meroë in November, 1906. It was so hot in the middle of the day that a standing camera scorched the hands. In the camera's spirit level, the liquid expanded until the bubble finally disappeared. Yet they did splendid copying there, with photographs and copies still of unique use. Breasted noted with dismay a "most barbarous treasure-hunting" at the pyramids of Meroë. The use of railroad ties to shore up heavy blocks of stone showed clearly that this was not plundering by the local Sudanese, and Breasted pointed the finger of blame at officials of the British Museum. This probably was the beginning of his intermittent controversy with Budge and Scott-Moncrieff of that Museum.

In the search for hieroglyphic inscriptions in the Fourth Cataract, the party drifted a hundred and thirty-five miles from Abu Hamed to Kareima. At one point, "we were surrounded by an inferno of raging water, twisting in yawning whirlpools. . . . The danger was, that in avoiding *one* rock, we should strike *another* below it. . . . The men pulled for dear life, two men to an oar, with the reis screaming time to keep them in stroke. We just grazed past." As it turned out, this perilous experience was only a preparation for the later attempt to shoot the rapids in the Third Cataract.

At the Gebel Barkal temples Breasted did do some excavating, despite his principles, but it was in the attempt to find inscriptions. Forty years earlier Mariette had removed royal stelas but had not bothered to record the exact find spot. An old sheikh was produced who remembered where the inscriptions had been found. Since this was along the southern front of the second pylon of the temple of Amon, logically, then, the unexcavated northern front of the same pylon should have similar inscriptions. The locals were employed at fifteen cents a day—half again the prevailing wage at that place—but a week's digging produced nothing. Ironically some years later Reisner was to find a wonderful stela of Thutmose III only a few feet away from Breasted's trial dig.

The great adventure of the expedition was the attempt, in January, 1907, to shoot the rapids of the Third Cataract. At the southern end of the cataract, the raises showed great ingenuity in *backing* their boats down through the rocky islands.

> Long ridges of granite, each an imposing line of huge boulders, sweep clear across the river. In such a barrier, which rises like a dam across the river-bed, the waters have forced a passage of any depth at *one place* only. These narrow sluice-like passages, which the natives call "babs" or "gates," are not opposite each other in the successive ridges of granite. In shooting through *one* there is great danger of being wrecked on the next ridge below where the "bab" is in another place. It is interesting to observe the method of these Nubian reises in navigating such difficult waters. They wait for a wind blowing against the current, which is fortunately the prevailing direction of the winds on the Nile. They then drift [north] with the current to the head of the cataract, where they hoist all sail. As the craft begins to feel the rush of the current, the reis heads her up-stream, taking the [north] wind directly astern. She begins to move slowly up-stream [south]. Thereupon the reis loosens his sheets, and the boat moves slowly down stream [north]. As she moves with the current, but *very* much more slowly than the current, she has plenty of steerage way. The reis now continues to spill the wind from his sails until she reaches the first rocks. If he is opposite a "bab," he continues to drop down slowly stern on till he passes safely through it. If *not*, he hauls down his sheets taut and draws slowly away from the rocks steering a little to the right or left as may be necessary to secure a position directly above the "bab." This position gained, he spills the wind again, till he has dropped through the "bab," when he must again haul taut his sheets to prevent running into the next line of rocks, and wrecking the boat. . . . The current is terrific, and it is sometimes wearing on the nerves to see the boat hovering above a ragged reef of rocks. . . . We often hung on thus for several minutes, with the rudder but ten feet from the hungry rocks, when a serious lull in the wind would mean total wreck.

With that danger skillfully passed, the boat moved downstream to the Kagbar Rapids, where the channel was so narrow and tortuous that sailing was impossible. It was necessary to hunt up fifty local workers to man ropes, whereby the boat could be slowly let down through a "bab" and then released in calmer water. And here came shipwreck.

Wed. Jan. 16, '07. . . . By noon the wind abated enough to make the attempt, and in an hour we had passed safely out of the lower "bab." The wind was still strong, and when the natives cast off the ropes, we were blown across the river [at] a high speed. Once across, the reis, instead of rounding, head to the current, and then again to the wind, to kill our motion, merely rounded into the shore. We struck heavily on a hidden rock, but rested immediately on a sandy shore. I heard a sailor say something about water in the boat, and looking down the forward hatchway, I saw the water spouting into the hold through a hole larger than my arm. . . . I soon had our four servants and helpers passing up boxes, for our entire winter's supplies were in the hold. . . . In ten minutes from the time we struck, the water was under our floor, and all our hundred boxes were out. . . . With her port quarter awash, and the waves rolling over the rail, our boat looks like a wreck. Only the two heavy lines from the two mastheads to the palms on the high shore, now prevent her from turning over into deep water and driving with the current, a total wreck. . . . To leave [the boat] now, would be a catastrophe for our winter's work, even if we could secure camels here, which is very doubtful.

After a dismal night, the next day brought relief. Breasted prepared a patch of tin, canvas, and asphalt varnish. All hands pulled on ropes; the hole was temporarily plugged with rags, and all hands bailed. The ship was finally on an even keel, with only a foot of water in the hold. Then, by one of those miracles of the desert, there appeared two young Englishmen, a surveying party, probably the only such party within hundreds of miles. With their help, the boat was careened and patched, inside and outside, with the hole between the patches filled with water-proof cement. Three months' work was saved.

There were other temples to visit farther north. The expedition went on, making only six miles in six days against the inexorable north wind. Toward the end of the month the weary Breasted noted in his journal that the gale had been blowing nine days and nine nights without interruption. Once within that stretch he trudged through the whirling sand to look at the three columns left of a temple at a place called "Sese" or "Sesebi." The name of Seti I had long been known here, and Breasted started his copy with little thought of anything new. A deeply cut sun disk at the top of each column puzzled him, and then suddenly, underlying the figure of the god Amon, he saw the erased figure of the heretic Pharaoh Akh-en-Aton—the characteristic long jaw, scrawny neck, and pot belly. On each of the columns Akh-en-Aton had been depicted worshiping the sun disk. Then, when his movement had been proscribed as heresy, the carvings had been hacked out and recut with a more conventional scene. The discovery of a temple of Akh-en-Aton five hundred miles south of Thebes was a major achievement of the expedition.

Near the Second Cataract, Breasted wanted to cross over to the island of Uronarti, which had a fortress of the Middle Kingdom, but there was no boat in the vicinity. Then a Nubian appeared with a float constructed of two bundles of dried reeds tied together. "When I had perched myself on this precarious craft, I was sitting a small two inches above the surface of the water. The native pushed it out, and holding it with his hands, propelled it across with his feet. He was a powerful swimmer and we went along very well, except that the heavy wind made an uncomfortable [trip]." The first question that Erman had given Breasted on his Ph.D. examination had been translation from Pyramid Texts. In those texts there are frequent references to a "double reed-float" as a means of crossing the waters of the next world. Now Breasted, in far-off Nubia forty-five hundred years later, was experiencing this primitive means of water travel.

On March 5, 1907, the expedition reached its northern goal at Wadi Halfa. In a little over four months they had covered nearly a thousand miles, had recorded nineteen temples, eleven stelas, one palace, and four groups of pyramids.

> Two of the hoped-for records we did not find: the frontier landmarks in the 4th cataract; and the missing stelae of the Nubian annals at Barkal (Napata). On the other hand three *unexpected* finds of importance were decreed us: the palimpsest columns of Sesebi, revealing the first temple and city of the great reformer Ikhnaton in Nubia; the great series of reliefs at Soleb recording the splendid jubilee of Amenhotep III; and finally in the same temple (Soleb), a whole pylon tower bearing reliefs of the revolutionary Ikhnaton, belonging to the short period *before* his religious revolution, a period from which it is the greatest surviving monument.

Wind, sand, rain, and human agency have damaged the monuments in both areas visited by the two Breasted expeditions. The excellent photographs and careful copies provided by his mission remain of inestimable value. Even though he did not carry out his dream of personally copying all the historical inscriptions in Egypt, this beginning was a triumph.

THE WANDERING SCHOLAR

Breasted's flashing enthusiasm, combined with attention to detail and unflagging industry, made him an excellent teacher. Yet $800 a year as his first salary at the University of Chicago was a real pinch. He had his

classes—no heavy load in Egyptology, but a constant regime—his staggering program of research and publication, and he was Assistant Director
of the Haskell Oriental Museum at the University. He had to fight for
position against the ambitions of the Professor of Assyriology, the President's brother, Robert F. Harper. That in all should have been enough to
occupy his time. But to supplement his income, he undertook an active
program of public lecturing: ladies' clubs, men's clubs, university extension groups, any group which would pay $25 and expenses, later in-
creased to $50 and expenses as his reputation grew. This turned out
to be steadily remunerative. He had a handsome appearance, an evan-
gelist's fervor, a fluent delivery, and the ability to transmit his enthusiasm
to others. When, in 1899, the Berlin Dictionary invited him to copy the
Egyptian inscriptions in the European museums on an expense basis only,
his small savings from lectures permitted him to accept the offer. He
and his family shuttled back and forth between the United States and
Europe, traveling third class on the European trains, living in dingy
rooms in obscure pensions, skimping on meals. It was a cold and drab
experience, but he came to know Europe well.

Naturally there were compensations for the scholar. That miserable
black stone in the British Museum which had been worn down by years
of use as a millstone—was it worth the time? Breasted "spent many stifling
summer days, sitting on a low stool under a window in the British
Museum endeavouring to reflect some light from the window above, by
means of a hand mirror, to the stone below." Suddenly he recognized
that the inscription had been written retrograde, so the hieroglyphs
reversed their normal position. Previous copyists had tried to read the
inscription backwards. The text proved to be unique, and Breasted published it as, in his opinion, "the oldest known formulation of a philosophical *Weltanschauung*," a judgment which has stood up well over the
past sixty years.

Meantime he was working on the translation of all the known Egyptian historical inscriptions from the beginning down to Persian times
and on a history based upon those texts. The *Ancient Records of Egypt*
has been evaluated by a British Egyptologist in these terms: "This, in-
volving as it did the copying of most of the historical inscriptions [in
Europe and] in Egypt also, and a vast deal of collation and reconstruction
of texts, would in itself have been a most creditable life-work." Yet
Breasted was to finish it before he was forty, and while engaged in the
task he wrote: "I am now laying plans to copy not merely the historical,
but *all* the inscriptions of Egypt and publish them." He probably would
have done it, if he had not been drawn off into other responsibilities.

In 1902 Breasted's dreaming produced a plan for an Oriental Institute for work in the Near East, which President Harper sent on to the office of John D. Rockefeller, Sr. It resulted in a contribution of $50,000 and the creation of the Oriental Exploration Fund at the University of Chicago. But Robert F. Harper's competing ambitions won out temporarily, and a Mesopotamian excavation took the field. Breasted had to wait until 1905, when President Harper found the funds to launch the two seasons of copying in Nubia.

Scribner's brought out *A History of Egypt* in 1905, and the University of Chicago brought out the companion *Ancient Records of Egypt* in five volumes in 1906. By resting on the *Ancient Records*, the *History* was able to let the ancient Egyptians speak for themselves and thus avoided long and distracting footnotes. These books still command admiration. I have already quoted a judgment on the prodigious *Ancient Records*. In 1935 one scholar called the *History* "brilliant" and "still the best book of its kind"; in 1961 another authority referred to it as "great" but "largely out of date." It is still the most lucid and persuasive writing about ancient Egypt in the English language and was translated into German, Russian, French, and Arabic and put into a Braille edition. Here was climactic triumph for a man still relatively young.

Yet there were other worlds to conquer. At Union Theological Seminary in New York in 1912 he delivered a series of lectures, which were then published under the title, *Development of Religion and Thought in Ancient Egypt*. Uncharacteristically these lectures were dry and detailed: he developed his argument with painful precision; but they were brilliant: "This book was epoch-making in its significance for the history of human thought." It was a thoughtful attempt to trace religious and intellectual process from earliest times to Christian days in Egypt. With Breasted, the word was not "process," but "progress," because his love of Egypt and his philosophical meliorism made him view the scene as an inspiring upper curve. It was still brilliant pioneering.

In Chicago, Breasted had a neighbor who was a partner in a textbook publishing firm. This man, Henry Hilton, urged Breasted to write a high-school textbook on ancient history. Breasted recoiled from the idea of "pure popularization," but was tempted by an income from royalties which might free him from the burden of outside lecture trips. It took four years, with writing and rewriting, but *Ancient Times* was finally finished in 1916. It became a sensation, an appealing and attractively written introduction to ancient history, directed toward teen-agers but exciting the interests of adults. Theodore Roosevelt reviewed it warmly in *The Outlook*. When the Rockefeller boys had the book in classroom,

John D. Rockefeller, Jr., came to know it and appreciate that Breasted was a gifted scholar, an appreciation which was to bear abundant fruit. So many schools used the textbook in the next fifteen years that the royalties poured in, and Breasted was finally relieved of economic worry.

In 1902 an appeal to the senior Rockefeller for an Oriental research program had resulted in funds which went chiefly to excavation in Mesopotamia. Breasted had had his two seasons in Nubia, and that had been the end of his field work. World War I came and went. Early in 1919 he wrote John D. Rockefeller, Jr., a proposal for an Oriental Institute, started at $10,000 a year as "a laboratory for the study of the rise and development of civilization." Mr. Rockefeller agreed to the proposal. A new career opened for Breasted.

THE LONG SHADOW OF A MAN

What kind of a scholar was James Henry Breasted? As his devoted student I have some difficulty in being objective. He was an admirable teacher, and even after administrative duties became heavy he found time to give to his students. He could make the pseudo-participle form of the Egyptian verb vibrant with significance as an invention of the human mind. He was persuasive: after forty years, I have some sense of apology if I cannot accept his high evaluation of the revolutionary Pharaoh Akhen-Aton or if I do not believe that conscience dawned for man preeminently in ancient Egypt. He offered his best for us to share.

He could be polemic. If we wanted to create a diversion in class, we might innocently ask him about his opinion of some French Egyptologist. That would be good for a fifteen-minute lecture on the easy but careless scholarship which he saw in most of his French colleagues. On the other hand, few Germans merited the same scorn. After the Nubian expeditions, he carried on an acrimonious argument with Scott-Moncrieff of the British Museum and was affronted when the editor of the only British journal on the ancient Near East refused him the last word. It is difficult to know the origins of his long coolness to his great American colleague, Reisner, but that feud certainly had misunderstanding and jealousy on both sides.

Although he had abandoned a preaching career, he retained an evangelical zeal, which was part of his charm and which certainly explained his ability to raise funds. A superb lecturer, he could hold an audience in silent thrall as he described his first sight of the tomb of Tut-ankh-Amon. Yet he could quite unconsciously drop into bathos in the same context. As he described the sensations of Herbert Winlock and himself as they stood awe-struck at the heaped-up treasures in the Tut-ankh-

Amon antechamber, Breasted said: "Gradually I became aware that Winlock beside me was muttering: 'My god! My god!'—and he said it reverently!"

With all his zest for talking, he could seclude himself and work hard. That had been his concentrated escape when he had been balked of his ambitions in his first years at the University of Chicago. He retained the knack after he became a world figure. In the 1920's, when he was in Cairo, engaged in frustrating negotiations with the Egyptian government, he was able to shut out his vexations, go into his hotel room, and take twenty minutes or two hours to work on the translation of a medical text. Without such concentration, he could never have achieved the volume of good work he produced.

A British colleague, after writing appreciatively of Breasted's scholarship, tried to characterize the man himself: "An unbounded enthusiasm, which a touch of naïveté rendered doubly infectious, gave a singular attraction to his conversation, and his handsome features and athletic figure added greatly to the pleasure afforded by his society."

A zest for life and a perennial youthfulness, harnessed to the methodical procedures of scholarship, made the man a great force.

8 GEORGE ANDREW REISNER AND THE FULL RECORD

As the crow flies, it is less than two hundred and fifty miles from Rockford, Illinois, to Indianapolis, Indiana. Within the space of two years there was born in Rockford one who would be acclaimed as the leading ancient historian of his day, James Henry Breasted, and in Indianapolis was born one who would be called the greatest excavator of his day, George Andrew Reisner. The two men were very different, yet each of them became an influential leader to good work in Egyptology.

Reisner's family had the means to send him to Harvard, where he followed his undergraduate studies with graduate work and a Ph.D. in Semitics in 1893. He was awarded a traveling fellowship to continue his studies in Germany, working on Assyriology at Göttingen and coming under the spell of Erman at Berlin. Although he served a brief instructorship in Semitics at Harvard and published some cuneiform texts, Egyptology had captured him, and in 1897 he went to Cairo to work on amulets and model boats for the *Catalogue* of the Museum. Two years later, when Mrs. Phoebe Hearst was making a tour of Egypt and had decided to support excavation there, the earnest young American was recommended to her as a field director. The Hearst Expedition of the University of California took the field at Deir el-Ballas in Upper Egypt and then moved to Naga ed-Deir in Middle Egypt. Reisner had had no field experience at the time but was associated with two men of some training, Mace and Lythgoe. Naga ed-Deir was an excellent ground for an apprenticeship, with cemeteries which covered the range of ancient Egyptian history.

A crisis came in 1904–5, when Mrs. Hearst decided that she could no longer support field work. Lythgoe had already left to organize an expedition for the Boston Museum of Fine Arts. There seems then to have been some scrambling for positions. It ended with Reisner appointed to an assistant professorship of Egyptology at Harvard and to the directorship of the combined Harvard-Boston Expedition at the Gizeh pyramids. Lythgoe and Mace shortly ended up with the Metropolitan Museum Expedition at Lisht in the Faiyum. On the surface, everything was amicable: "Harvard saw advantage to the University in taking part in scientific excavations in the interest of scholarship and the advancement of learning; the Museum desired to add to its collection of authentic and documented works of art. Reisner himself was alive to the value of being associated with one of the world's greatest universities and one of America's leading museums, and with the assurance of adequate financial support for his work which would result." Feelings were hurt at the time, however. "At about this period there must have developed an intriguing streak in Reisner's makeup, for he rowed with many of his old cronies, and even after the first World War his feud with Breasted, who was then trying to reorganize the entire set-up of digging in Egypt, and with Howard Carter, when the latter was working in the tomb of Tut-ʿankh-Amūn, are not tales of Christian charity." Yet the appointment to head the Harvard-Boston Expedition released Reisner's energies for some of the finest work ever done in Egypt. We shall discuss his work at Gizeh later.

THE LAND OF CUSH

In the period 1906–10 Reisner was responsible for three field jobs: the Harvard-Boston Expedition at the pyramids, a Harvard expedition at Samaria in Palestine, and an archeological survey of Nubia for the Egyptian Survey Department, to study the area which would be inundated by the first raising of the Assuan Dam. We shall deal here with the work in Nubia and its later extension into the Sudan.

The survey of an extended area which is soon to be lost under rising waters is a different proposition from the excavation of a single site. There must be a total description of the general evidence in the entire area, and there must be hasty excavation at those points which show highest promise. Reisner laid down the methods and principles of such a survey in terms that are still valid today, and he described the sequence of cultures there—cultures parallel to, but different from the phenomena in Egypt itself—in terms which have since been supplemented and modified, but which are still generally valid. The present archeological work in Nubia owes much of its structural framework to Reisner's pioneering.

Just before World War I Reisner moved into the Sudan proper, where he had a dozen very profitable years: at Semneh and Kummeh at the Second Cataract, at Kerma near the Third Cataract, at Napata—Gebel

Barkal, el-Kurru, and Nuri—near the Fourth Cataract, and at Meroë between the Fifth and Sixth Cataracts. Again, understanding of what happened in the ancient history of Cush rests upon Reisner's work.

For the northern part of the region he established the names and succession of the Egyptian viceroys who were sent to control Nubia on behalf of the Egyptian Empire. For the southern part he brought into succession the Cushite kings from the eighth century B.C. to the fourth century A.D., a truly remarkable task, based essentially on inscriptions but also on typological development of materials. Painstaking methodology paid off generously. Finds ranged from an important historical stela of Thut-mose III at Gebel Barkal to a handsome Hellenistic silver cup from Meroë, showing in high relief a judgment scene before some ruler.

Of all this detective work the most remarkable adventure was at Kerma, on the east shore above the Third Cataract. The Egyptian Middle Kingdom held the territory as far south as the Second Cataract by a series of fortresses. Yet the trade from the Sudan apparently justified going beyond that. South of the Third Cataract the Egyptians built a great fortified trading post, "The Walls of Amen-em-het." It seems to have been like one of the blockhouses out in Indian territory during the development of the American west. In a great tumulus nearby Reisner excavated an extraordinary scene, a mass burial.

> A great funerary feast was made at which over a thousand oxen were slaughtered and their skulls buried around the southern half of the circle outside. The body of the prince was then laid to rest in the vaulted chamber, with his offerings; and the wooden door was closed. The sacrificial victims, all local Nubians, either stupefied during the feast by a drug, or strangled, were brought in and laid out on the floor of the corridor—from two to three hundred men, women and children. With these Nubians were placed a few pots and pans, occasionally a sword, and often their personal adornments. Then the corridor was filled in with earth, forming a low, domed mound.

Within the tumulus were found the fragmentary statue of an Egyptian noble named Hep-zefi and the statue of his wife Sennui. Now Hep-zefi (or Djefa-Hapi, according to another reading of his name) was well known to Egyptology. At Assiut he had constructed a large tomb, carved with texts providing for eternal services at that spot. Yet here his statue was, hundreds of miles south of Assiut, buried in a strange mound with barbaric rites. Reisner argued that Hep-zefi must have been the local high commissioner and trading agent for Egypt in this out-of-the-way place, and when he died, he was buried here with savage ostentation. That may be, but scholarly caution has retreated from Reisner's conclusion. It is also possible that the local Nubian ruler at that time, in addition to ordering the greatest suttee burial possible, was sufficiently aware of burial customs in Egypt to want the proud dignity of funerary statues. He may therefore have purchased—Egypt may have traded—the statues of Hep-zefi and his wife to ornament his tumulus in a distinguished way. Perhaps we are trying to exculpate the Egyptians from the practice of suttee, but we do need other evidence that Hep-zefi was actually commissioner at Kerma and was buried there.

HARVARD CAMP

On the pyramid plateau at Gizeh the three great pyramids loom up on the eastern face, and the Second and Third pyramids are each slightly set back from their northern neighbor. Behind the Great Pyramid lies a city of the dead, white streets of limestone mastabas, the resting places of the Old Kingdom nobles. Off to the west behind the Great Pyramid one climbs a slow rise and comes to the site of Harvard Camp, one of the truly thrilling locations in the world. A simple terrace facing south is backed by unobtrusive mud-brick buildings, shaped into a quadrangular compound. From this terrace one looks east and southeast across the mastaba city to the three pyraminds. Dominating the view is the Great Pyramid, a mass of different character at every hour of the day: somberly gray against the sunrise, too bright to look at fixedly at noontime, vibrantly rosy in the sunset, and endlessly massive in the moonlight. Just at dusk the streams of tourists have left, and a fox comes out of a crevice in the pyramid and looks around to see whether it is safe to descend to the desert. On most winter days the cloud patterns play experiments in design around the peaks of the pyramids.

This was the place that Reisner loved. Even after his eyesight was nearly gone he would come out on the terrace and sense the excitement of a sunset. This was a place which was a powerful influence for good archeology. The Gizeh Plateau was so accessible that every archeologist visited Harvard Camp, and many tourists found their way there. The high standards of "the Doctor," or "Papa George," were very clear, and every digger hoped for his approbation. Particularly the other excavators in the pyramid area were dependent upon his praise and advice. The range of visitors to a Sunday tea at Harvard Camp had broad and interesting coverage.

Certainly Reisner was a great man. Winlock, who was an excellent judge of good archeology and who was not prejudiced in favor of Reisner as a person, wrote: "There is no question but that Reisner was the greatest excavator of Egyptian antiquities then alive and both his luck and his judgment were phenomenal." Essentially he was the great recorder. Dows Dunham outlines his methodology.

> Reisner used to say the records of a well conducted excavation should enable future scholars to reconstruct in every detail the conditions found by the excavator. This ideal, though seldom if ever completely attained, was at least approached in the records of our Expedition. They were essentially as follows: *first* came the Diary, which was written up every day by the head of the Expedition, and which recorded exactly what work was done on that day, by whom done, the conditions observed and the objects unearthed, and with comments on what, at that stage, appeared to be the significance of the work. This Diary often included sketches and measurements to help explain to others what was verbally described. *Second* came photography, done by specially trained Egyptians under the direction of the excavator. Every stage of the work, every object found was visually recorded at the time, and as objects were removed from the ground they were again photographed, sometimes from several angles. *Third*, there was what was known as the Object Register. This was a large ledger, kept in duplicate, in which every single object or fragment—potsherds, beads, scraps of every kind as well as important objects—was entered with an identifying number, a careful verbal description, usually a measured drawing, measurements, date, place of finding, and a note of photographs taken. In addition to these day-by-day records, maps and plans of the site and of individual buildings had to be made, and the supervision and direction of the workmen had to be seen to.

Much of this is accepted routine in current digs but was not when Reisner worked out his method, and no one else was more careful than he to follow a step-by-step procedure. It was said of him that when his eyesight was nearly gone, his staff would make a sketch of some object in white chalk on black paper and hold it up to his dim sight. The precision of his mind gave him an awesome memory. He could make out the outlines of the object; his mind would begin working; and he would tell them that the object had been found near the entrance of such and such a tomb; it should be in the Diary near the end of such and such a month in such and such a year.

Such precision, based on the knowledge that archeology destroys when it removes materials from their location and association, did not make easy writing in the final publication. A fellow Egyptologist once jested that he had spent months excavating Naga ed-Deir, and he meant untangling the analysis in Reisner's books: painstaking detail thrust at one with endless precision. Yet no one could gainsay the truth that this was the only honest method of presenting all the evidence so that others might make independent judgments.

The British Museum scholar, H. R. Hall, writing in the article on "Archaeology" for the *Encyclopaedia Britannica*, was rather snappish about Reisner. He acknowledged the value of Petrie's insistence upon careful method. Then he wrote:

> But this method may be too rigid. In many excavations now it is an impossibility to record and catalogue everything found, still less to publish everything found, to illustrate as well as describe everything. Reisner has tried to do the latter; [Sir Arthur] Evans has not. Reisner's method of publication is that of the scientific catalogue. Evans writes a readable book. . . . How would it be possible to publish Knossos in Reisner's method? And would it serve any good purpose to do so?

That question can be answered now, since some belated doubt has arisen about Evans' recording at Knossos, a misgiving difficult to answer fully and finally. With Reisner's system there certainly was not the same verve of excitement, but there was no question at the time or in the future.

It was stated above that the photographers on the Harvard-Boston Expedition were Egyptians. An outstanding factor in Reisner's direction of work was his relation to his native working staff. Petrie, in the early 1890's, had settled upon the men of Quft to be trained as skilled diggers and overseers. Reisner carried this trust several steps further. His Arabic was excellent, and he took a family interest in his Quftis. They did his photography for him. He gave their sons educational opportunities, and these young men ultimately kept some of his records. They felt themselves to be members of the archeological staff. His interest in them was returned by their devotion to him and their fierce pride in working for him.

Reisner spent most of his time in the field and rarely returned to Harvard for a stretch of teaching. Egypt became his home, and he began to identify himself with the hopes and ambitions of the Egyptians. There is no doubt that he was friendly to the fellahin from the beginning. As early as 1901 he gave the locals at Deir el-Ballas permission to take the fertilizing *sebakh* from the dump of the California expedition. In gratitude one fellah came to the camp with a papyrus to give to the Doctor. It had been found near the site two years earlier. Although the outer columns had flaked and crumbled, because it had been tied up in a headcloth, most of the text was intact. It proved to be a valuable medical papyrus of the Eighteenth Dynasty. Reisner named it in honor of his patroness and published it as the Hearst Medical Papyrus.

Reisner's sympathies for the Egyptians colored his relations with the British and with his fellow Americans when he felt that they were pushing the Egyptians too hard. That was undoubtedly a factor in his criticism of Howard Carter, when the latter sued the Egyptian government to claim a division of the finds from the tomb of Tut-ankh-Amon, and of Breasted, when the latter tried to persuade the Egyptian government to accept an internationally controlled institute of Egyptology. Reisner was entirely sincere in his sympathies and hostilities. In return the Egyptians liked and trusted him. He received his reward in a generous division of the finds from the Harvard-Boston excavations. That the superb painted limestone bust of Ankh-haf was assigned to Boston in 1927 was exceptional in a time of increasing nationalism. Few other foreign expeditions in Egypt could have expected such generous treatment.

The work at Gizeh took more than a generation. The actual earth moved may not have bulked large over so many years. The results were admirable. The sculptured pieces from the mastabas gave a comprehensive repertoire for the Old Kingdom. From the remains of the period of the three great pyramids, Reisner's analysis picked out two schools of sculpture: Sculptor A and his school, characterized by a severe style in which all faces were brought toward a standardized type; and Sculptor B, a realist who used a softer modeling for an approach to portraiture. In the period we are examining, the Harvard-Boston work focused on the Third Pyramid and resulted in the volume, *Mycerinus*. But the range of the work was already the entire Old Kingdom.

As we shall see later, this stocky, rumpled scholar, with a pipe always thrusting from a combative jaw, mellowed in later years and won the affectionate title of "Papa George." From the beginning he was a figure to respect and emulate, an excavator who took certain of Petrie's principles and methods and advanced them to rigorous standards of control. On top of that precision, he had a magic thumb for getting results and the imagination to illuminate his findings with high interest.

A HOST OF WITNESSES

The generation of scholars from 1895 to 1920 was becoming responsibly professional in every phase of Egyptology. To be sure, Theodore M. Davis was continuing his partisan patronage up to World War I. Budge was in the field and produced three works which had so massive an air of authority as to check other works in the same field: *First Steps in Egyptian*, in 1895; *The Chapters of Coming Forth by Day*, a translation

25*a* Breasted crossing to join his photographer above the temple of Abu Simbel

25*b* The Kagbar Rapids in the Third Cataract, where the Breasted expedition was wrecked in 1907

26 The working party for the tomb of Tut-ankh-Amon, lunching in a neighboring tomb. *Left to right*: Breasted, Burton, Lucas, Callender, Mace, Carter, and Gardiner

27b   Visitors to the tomb of Tut-ankh-Amon. Lord Allen-by is at the right; Breasted, bareheaded, is talking to Lady Allenby, seated.

27a   Howard Carter, with the walking stick, super-vising the clearance of a bust from the tomb of Tut-ankh-Amon

28*a* George A. Reisner in 1935

28*b* The carrying-chair of Queen Hetep-heres, as reconstructed

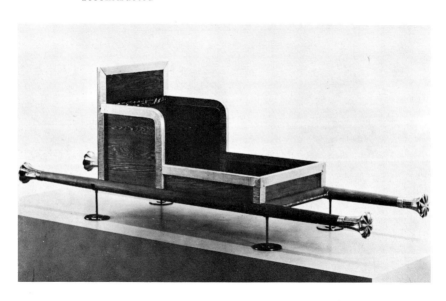

29*a* The pyramid plateau at Gizeh. The long shadow in the center points toward Harvard Camp.

29*b* Chicago House at Luxor, shortly after it was built in 1931

30 Herbert E. Winlock (*foreground*), sorting fragments of the Hat-
shepsut statues found at Deir el-Bahri

31a   Fragments of a red granite statue of Hat-shepsut, as pieced
       together

31b   The same statue, restored and exhibited in the Metropolitan
       Museum of Art, New York

32a   One of the first classes of Egyptians in Egyptology, about 1925. Breasted, in the center, is flanked by two of the professors—Golenischeff, on the left, and Graindor, on the right.

32b   *Left to right:* Junker, Reisner, Breasted, and Borchardt in Cairo in 1935

of the Book of the Dead, in 1898; and *An Egyptian Hieroglyphic Dictionary*, in 1920. It is certainly invidious to brand such widely used and influential books as encumbrances to Egyptology, but they were brusque, single-handed efforts which ignored the progress of the science as worked out by others. Often they rested upon Budge's authority alone, without adequate references to control the translation.

Griffith, however, was at the height of his powers. He published a study of demotic papyri which marked a solid milestone in the understanding of that difficult script. He worked out the essentials of the Meroitic writing, a sheer feat of analogical genius. To the excellent eleventh edition of the *Encyclopaedia Britannica* (1911), he contributed forty-five basic articles. And in 1910 he went off to dig for further Old Nubian and Meroitic texts at Faras, in Lower Nubia.

Three other British scholars deserve praise in this period. We shall have more to say about Gardiner in a later chapter. T. Eric Peet was an Englishman of modest means who went from a specialization in mathematics to excavation in Italy and then in 1909 to a dig in Egypt. Gardiner read Egyptian with him, and later Peet took the field for excavations of his own directing. He was a well-rounded Egyptologist, an experienced and competent excavator and a first-class philologist, specializing in hieratic of the late New Kingdom. Peet's death in 1934, just after he had been appointed to the chair of Egyptology at Oxford, robbed England of a man who could have been the respected and trusted leader of his fellows.

A third British archeologist exerted his force essentially in a negative way. Somers Clarke was an architect who had participated in excavations in the 1890's. In 1902 he retired and built his own house near el-Kab in Upper Egypt. Visitors were welcome, but they were subjected to a detailed commentary on what was good work and what was not. "His remarks on the injuries done in the name of archaelogy to architectural history by excavators and restorers were many and pungent."

The Americans were also coming in responsibly. We have already seen that Lythgoe and Mace went to Lisht on behalf of the Metropolitan Museum in 1907. After work in the Oasis of Khargeh and at the palace of Amen-hotep III in southern Thebes, the Museum settled down in 1910 near Deir el-Bahri for those years of brilliant success which were to make Herbert E. Winlock famous. That is a story for a later chapter. The Eckley B. Coxe, Jr., Expedition of the University of Pennsylvania did solid but unsensational work in Nubia and then moved north to Dendereh and Memphis. In 1901–2 a young graduate of Yale, Robb de Peyster Tytus, joined Newberry in excavating the palace of Amen-hotep III at

Thebes. When he died a few years later, his mother financed in his memory the "Tytus Memorial Series," under the editorship of the Metropolitan Museum. Here Davies gave splendid examples of his gifted copying, as in the brilliant *The Tomb of Nakht at Thebes*.

Lord Carnarvon and Howard Carter started work at Thebes in 1907. Ludwig Borchardt made his first preliminary digging at Tell el-Amarna in the same year, beginning significant work which was to include the discovery of the famous head of Nefert-iti. Both of these expeditions belong, in their development, to later sections of this book.

These were the years when the gifted American artist, Joseph Lindon Smith, and his energetic wife, Corinna, were visiting Egypt nearly every winter. Smith developed that extraordinary sculptured line in painting to copy Egyptian wall scenes. As we have seen, he also participated in some of the great finds. While he was painting and helping excavators, Mrs. Smith built an independent career, with a study of the Koran and the Muslim traditions and a concern about international smuggling. The Assuan Dam now kept the soil of Egypt moist over a larger part of the year. Thus a certain snail was able to survive throughout the land. This snail was the host for a parasite which caused the debilitating disease, bilharziasis. With a large proportion of the fellahin weakened by this ailment, they took up narcotics on a large scale, particularly hashish. The Smiths' friendship with Russell Pasha of the Egyptian police gave Mrs. Smith a lifelong interest in the problem of smuggling narcotics, on which she became an authority respected by the League of Nations.

ARCHEOLOGY IN OTHER COUNTRIES

Excavation performance was uneven in competence elsewhere in the Near East. Work in Mesopotamia, like that in Egypt, had had sufficient experience to reach a respectable maturity. At Babylon the Germans under Robert Koldewey began a careful clearance of the huge mound in 1899 and continued until the first World War. The British, with L. W. King and R. Campbell Thompson, returned to Kuyunjik (Nineveh) to carry out a far more systematic job than had been normal practice in the days of Layard or George Smith. Up in the hills toward Iran the French under de Morgan continued their generations-long dig at Susa and were spectacularly rewarded in 1901–2 by the discovery of the stela carrying the law code promulgated by Hammurabi. The University of Pennsylvania's later work at Nippur in Babylonia was rewarded with statuary and a great quantity of cuneiform tablets, upon which scholars are still at work.

Not all of the work was of high quality. The University of Chicago started excavation at Bismayah in southern Mesopotamia in 1903–4 under Edgar J. Banks. This was the expedition under the Oriental Exploration Fund which had competed with Breasted for Rockefeller funds. The diggers were inexperienced and their relations with the Turkish authorities degenerated from month to month, with charges that the Americans were smuggling antiquities out of the country. After two seasons the dig was closed down. For years thereafter Banks sold cuneiform tablets to clergymen and professors from his private collection.

Sayce had made clear the importance of the Hittites in ancient history. He tried to interest the British authorities in an Anatolian excavation at Boghaz Keui, which gave promise of being the Hittite capital. The Germans moved more rapidly and forcibly, however, since they persuaded the Kaiser to intervene on their behalf in Istanbul. In 1906–7 Hugo Winckler, a German philologist, and the Turk, Théodore Macridy Bey, began work at Boghaz Keui. The results were sensational; the methods were shocking. Ultimately they found up to ten thousand cuneiform tablets of the Hittite royal archives. A Kurdish overseer unearthed the tablets and delivered them in baskets to Macridy, who carried them to Winckler, who remained in his chilly wattle hut, studying each document as it was presented. There was no systematic oversight of the dig or recording of the precise location of the objects. Publication, however, proceeded with commendable promptness. Some of the tablets were written in Akkadian (Babylonian) cuneiform and could be read with dispatch. Others used the cuneiform script for unknown languages. The most important of these was deciphered in 1915 by the Czech scholar Bedřich Hrozný as Hittite, a language belonging to the Indo-European family. A brilliant new chapter of ancient history was thus opened.

The British Museum sent D. G. Hogarth, Leonard Woolley, and young T. E. Lawrence to Carchemish on the Euphrates, just before World War I. They brought to light a Hittite culture several centuries later than that at Boghaz Keui, a culture marked by a body of Hittite hieroglyphic inscriptions. Woolley and Lawrence also made an archeological reconnaissance of the Sinai Desert which was of real value to the British forces when they crossed that wilderness a few years later.

Work in Palestine increased in volume, but was not of uniform quality. We have already mentioned the Harvard work at Samaria, and of course Reisner was a guarantee that standards there would be high. At Gezer from 1902 to 1909 the Irish scholar R. A. S. Macalister ran a careful dig, which was well published and for several years was the reference point for excavation elsewhere in Palestine. The trouble with work in that country arose out of several factors. Excavation inevitably sought biblical objectives, which could not readily be brought to light. In contrast to Egypt and Mesopotamia, Palestine had a paucity of written materials which could serve as constant guideposts for the work. And Palestinian buildings were built and rebuilt and overbuilt in stone, which made a distressing jumble to the inexperienced excavator. The Germans and Austrians tried to untangle the tangled evidence at Megiddo, Taanach, and Jericho, but only brought to light complexities which had to be sorted out by others in later years.

Jerusalem was the scene of a disreputable operation in 1909–11, when a wealthy British adventurer, Captain the Honorable Montague Parker, bribed the custodians of the mosque inclosure to carry on clandestine excavations in the hope of finding temple treasure. The expedition was guided by a crystal ball, and a yacht was anchored at Jaffa for escape purposes. His activities were essentially fruitless and led to a hasty flight when they were discovered. They did start the brilliant career of a young French cleric, L. H. Vincent, who was permitted to study the pottery and other "insignificant" finds. Père Vincent went on to eminence as the beloved head of the École Biblique for nearly half a century, a great force for scholarly good in a land where archeology was always difficult.

Another valued force in Palestine was launched in 1900, when the American Schools of Oriental Research started the School in Jerusalem. The sober annual work of this institution, particularly in the post–World War I regimes of William F. Albright and Nelson Glueck, brought great credit to the Americans.

Out in the Mediterranean a new culture sprang into exciting being through the work of one man. Arthur Evans was a museum curator at Oxford. In 1896 he enunciated his "Cretan hypothesis," the idea that the island of Crete had preceded and shaped the classical Greek culture. At the moment there was no way to test this hypothesis. Then in 1896–98 Crete revolted and broke away from the Turkish Empire. Evans went to work excavating in Crete in 1900, kept on until 1908, then resumed after World War I with several years of fruitful digging. The palace of the legendary King Minos at Knossos was his prize display, and it was indeed a prize. The Cretan culture was colorful and lively; it was monumentally impressive. Evans published it, reconstructed by his genius, in attractive brilliance. It retains that charm which he found there and published with such liveliness. Even though it has now become necessary to recede somewhat from the "Cretan hypothesis" and to modify some of the sweeping conclusions that the work seemed at first to justify, Sir

Arthur Evans brought to light an important independent culture of great importance.

In the Minoan culture of Crete and the Hittite empire of Anatolia, ancient Egypt was acquiring neighbors and competitors to enlarge her setting in the eastern Mediterranean.

Nefert-iti's Head and World War

In 1907 the Deutsche Orient-Gesellschaft received a concession to dig at Tell el-Amarna, and from 1911 on Ludwig Borchardt had great success in excavating and describing the villas of the nobles at that heretic capital. The houses of General Ra-mose, of High Priest Pa-wah, and of the sculptor Thut-mose were particularly fine. In Thut-mose's studio were found works of art in various stages of carving and a fine series of plaster masks of royalty and nobility, for the teaching of art students. In the course of time the prize piece was seen to be a painted limestone bust of Queen Nefert-iti, Akh-en-Aton's wife. This gracious and moving work of art has come to be one of the best known products from ancient Egypt, both because of its esthetic appeal and because of the controversy as to whether it properly belongs in Cairo or in Berlin.

World War I cut short the German excavations at Amarna, and Borchardt did not publish the head of Nefert-iti until 1923. Immediately a storm broke out in Cairo over the title of the Germans to this bust. How could such an outstanding work of art have been conceded to them in the division at the end of a season's campaign? The implication was that there must have been some kind of devious activity which prevented Egypt from retaining the treasure.

Borchardt's publication seems to anticipate protest. It states that there were two outstanding objects found in the 1912–13 season and that one of them, a fine painted limestone altarpiece depicting the Amarna royal family, went to the Cairo Museum, whereas the other, the Nefert-iti bust, was assigned to Berlin. Clearly the implication is that there was a division of paired values and that the official who made the division for the Egyptian government selected the altarpiece as better serving the needs of the Cairo Museum, and as a counterpiece, conceded the head to the Germans. The official records on the division corroborate that the German share of the finds included the head, but the officer for the Egyptian Service of Antiquities had no memory of the exciting quality of the piece, so it is unlikely that he thought of it as one of two outstanding objects which might be considered against each other, with the interests of Egypt guarded by retaining any piece which was unique. A protest was raised in Cairo after the 1923 publication of the head. The advance of nationalism now imputed to the Westerner the spirit of exploitation; it was implied that Nefert-iti's head had left Egypt either illegally or by some hocus-pocus practiced by Borchardt at the division.

Borchardt's brief description of the excavation of the piece shows that the Germans were immediately aware of its high value. On December 6, 1912, in a room of the house of the sculptor Thut-mose, the head was found lying in the debris, apparently fallen from a wall bracket. It was nearly intact, with one inlaid eye and pieces of the ears as the only missing parts. The satisfaction with which Borchardt wrote that they had in their hands *"das lebensvollste ägyptische Kunstwerk"*—the most charming Egyptian work of art—shows that they knew that they had a prize.

What actually happened at the division? Probably we shall never know. It seems unlikely that there was open dishonesty. It is possible that there was a kind of verbal sorcery practiced upon the young Frenchman who came to make the division. It is not unknown for archeologists to try to safeguard their most cherished pieces by pretending that their greatest interest is in objects of lesser merit, in order to direct the attention of the government man away from the prizes. This is a well-known bargaining technique in the Orient. At any rate the official for the Service flatly said that he had not passed the head of Nefert-iti.

One hears various stories, now colored by emotion. A German scholar who was present recollects that Borchardt must have been aware of the high value of the piece because he offered the handsome bakshish of £5 to any workman who might find the missing eye. This witness remembers that the French official who supervised the division for the Egyptian government was indifferent whether Cairo received the bust or the altar. He also recalls that the official release documents described the limestone bust of the queen as the head of a princess in plaster, thus committing two errors of record. Perhaps it was not so much verbal sorcery as official laxness. We shall never know. At any rate, after the head was published, the Egyptian government demanded its release and refused any archeological concessions to the Germans until it should be sent back to Cairo.

A stalemate resulted for nearly a generation. Even a trial attempt to work out an arrangement which would save face on both sides failed. The Germans were to insist upon their legal title to the head but, in the interests of amity, were to offer it as a gift to Egypt. Egypt was to insist that it would return rightfully to Cairo, but in view of the German relinquishing of title, Berlin might be rewarded by the gift of some Old

Kingdom statues from the Cairo Museum. This scheme failed. The bust of Nefert-iti had become a cult object in the Berlin Museum, with reverent visitors laying bouquets of flowers before it. The German populace refused to trade their queen for a couple of commoners. A later attempt at exchange was vetoed by Hitler himself.

Shortly after World War II, I called upon the Undersecretary of Education in Cairo. He waved in my face a sheaf of papers which contained a proposal that the Dendereh zodiac be returned by France to Egypt. But, he protested, the American Army had discovered the bust of Nefert-iti in its hiding place in western Germany toward the end of the war and had returned it to the Germans without recognizing the higher Egyptian claim. It was futile for me to argue that our army's fine-arts specialists could not go back farther than the appropriation of works of art by Hitler, Goering, and Mussolini. For him, Nefert-iti was Egyptian and should remain Egyptian; the argument was ended. The head now rests in a small museum in Dahlem in the Western Zone of Germany.

More than the Dendereh zodiac, more than the pieces smuggled out by Budge, the head of Nefert-iti represents to Egyptian nationalism the powerful exploitation of their assets by Western scholars. This famous case was responsible for much of the restrictive and retentive attitude of the Egyptian Service of Antiquities from the late 1920's until 1960, when the needs of the Nubian campaign induced Egypt to offer more hospitable terms to foreign archeologists.

World War I played in two ways in this unending competition between the excavator and the licensing government. On the one hand, the war provoked additional anti-Western feeling among the Egyptians, who saw the Muslim Turks fighting the Western Christians and who suffered the indignity of far tighter British control under war conditions. The riots and demonstrations after the war erupted from this newly aggrieved nationalism, which cast a suspicious eye upon all Westerners active in Egypt, whether soldiers, diplomats, businessmen, missionaries, or archeologists. Gaston Maspero, sixty-eight years old and in poor health, resigned as Director-general of the Service of Antiquities in 1914. As in the case of Lord Cromer, the retirement of such a figure marked the end of an era. No successor could wield Maspero's authority, which, in his day, seemed to serve both East and West. Thereafter, the Frenchman who carried out the tradition by serving as Director-general, first Pierre Lacau and then Étienne Drioton, had to keep his attention cautiously upon the interests of Egypt and upon the outcry which would arise if there were any suspicion of favoritism for a Western expedition.

On the other hand, the 1920's were a most active period for archeology in the entire Near East. The Arab countries were no longer ruled by the Turks, and a series of Western mandates brought in European directors or advisers to antiquities services in those lands. The new professionalism of archeology, the mature recognition of the essential problems in ancient Near Eastern history, and the material prosperity of the 1920's produced an age of many explorations and excavations. Egypt also experienced the same profusion of expeditions, as we shall see in the next chapter, even though the political setting in Egypt differed from that in Palestine, Syria, or Iraq. The decade from 1922 to 1932 was very active. Then the depression limited finances everywhere, while the rising demands of nationalism were inflamed by political circumstances, by the furor over the head of Nefert-iti, and by the covetous rivalry over the objects from the tomb of Tut-ankh-Amon. But that is a later story.

9 TUT-ANKH-AMON
AND INDEPENDENT EGYPT

The struggle between the Egyptians and the British in the period 1919–36 was a deadlock of obstinacy. Great Britain would have been glad to see a stable regime in Cairo and thus to cut down upon her constant troubles in that country, but no British government was willing to give the Egyptians all that they demanded. Egypt wanted increasing sovereignty and might have received it piece by piece, but no Egyptian leader dared to accept the limited concessions which Great Britain was willing to offer at any one time. In the passion of nationalism, the Egyptians demanded the future now. In the increasing dissatisfaction in Cairo, moderates soon found themselves out of popular favor, and the power of the extremists increased apace.

Zaghlul Pasha in 1919 requested that his *wafd* be permitted to go to London to plead for independence. When London refused, there was disorder, and Zaghlul was deported to Malta, whereat the disorder became violent rebellion. Lord Allenby was made Special High Commissioner in Egypt, and negotiations dragged on. Finally, in February, 1922, Great Britain declared Egypt an independent sovereign state, reserving the right to defend the land against foreign aggression, to protect foreigners resident in Egypt, and to defend the rights of minorities—in other words, to maintain the British army on Egyptian soil. The sixth son of Ismail was to become Fuad I, King of Egypt. No Egyptian politician would openly accept this British offer, but they tacitly went ahead to form governments under it. In 1924 there seemed to be some hope of compromise, when Zaghlul finally became Prime Minister in Cairo, and Ramsey McDonald formed a Labour government in London. The British did make concessions, but McDonald refused to promise the withdrawal of British forces from Egypt or to relinquish the right to defend the Suez Canal. Zaghlul made no concessions and as a result became stronger than ever at home.

The crisis sharpened in November, 1924, when Sir Lee Stack, the Sirdar (Commander-in-chief of the Army) and Governor-general of the Sudan, was cold-bloodedly assassinated in Cairo. Great Britain responded with her former vigor. Egypt had to apologize and pay an indemnity. Zaghlul was forced to resign, and the Egyptian Parliament was dissolved.

Yet it was a losing game for Great Britain. Forces had been released in Cairo which could not be stopped. When Zaghlul died in 1927, he was succeeded as leader of the Wafd party by Mustafa Nahas, a man of equal stubbornness but not equal gifts. Egypt continued in unrest. School-boys who had tasted the pleasures of political agitation would now, on the slightest provocation, take to the streets in a riotous demonstration. A new striking force was the Muslim Brotherhood, a reactionary group founded in 1928, which perhaps took off from the teachings of al-Afghani and Mohammed Abduh in wishing to strengthen Islam by purification, but which reached a point of political-religious fanaticism which could justify the assassination of any Egyptian politicians willing to compromise.

It became a standard device of the politicians to call out the Cairo populace for a noisy demonstration in the square in front of Shepheard's Hotel and the Continental Hotel. For a time such demonstrations had the ingenuous atmosphere of a public holiday. The Westerners sat calmly on the hotel terrace, ostentatiously occupied with their whiskies or their teas, while the mob happily followed some orator denouncing the Westerners. Once the demonstration lost its fervor through bad timing. The mob had poured into the square, and the orator had commenced his harangue. On that day the first sugar cane of the season had just reached the Cairo market. The street hawkers brought the first succulent sticks of cane to this great concentration of customers. Not only was the throng distracted from a responsive attention to the oration, but because it is difficult to express grievance when you are enjoying a fresh treat or to shout slogans when your mouth is full of sugar cane, the affair was a good-humored fiasco. By the 1950's the rioters would become more single-minded and better disciplined.

Early in 1936 Fuad died. He had disliked the Wafd, because every Wafd prime minister had been more powerful than he. Fuad was succeeded by his son Faruq. Nahas Pasha became Prime Minister with strong popular support. At the time Mussolini was invading Ethiopia, and Great Britain desperately needed peace in Egypt, with a firm control of the eastern Mediterranean and the Suez Canal. In August a treaty of alliance was signed between Egypt and Great Britain whereby the independence of Egypt became more nearly a fact. The British army was to leave Egypt proper and to remain in the Suez Canal Zone only, until the Egyptian army might be trained to take over the defense of that waterway. British officials in Egyptian service were to be withdrawn. The Sudan, which had been controlled by Britain alone since 1924, was once more to be a condominium of joint control. Within a year, that final vexation, extraterritoriality, whereby foreigners could be tried by their own courts, was also abolished. Egypt had won all—nearly all—of her goals. British soldiers were still on Egyptian soil, and they were the only really effective force in the country.

Meanwhile the population of Egypt continued to increase at an alarming rate, going up more than 3 million from 1917 to 1937. Part of the dissatisfaction of the Egyptians arose out of an overcrowded land, in which the soil could not adequately feed all the demanding mouths.

Within this frenzied political setting, Egyptian archeology had a decade of remarkably vigorous and fruitful work. The Egyptologist was interested in things thousands of years old. Normally his work took him through Alexandria and Cairo and then out into some remote province, where the political tensions did not seem to matter. But they did matter. He was legally accountable to officials of the Egyptian government, who became increasingly responsive to the political tensions in the land. Those officials felt obliged to answer to the Egyptian Parliament and press. As we shall see in the next chapter, many archeologists found the atmosphere inhospitable and withdrew from work in Egypt.

THE TOMB OF TUT-ANKH-AMON

George Edward Stanhope Molyneux Herbert, Fifth Earl of Carnarvon, was a man of many interests. He owned a famous racing stable, was a fine hunter, a skilled amateur photographer, and an art collector of taste and discrimination. He was one of the early devotees of the automobile, and he liked to drive at full speed. On a rural road in Germany he was suddenly confronted with two bullock carts and smashed up his motor car and himself. For the rest of his life he suffered recurrent illnesses. His physicians advised a life free from exertion or excitement. Then in 1903 he went to Egypt and was entranced by field archeology. Eventually he was assigned a concession in a part of the Theban necropolis where it was assumed that he could do no serious harm. On Maspero's advice he secured the experienced services of Howard Carter as his excavator. For several years they had a life free from exertion or excitement: a few modest finds each season, but nothing which caught public interest. The slow-going pace of archeology seemed to be good therapy. Carnarvon's health was so precarious that he had a personal physician in constant attendance.

When Theodore M. Davis relinquished his concession to the Valley of the Kings, Carnarvon and Carter put in an application to work in that area. Although Maspero agreed with Davis that the Valley was exhausted, he did permit the concession in 1914. Then the war intervened. Carter was stationed in Egypt and was able to do a little each season, with a full resumption of work in 1919. They were looking for Tut-ankh-Amon. From Davis' excavations they had three points of reference suggesting that Tut-ankh-Amon had been buried in the Valley: a faïence cup bearing the royal name, a pit containing the name on fragments of gold leaf, and the cache of pots and bundles, which Winlock ultimately recognized as the burial equipment for Tut-ankh-Amon. Yet for six seasons they followed these leads without success. The 1922–23 season was to be the last for that particular search.

The area of excavation had been narrowed to a triangle on the west side of the Valley only about a hundred and fifty feet on a side, defined by the tombs of Ramses II, Mer-ne-Ptah, and Ramses VI. That seemed to be small enough, but the dumps of previous excavators were massive, and these overlaid a critical obstacle, the original quarrying dump from ancient times. Each of these royal tombs had been tunneled out of the hillside, and below its mouth lay a great pile of stone chips, the product of the quarrying. That pile had been the visible sign of a tomb to the eyes of ancient and modern robbers and of modern excavators. In the twelfth century B.C. and in the twentieth century A.D., nobody had realized that the large tomb of Ramses VI (1140 B.C.) was immediately above the small tomb of Tut-ankh-Amon (1340 B.C.), so the quarry pile of Ramses VI concealed the tomb which Carter and Carnarvon were seeking. This same pile had fooled the ancient tomb robbers, so the tomb of Tut-ankh-Amon had remained essentially intact down to our day.

Carter started the work of that final season on November 1, 1922. Three days later his workmen reported to him a step cut into the rock and leading down, as if to a stairway. At the bottom of sixteen steps there was an intact sealed doorway. Lord Carnarvon in England was alerted by cable, and Carter paused to await his arrival.

On November 26 a lower sealed door was breached, and Carter peered into the antechamber through a small hole. It is difficult to improve upon his words.

> As my eyes grew accustomed to the light, details of the room within emerged slowly from the mist, strange animals, statues, and gold— everywhere the glint of gold. For the moment—an eternity it must have

seemed to the others standing by—I was struck dumb with amazement, and when Lord Carnarvon, unable to stand the suspense any longer, inquired anxiously, "Can you see anything?" it was all I could do to get out the words, "Yes, wonderful things."

This is not the place to catalogue the treasures found in the tomb of Tut-ankh-Amon. Structurally it was a small and insignificant tomb, hastily scooped out of the foot of the cliff, but every room was packed to the ceiling with treasure: furniture, inlaid boxes, jars of metal, of faïence, and of alabaster, statues, chariots, walking sticks, bows and arrows, scarabs, bouquets, gloves, scarves, and a nest of golden shrines. It is still an exciting experience to view the display as presented in the Cairo Museum. For forty years since that time every striking archeological discovery has been evaluated as "one of the greatest finds since the tomb of Tut-ankh-Amon." And so, back in 1922–23, the London *Times*, the *New York Times*, and the *Illustrated London News* played up the discoveries week by week. And so, everyone who could travel to Egypt made the pilgrimage to the Valley of the Kings. Thousands of them presented their cards or letters of introduction to Carnarvon or Carter, hoping to be permitted inside the tomb.

The astonishing nature of the tomb and of its materials does not completely account for the public excitement. Yes, of course, there was the romantic story of a nobleman on a treasure hunt coming upon vast quantities of gold. There was the mystery of untouched survival for nearly thirty-three hundred years. For those who knew their history, there was the tie-in of Tut-ankh-Amon with the family of Akh-en-Aton and Nefert-iti, about whom romancing may be endless. Tut-ankh-Amon was Akh-en-Aton's son-in-law. The London press felt a vested interest in a British discovery; and I have heard that the managing editor of the *New York Times* had a hobby of reading Egyptian hieroglyphs and felt a personal pride in the story. It was a continued story, with new treasures emerging week after week, with the sudden death of Lord Carnarvon and then the fantastic rumors of the "curse of King Tut." Further, it came at a time when public interest craved something exotic and non-controversial. The League of Nations, reparations from Germany, Home Rule in Ireland, disarmament, prohibition and bootlegging—these were vexatious problems in a world which had reacted from World War I with the desire to be rid of tensions—"King Tut's tomb" was interesting, amusing, and imposed no strain upon the conscience. Everyone wanted to see it.

It was a great stroke of fortune that Howard Carter was the man responsible for the clearing of the tomb. For some one else the temptation to hold press conferences, to pose for the camera, to clear the tomb in a sensational hurry, would have been a great temptation. With physical materials Carter was a patient and careful craftsman; he went one step at a time. He and his staff did the manual work in the tomb, refusing to be bothered by officials, tourists, or journalists. Carnarvon took care of public relations, and, as it turned out, he had the harder job.

Carter was a gifted water-color artist who had worked with Petrie thirty years earlier, had made admirable copies of the beautiful carvings in the temple of Deir el-Bahri, and in 1899 had been appointed Inspector of Monuments in Upper Egypt and Nubia. He was vigilant enough in that post to earn the resentment of clandestine diggers and of dealers. Shortly after he had been transferred to the inspectorate at Sakkarah, he supported the native guards at a tomb when they refused to admit a group of intoxicated Frenchmen who lacked the proper tickets. One of the Frenchmen was knocked down; there was a formal protest; Carter refused to apologize and had to resign. He had been knocking about from one temporary job to another until he was recommended to Lord Carnarvon in 1907.

Carter had a very British face, round with a full moustache, and when not at work, a neat formality of dress. His lonely years had made him very much an individualist. He was accustomed to work alone, and he worked best alone. When he had to have assistants, he was explicit enough in his instructions to them, but otherwise treated them with conspicuous disdain. He could be a brute, but he was superb in his handling of antiquities. It took ten years to clear out the four small rooms of the tomb, record the objects as they appeared, clean and restore them, and then pack them for shipment to the Cairo Museum. His meticulous care saved a great deal of the evidence.

In the 1922 emergency he assembled a good staff. An engineer handyman, A. R. Callender, was summoned from nearby Armant. The Metropolitan Museum generously loaned him the experienced excavator, A. C. Mace; the skilled photographer, Harry Burton; and two draftsmen, Lindsley F. Hall and Walter Hauser. One of the ablest new members of the staff was Alfred Lucas, who had just completed service as chief chemist to the Egyptian Survey Department. Lucas came to be the leading authority upon ancient Egyptian materials and their uses. There could have been no one better fitted for the preservation of the valuable objects coming out of the tomb. Further, in the expectation that the tomb would provide inscriptions, Carter asked two philologists to stand by, Breasted and the skilled Alan H. Gardiner of England. These composed the essential staff, along with the patron Carnarvon, who handled public relations.

In that first year tragedy struck. Carnarvon neglected to treat a mosquito bite; it became infected; pneumonia set in, and he died in April, 1923. Out of that sad fact the superstitious carrion made a feast, with the "curse of King Tut." It was claimed by these scaremongers that the tomb had been inscribed with an ancient curse, something on the order of "Death shall come on swift wings to him who shall violate this tomb." One otherwise reputable scholar wrote that he had seen the curse inscribed over the door. Those of us who have read the few inscriptions in the tomb know that there is no such text. For some years two smug scoundrels toured the lecture clubs in the United States, each of them claiming that of the twenty-three workers on the tomb of Tut-ankh-Amon twenty-two had died in strange and terrible ways and that the lecturer alone was left to tell the tale. Neither of them had ever worked on the tomb or was even an Egyptologist. A British Egyptologist, Weigall, let reporters understand that he was feeling under some malign influence and enjoyed a brief spurt of prominence as another victim of the curse. He happened to be one of the many with whom Carter had quarreled, and he had been forbidden entry into the tomb! In statistical fact it could be argued that working on the tomb extended life expectancy. Of the ten staff members I have named above, two were still alive after forty years. Five others survived the finding of the tomb by an average of twenty years. But what are statistics to those who want to believe a childish sensation?

The Carnarvon estate continued to support work on the tomb of Tut-ankh-Amon, and in 1923–24 Carter had the delicate and difficult task of dismantling the golden shrines around the sarcophagus, lifting the granite lid, and finally viewing the burial within the sarcophagus on February 12, 1924. Carter was exhausted and on edge when he received a brusque telegram the next day from the Minister of Public Works forbidding him to show the tomb to the wives and families of his collaborating experts and stating that the police had been instructed to prevent their entry, by force if necessary. Carter blew up and posted a notice saying that the tomb was closed, "owing to the impossible restrictions and discourtesies on the part of the Public Works Department and its Antiquity Service." The government thereupon forbade him to enter the tomb again and formally seized possession of it. There ensued a long legal wrangle. At stake was not only the right to carry on scientific work without bureaucratic interference; at stake was the question whether any of the treasures might come to the Carnarvon estate by a division of the finds.

The concession which Carnarvon and Carter held for work in the

Valley of the Kings stipulated that if they found an intact tomb, the uniform collection of objects must remain in Egypt; if, however, the tomb had been plundered, its surviving materials would be subject to division between the Egyptian government and the excavators. All tombs in the Valley had been pillaged in the twelfth century B.C. Now Carter had discovered unmistakable evidence that the tomb of Tut-ankh-Amon had been robbed of a few pieces shortly after the young king's death, had been resealed by the cemetery authorities, and had remained intact until the present time. Was it then a plundered tomb, subject to division, or was it essentially intact, and therefore all to be held in Egypt?

Breasted served as mediator between the Egyptian government and Carter and his lawyers and worked out a compromise which would have salvaged the dignity of both parties and permitted resumption of work on the tomb, when suddenly Carter's lawyer in court asserted that the Egyptian government had seized the tomb "like a bandit." This insult resulted in the breaking-off of all negotiations, and the Carnarvon estate felt obliged to drop its lawsuit. Carter might never have resumed his superb technical activity in the tomb if the assassination of the Sirdar in the autumn of 1924 had not precipitated a complete change in the Egyptian government, so, without fanfare, Carter was permitted to return to the tomb and continue.

The young king Tut-ankh-Amon still lies in his sarcophagus in the Valley of the Kings, little, lonely, but somehow dignified and impressive. The Cairo Museum's most stunning display is the tremendous collection of objects from that small burial. But Egyptology was slow to recover from the passions and suspicions aroused by the controversy over the discovery. To the Egyptians it was another example of Western self-arrogation. They vowed that nothing from the tomb of Tut-ankh-Amon should ever leave Egyptian soil. For nearly forty years they held to that resolve. Only in the present years did the little Tut-ankh-Amon traveling exhibit come to the United States to publicize the archeological crisis in Nubia. Breasted, who had tried hard to persuade the Egyptians to make freewill gifts of a few duplicates to the British Museum and the Metropolitan Museum, would have been pleased to see these objects temporarily on American soil.

THE QUEEN REBURIED

At Gizeh the Harvard-Boston Expedition enjoyed a series of valuable discoveries, enabling Reisner to reconstruct names and relationships of the royal family in the Fourth Dynasty. Then an accident on February 2,

1925, led to a critical discovery which in many ways was as exciting as the tomb of Tut-ankh-Amon.

Reisner happened to be in the United States at the time. The expedition was carrying out a systematic clearance of the well-trodden area east of the Great Pyramid, a section known so long that it offered little promise. The photographer was setting up his camera on an apparently clear surface, when one of the legs of the tripod sank into a soft spot, which was clearly not native rock. A white scar appeared on the pavement. This proved to be part of a cunning patch of plaster, leading to a deep shaft, ultimately ninety feet down. Here was a secret tomb. At the bottom a burial chamber led off, and the excavators could see an alabaster sarcophagus and a great crumpled mass of gold, alabaster, and decayed wood. In a cartouche appeared the name of Snefru, the father of Khufu, builder of the Great Pyramid. A cable went off to Reisner at Harvard, and he answered tersely that the burial could not be that of Snefru and that the tomb was to be closed again pending his arrival.

When work resumed it took about twenty years and included the fascinating detective work of clearing the tomb, of reconstructing the furniture, and of building a theory which could account for the condition of things as found. There was a single chamber, seventeen feet long, nine feet wide, and six feet high. The floor was littered with an utter confusion of tumbled and crumbled objects. At first scarcely more than one man at a time could work in this cramped space at the bottom of the deep shaft. Reisner had decreed that the work should progress so systematically that every object could be reconstructed and returned to its original place. The decay of the wood meant that the furniture had collapsed, strewing gold fittings, vessels, and implements over the floor in a matted confusion. Reisner, Dows Dunham, and Noel Wheeler spent more than ten months in 1926 sorting out this tangle, working right through the hot summer days. If you could note exactly how each fragment lay in relation to all of its neighbors, you might be able to state that these twelve pieces were all parts of one object, whereas fifteen other pieces which were intermeshed with them belonged to a second object. Theoretically that was reasonable, but only a kind of superhuman patience could check and countercheck, to separate out a chair from a bed or a canopy. The characteristic Reisner record was 1,701 pages of notes, plans, and sketches, and 1,057 photographs.

A later stage was physical reconstruction of the collapsed furniture. For example, a wooden armchair had had gold sheeting and legs sheathed in gold. With the decay of the wood, the gold had fallen straight down. Even though it had flattened out somewhat, it still retained form. Faint marks showed where the gold sheets had overlapped each other. Dowel-holes showed where the sheeting had been fastened to the wood. Some of the furniture had had an inlay of golden hieroglyphs. By careful comparison these could be reconstructed into an inscription giving the titles and name of Queen Hetep-heres, mother of Khufu. Reconstruction of the scattered scraps into beautiful and dignified furniture was a fascinating game which was not finished until 1939. There was very little analogy of Fourth Dynasty furniture to serve as guide. The very appealing and convincing results may be seen today in the Cairo and Boston Museums.

As many high officials and Harvard-Boston staff members as could crowd into the little room—eight persons—assembled at Gizeh on March 3, 1927. They were lowered down the vertical shaft in an armchair attached to a pulley. In their official presence, the lid of the alabaster sarcophagus was carefully raised, to view the remains of the mother of the builder of the Great Pyramid. The sarcophagus was empty.

Why then this chamber crowded with her funerary furniture? Why then the deep and concealed pit? Why then the crowding of mortuary objects into so constrained a space? When Khufu had this secret tomb prepared beside his pyramid had he known that his mother's sarcophagus was empty? We shall never know the answer to these questions, but Reisner composed an ingenious theory to embrace all the facts. The husband of Queen Hetep-heres, King Snefru, had been buried at Dahshur, fifteen miles south of Gizeh. It is reasonable that she herself was first laid away beside her husband at Dahshur. Then her son Khufu transferred his attention to his own burial place, the Gizeh Plateau. Dahshur was abandoned under the protection of the funerary priests and cemetery guards. Perhaps then human greed entered; the responsible guards and priests obligingly looked the other way, and robbers violated the Queen's tomb. They seized upon the mummy, carried it out somewhere into the desert, and stripped it of the jewelry and ornaments on the body. Then some one not in on the conspiracy hastily reassembled the things in the tomb, put the lid back on the sarcophagus, and reported to the King. In terror of his life, this informant dared not say that the Queen's body had disappeared. He perhaps reported that robbers had attempted an entry, had been caught in the act and killed. He recommended that Hetep-heres be reburied in a place of greater safety.

Following the theory, Khufu accepted the statement that his mother still lay in her sarcophagus and ordered a secret and hasty reburial beside himself at Gizeh. No one, up to the Vizier himself, dared risk his life by telling the King that her body was missing. In all solemn secrecy, the sarcophagus, the funerary equipment, the carrying chair, the two armchairs, the bed and its canopy, the various boxes, jars, and tools were brought from Dahshur and reburied in the little chamber in Gizeh, to rest for forty-five hundred years. It is a theory of beautiful reasoning, which, alas, cannot be tested as a modern detective might follow up his reasoning.

Reisner continued his work at Gizeh up to his death, but the discovery of the tomb of Hetep-heres was a crown upon his career. His eyesight began to fail badly, but he insisted upon continuing both field work and publishing, remaining at Harvard Camp into the days of World War II. He became more tolerant of his fellow men and even sought out their company in the clubs of Cairo. In November, 1935, he and Breasted had a cordial visit at the Continental Hotel in Cairo, a tacit burying of the hatchet by each of them. His last years were marked by extraordinary courage in the face of physical deterioration and by the utter devotion of his remaining staff and Qufti workmen. When he knew that he was going to die, he asked to be taken from a Cairo hospital back to his beloved pyramids. He left his archeological notes to the Boston Museum, and to Harvard he left a collection of thirteen hundred detective stories.

"Go Down into Egypt"

World War I had been an enforced breathing spell. The former dilettantism in archeology was dying; the new professionalism was coming to the fore. An increased consciousness of the goals of archeology, the hospitality of most of the Near Eastern countries to excavation under new governments, and the prosperity of the 1920's combined to give a decade of very active work. Before the war, one might count the active foreign expeditions in Egypt on one's fingers; in the 1920's they had increased greatly in number. They worked in all parts of the land, at every type of interest from copying to excavation to restoration of monuments, from the early prehistoric to the Christian.

It would be different in the 1930's, after the depression had cut down upon financial resources and when the tightening restrictions of nationalistic Egypt made field work subject to constant tensions and made the expectation of a good division of the finds a false hope. Then the brief-term expeditions no longer came to Egypt, while some of the long-standing enterprises packed up and departed, leaving only a few traditional missions carrying on limited work. In the stretch from 1919 to 1936, we are here chiefly concerned with the more active earlier period.

The French scholar, Pierre Lacau, was Director-general of the Service of Antiquities from 1914 to 1935. A very able philologist and a man of high personal integrity, he was in an impossible position as an administrator. If he permitted the Western scholars the latitude which they felt necessary for their work, the Egyptian nationalists would raise a bitter and effective outcry. If he imposed upon the Western excavators all of the suspicious limitations which nationalism demanded, excavation in Egypt would be limited only to inexperienced Egyptians and the all-too-experienced antiquity dealers. He had to sit on the fence, which seemed to each side an evasion of a necessary and proper commitment. Lacau and his successor, Canon Drioton, were caught between the French demand that they continue to direct archeology in Egypt and the Egyptian demand that the Service of Antiquities be taken over by their own nationals.

Under the circumstances, the brilliant showing of the many expeditions is a tribute to all parties. We cannot name all of the enterprises. For the British, the Egypt Exploration Society took over at Tell el-Amarna with a series of successful seasons. Their most colorful offering was the bright painted decoration in private homes, so different from the temple and tomb art. For the Austrians, Hermann Junker supplemented valuable work in the Gizeh necropolis with explorations in the Delta, which brought forth an interesting prehistoric settlement at Merimdeh Beni-Salameh. Meanwhile, Gertrude Caton-Thompson found equally primitive evidence on the beaches of the Faiyum, and in Middle Egypt with Guy Brunton, established an early predynastic culture, Badarian. These two operations by the British School of Archaeology in Egypt gratified Petrie, for they extended the predynastic cultures which he had defined back into more remote times. The French Archeological Institute of Cairo was carrying on a perennial investigation of the tombs and the workmen's village at Deir el-Medineh in western Thebes. In the long run this would provide basic information on the lives of the Egyptian working class three thousand years ago. In the northeastern Delta, Pierre Montet of the University of Strasbourg began excavations at Tanis, one of the most important cities of ancient Egypt. After some years he found there the royal tombs of kings of the Twenty-first and Twenty-second Dynasties, rich in gold and silver and jewelry, but showing a degeneration in style and craftsmanship from the days of Tut-ankh-Amon. At Karanis (Kom Ushim) in the northern Faiyum the University of Michigan dug for papyri of Greco-Roman times.

Then there was also an explosion of activity by the Oriental Institute of the University of Chicago. The modest financial beginnings of this institution soon expanded into an empire of field expeditions throughout the Near East. In Egypt alone there were seven enterprises. One of them Breasted called "the *most* formidable task I have ever undertaken." This involved copying Coffin Texts, the largest body of unstudied inscriptions from ancient Egypt, mortuary texts written on the wooden coffins of the Middle Kingdom. Pierre Lacau had been busy on these since 1904, and at first it was proposed that Breasted and Gardiner collaborate with him for further work. But so many coffins, filled with a cramped and scratched writing, scattered through the museums of six countries, demanded a more uniform attack. Adriaan de Buck of Holland was charged with the task in 1924. No better scholar could have been found for the work. Before his death in 1959, de Buck had produced seven masterly volumes of copies, which will provide a storehouse for study of the mortuary literature between the Pyramid Texts and the Book of the Dead.

Breasted's next objective was that old dream of his, the copying of all the inscriptions of ancient Egypt, an extension of the work of his two Nubian years. The great temple of Ramses III (built about 1200 B.C.) at Medinet Habu in southern Thebes was chosen as the first objective because it provided the best example of a unified and relatively intact temple in the New Kingdom. In 1924 an epigraphic expedition was formed under the directorship of one of Breasted's former students, Harold H. Nelson. Experiment in the exact copying of a vast area of wall surface, packed with detail of scenes and texts, developed a method of checking and counterchecking, using the photographer, the draftsmen, and the Egyptologist, a procedure so painstakingly controlled that the complex of buildings at Medinet Habu has still not been finished. The Epigraphic Survey at Medinet Habu and Karnak has set a standard of copying work unsurpassed in careful control. Chicago House at Luxor, with its Egyptological library and its beautiful location on the Nile, has been a magnet for visiting scholars for more than thirty years.

The full study of Medinet Habu demanded an architectural description, which in turn demanded excavation. Despite the fact that the earth around the temple had been raked over ever since Mariette's day, there had been no complete and systematic clearance. An architectural historian, Uvo Hölscher of Hannover, was entrusted with this task, and we now have a type description of an Egyptian temple, with its complex of ancillary buildings and storage and service rooms.

Breasted had always been interested in origins; he wanted to know about the earliest human settlement in the Nile Valley. For generations people had picked up surface flints, some of which went back to Palaeolithic forms, but these lay casually on the desert floor, without stratified context. In 1926 Kenneth S. Sandford, a geologist of Oxford, was charged with the responsibility of analyzing the geological and paleontological history of the Nile Valley. Sandford and W. J. Arkell, in a light British motorcar, ranged the edges of the Valley, penetrated up into the cliffs, and gave a documented analysis of the development of the terraces fringing the Nile and the earliest stratified evidence of man's appearance. Their main theory of development remains a basis for the constant amplification and modification of their findings since that time. Sandford also joined a 1932 expedition of the Royal Geographic Society in a bold exploration of the western desert, reaching as far south and west as the Oasis of Uweinat.

In the spring of 1929 Breasted accompanied John D. Rockefeller, Jr., on a visit to the Near East, specifically to the Oriental Institute expeditions there. Before they left America, Breasted was asked by an official of the Rockefeller Foundation not to seek any additional financial support from his patron during the trip. Breasted conscientiously followed this charge. But he was a man of such bounding enthusiasm and vision that his guidance through areas of interest was highly infectious. Mr. Rockefeller was attracted by certain opportunities and generously volunteered to support three new copying projects. No one could fail to be charmed by the lovely water colors which Nina M. Davies had made in the Egyptian tombs. Two superb volumes of colored reproductions appeared. In the beautifully carved temple of Seti I at Abydos, a Canadian woman, Amice M. Calverley, was copying for the Egypt Exploration Society, but no funds were available for publication. A sum of money was provided for volumes of copies from this temple. At Sakkarah the Old Kingdom mastabas were always an excitement, but there had been very little modern copying there which used the new techniques. The Sakkarah Expedition of the Oriental Institute was organized under Prentice Duell. It succeeded in copying and publishing most of the tomb of Mereru-ka within the allotted grant of money.

The profusion of Breasted enterprises in Egypt and the comfortable living quarters provided for the expeditions provoked some natural criticism from scholars who were living and working nearer Petrie's standard of austerity. Breasted recalled the penny-pinching days of his first visit to Egypt or of his two Nubian expeditions and responded that there was no justification for working under such primitive conditions that physical and mental health were affected. An expedition should have adequate quarters and adequate resources, in order to permit concentration upon the archeological job to be done.

ARCHEOLOGY IN OTHER COUNTRIES

The Turkish Empire no longer ruled the Arab countries. Palestine and Iraq lay under British mandates; their antiquity services had British directors; Syria and Lebanon were under French authority. In Turkey itself and in Iran there came into being new westward-looking regimes. The times were ripe for a vigorous archeological development.

In 1927 Petrie took his British School of Archaeology in Egypt "over the border." He explained briefly that it was important to extend the search for Egyptian evidence into neighboring countries, so he had chosen to move into southwestern Palestine; but it had been obvious for some time that he was not happy under the new regime in Egypt. That he had also been bitterly critical of Maspero's regime is immaterial; after years of discontent over the relations between the excavator and the government, he was seeking new and potentially more satisfactory fields. His successive sites in Palestine had their value, but he never succeeded in recapturing that spectacular series of successes which had been his in Egypt. In part, he was too old and too fixed in his ways to adjust to radically different conditions; in part, the archeology of Palestine itself demanded a totally fresh look, without preconceptions transferred from another area.

A similar statement may be made about the work at Jericho by another Englishman who had learned his archeology in Egypt, John Garstang. It is clear from his publications that he was interested in tying Jericho into Egyptian history and in finding walls overthrown in Joshua's time. Some of his conclusions had to be challenged because they were tendentious. Jericho has subsequently been found to be interesting enough in its own right, and the more recent findings have made it a type site for other very early cultures.

The University of Pennsylvania work at Beth Shan on the upper Jordan did not suffer the same disadvantages, both because the Egyptian evidence there was clear and decisive and because the director of the expedition, Clarence S. Fisher, was a man trained by Reisner, taught to take the evidence as it came. Perhaps the best example of learning the archeology of Palestine for its own sake was at Tell Beit Mirsim, a mound about twenty-five miles southwest of Jerusalem. There William F. Albright, of the American School of Oriental Research, began a dig in 1926 with a care which made the mound a type site for subsequent work in Palestine, particularly in Bronze Age and Iron Age pottery. Albright and Père Vincent emerged at this time as the two clear and authoritative voices on Palestinian archeology.

Up the Phoenician coast at Byblos, the French under Pierre Montet began an important excavation, uncovering princely tombs and ample evidence of connections with Egypt from early historical times. The dig unfortunately was not well supervised. The French dumped the debris into the Mediterranean, and a local sheikh reaped a rich harvest of small objects by sending out a boat at night to rake over the discarded earth. Many of the fine alabaster pieces with hieroglyphic inscriptions of Egyptian kings, sent as gifts to the ruler of Byblos, ended up in the Museum of the American University of Beirut when the sheikh decided to sell his loot.

Farther north on the Phoenician coast a peasant was plowing a field in 1928 and drove his plowshare into the top of a tomb. The next year the French moved in, under the direction of Claude F. A. Schaeffer, and enjoyed a series of spectacularly successful seasons. The site, modernly called Ras Shamra, proved to be ancient Ugarit. The most important finds were clay tablets written in a script which was alphabetic and Semitic but used cuneiform signs. There were long mythological poems about gods and heroes, which were promptly recognized in form and allusion to have strong parallels in the Old Testament. Scholars have been reaping a rich harvest from them ever since.

In the spring of 1920 Breasted was leading a survey party through the Near East and was in Baghdad in the month of April. Here he was advised that the British army had been digging machine-gun emplacements at a place called Salihiyeh on the Euphrates, some two hundred and fifty miles northwest of Baghdad, and that they had uncovered some ancient wall-paintings. Since the British line was now to be pulled back from that region, it was important that some scholar go and record the paintings. Would Breasted oblige? Breasted agreed, provided that the British would sanction an attempt by the American party to continue through the no man's land of the Upper Euphrates to Aleppo in northern Syria. The permission was given, and the party successfully made the hazardous traverse, on the way making notes and photographs of the Salihiyeh paintings. These called attention to the site, identified as Dura-Europos, the seat of a Roman garrison and an important city from the second century B.C. to the third century A.D. In 1928 Dura-Europos was occupied by a joint expedition of the French Academy and Yale University, under the directorship of Mikhail J. Rostovtzev of Yale. The most remarkable find was a Jewish synagogue of the middle third century A.D. with well-preserved frescoes, which now ornament the Museum of Damascus.

The prehistory of Mesopotamia was coming to light in the years we are considering. In 1919 H. R. Hall of the British Museum isolated a primitive culture at Tell al-Ubaid, near Ur in southern Mesopotamia. In 1927 members of the Deutsche Orient-Gesellschaft, under Julius Jordan, began work at Warka (Uruk), also in the south, and were rewarded with another prehistoric culture, marked by imposing temple architecture with mosaic design. In 1922 a joint expedition of Oxford University and the Field Museum of Chicago settled in at Kish, not far from the site of Babylon, and in a few years they isolated another culture near the dawn of history, Jemdet Nasr. The successive series on toward history— al-Ubaid, Uruk, and Jemdet Nasr—is now an accepted sequence, but these cultures all emerged out of the unknown within a few years of each other. These were all in the Babylonian territory. Up north, in the Assyrian area, the University of Pennsylvania, under E. A. Speiser, began in 1927 to dig a high mound named Tepe Gawra. The very satisfying results provided a prehistory for the north which could be put into correlation with that appearing in the south.

The most sensational work in Iraq was that of Leonard Woolley at Ur, beginning in 1922, on behalf of the British Museum and the University of Pennsylvania. Woolley was a rare combination of sound excavator and imaginative showman. His work at Ur was rewarded with a superb treasure of gold and jewelry from a "royal cemetery" which had mass burials of human victims like those we saw at Kerma in Nubia. Woolley's excellent results were clouded for other scholars by the slogans he used in his popular writings: "Ur of the Chaldees" and "Abraham's Home Town." Above all, other diggers were annoyed by his claim that a sterile level of clean silt at Ur represented the biblical Flood. This created great interest back home, but excavators at other Mesopotamian sites, who had also found sterile layers of sediment or sand at different archeological levels in their mounds, were understandably vexed by Woolley's successful publicity. There was no one flood period for all Babylonia.

Going further afield, in 1922 John Marshall began excavations in the Indus Valley and developed two very early sites, Mohenjo Daro and Harappa, which go back to the third millennium B.C. Thus the subcontinent of India was added to the great early Oriental cultures.

The Oriental Institute was also in western Asia with six new expeditions. On the southern side of the Plain of Esdraelon in Palestine, the ancient town of Megiddo guarded a pass through the Carmel Range. It was so frequent a battleground in antiquity that the Book of Revelation in our Bible locates the final struggle between good and evil at Armageddon, that is, "Mount Megiddo." Megiddo had frequent appearance in the Egyptian records, and it was an obvious place for a modern excavation. The Oriental Institute began work there in 1925, under the field directorship of Clarence S. Fisher. Unfortunately there were frequent changes in command. For the first two seasons the plain in front of Megiddo was cursed with malaria; later the tensions growing out of Arab-Jewish relations in Palestine infected the members of the staff. There were excellent discoveries at Megiddo: a fortified gate, a palace, an underground water system used in case of siege, a fine collection of carved ivories, and a series of horse stables, originally dated to the time of Solomon, but quite possibly a few generations later. A final trench down to bedrock produced a primitive shrine and curious rock carvings. The pottery of Megiddo was well described in publication. Yet the excavation has had an element of disappointment. The dating of the levels at Megiddo has been subject to criticism. Again it might seem that when a Palestinian mound is approached in the expectation of certain specific results the psychology of the diggers is at fault. Palestine must be taken for itself before any relations are sought.

Theories about the emergence of the Hittite culture in Anatolia had been based upon limited evidence, and that area seemed to offer great promise. The Oriental Institute launched an exploration in 1926 and in the following year settled down to excavate the mound of Alishar, well to the east of Ankara. Again the results were at first valuable as type material, but as time has gone on, Alishar itself no longer seems clear, consecutive, and typical enough to serve for comparison elsewhere.

No similar charge need be leveled against the Oriental Institute results from the Amuq Plain of northwest Syria (now a part of Turkey). The work which began there in 1932 sampled several mounds without preconceived ideas, and in part because of careful analysis and in part because it remains the chief sequential work in the area, the results remain basic for this bridge between Syria-Palestine and Mesopotamia.

The Oriental Institute's work in Iraq, under the genial direction of Henri Frankfort from 1929, was also critical and important. Northeast of Baghdad the expedition worked on four mounds, which ran from the Uruk period well on into historical times. The emerging picture clarified the transition from prehistory through the early dynastic ages and down into well-documented times. The actual illustrations of the process were many: Tell Asmar, a fair-sized city in its corporate elements, a fine cache of early votive statutes, a temple complex mounted upon an oval mound at Khafajah, evidence which fixed the dates of the newly found Indus Valley culture, and so on. This Babylonian expedition pulled together what had already become visible in other separated sites of Mesopotamia and put it in orderly sequence.

To the north the Institute's Assyrian expedition excavated the imposing mound of Khorsabad, royal residence of Sargon II (721–705 B.C.). One heroic enterprise is worth recording here. A colossal winged bull of stone, thirty to forty tons in weight, had been the ancient guardian of a royal doorway. Rain seepage in the wall behind had apparently thrown it down, and it lay buried and broken into three major pieces, the largest about fifteen tons in weight. In 1929 the best transportation medium for the twelve-mile trip from the mound of Khorsabad to the Tigris River was a three-ton truck. A trailer was built of iron, with wheels taken from wartime cannon. When loaded with the largest piece, this trailer frequently collapsed. On the fifth day of the journey, the truck itself broke down completely, three hundred yards from the waiting boat on the river. Cables were run out from the boat so that its donkey engines might drag the heavy weight down to the bank. In the process, the boat pulled itself out of the river and up onto the bank. It then had to put out anchors to haul itself back into the stream. All in all it took Pinhas Delougaz nine hot and frustrating days to move that one piece twelve miles. Its majestic dignity in the Oriental Institute Museum at Chicago fully justifies the painful effort.

Finally, the Oriental Institute in 1931 took over work at one of the noblest sites of the ancient world, the palace terrace of Darius and Xerxes at Persepolis in Iran. The excavation, first under Ernst Herzfeld and later under Erich F. Schmidt, was chiefly concerned with beautifully sculptured reliefs, although the Elamite cuneiform tablets from the palace treasury continue to give valued information on the economics of the Persian period.

From 1936 on, the Oriental Institute had to trim its financial sails, and most of its expeditions terminated their work within a few seasons. The major enterprise continuing to the present time has been the copying expedition at Luxor. Breasted's first and major interest has been continued.

This tedious catalogue of places, persons, dates, and discoveries has its solemn purpose. A record of American archeological work in Egypt needs to be put into perspective—the work of other agencies in Egypt and the parallel archeological developments in neighboring countries. All were part of a progressive curiosity about the beginnings of human history in the ancient Near East.

10 HERBERT E. WINLOCK: THE PIECES FALL INTO PLACE

INSTITUTIONS AND INDIVIDUALS

In the development of any field of study, it is common experience that the generalists are followed by the specialists. Thus the natural history and natural philosophy of a century ago soon subdivided into physics, chemistry, zoology, botany, and so on. Now the physicist has become a specialist on nuclear particles, crystallography, high temperature, and so on. The teaching of "general physics" may be a specialty in itself. Similarly, in the field of Egyptology, the Lepsius or the Mariette or the Maspero, who spoke with authority on the entire field, was followed by the Petrie or the Carter or the Winlock, whose basic concern was excavation and its results, and by the Erman or the Griffith or the Breasted, whose concentration was upon the texts and their meaning. As time went on, the greater volume of information and the more demanding techniques of study produced further specialization: the excavator who was primarily concerned with primitive cultures, the architectural historian, and the philologist who was skilled in the later stages of the language. That even broke down into specialists on administrative or legal texts, on literary texts, or on religious texts. Egyptology had become too large and too exacting in standards for one scholar to command authority in every aspect of the field. Once the master scholar could stand upon a single peak and seem to be a giant. Now there are so many peaks that their relative heights seem far lower.

The scholar is thus faced with the choice of publishing his conclusions in a specialized work which would be appreciated by a limited number of other specialists or of joining with others in a co-operative production in which each author contributes his expertness to a composite whole.

Eduard Meyer and Gaston Maspero had written ancient Oriental histories and Breasted had written his high-school textbook with singlehanded skill. After World War I, when Cambridge University constructed the *Cambridge Ancient History*, it seemed obvious that the work

178

must be a collaborative effort. Greater authority at every single point would more than compensate for the loss of continuity and consistency. The contributors on early Egypt, H. R. Hall, T. Eric Peet, and James H. Breasted, had very different attitudes toward certain aspects of the history, which was both a strength and a weakness.

The Berlin Dictionary of hieroglyphic had been a collaborative effort from the beginning. World War I, however, withdrew the financial support which had been expected from the German government. When Erman's health and eyesight began to fail, it was the steadfast diligence of Hermann Grapow that brought the work to publication. The first volume appeared in 1925, and Erman wrote in the Introduction: "We thank our friends abroad, above all Mr. J. H. Breasted and Mrs. Ransom Williams, that the Dictionary has not been forced to stop in the post-war period. Now Mr. John D. Rockefeller, Jr., through a generous contribution, has made it possible to bring out the work in the present form and at a reasonable price." The Dictionary has had its critics, but it is a working tool which every Egyptologist uses with profit every day.

An example of a personal tour de force production was W. E. Crum's *Coptic Dictionary*, upon which he began work about 1905 and which was published from 1929 to 1939. Although it was really a tremendous effort by a single man, Crum expressed his gratitude to the many collaborators from different countries.

The daring Breasted, with his Assyriological colleague, D. D. Luckenbill, was not daunted by the perils of dictionary-making. In the early 1920's they launched work on a historical dictionary of the Assyrian (or Akkadian) cuneiform. It is one thing for a government or a national academy to undertake such a mammoth enterprise. It was even bolder for the Oriental Institute, a part of a private university. Despite generous collaboration from scholars everywhere, the sheer labor of collecting, parsing, and analyzing texts took a generation of unremitting drudgery. The first volume did not appear until 1956.

Another singlehanded masterpiece was the grammar of the classical stage of the Egyptian language published by Alan H. Gardiner in 1927. This gifted Englishman had started the study of hieroglyphs quite young, had been encouraged by Griffith while still a schoolboy, had studied with Erman at Berlin, and had been accepted as a foreign collaborator on the Berlin Dictionary from its beginning. Although he expressed indebtedness to Kurt Sethe and Battiscombe Gunn, the *Grammar* was essentially based upon his own collection of examples. One grateful scholar has written:

There is no exaggeration in stating that Egyptian grammar was canonized by this superb work and that all present and future students of the language can only benefit from Gardiner's concern as a teacher in designing a text which is unequaled in the entire Near Eastern field as a felicitous combination of an exhaustive reference grammar and a graduated lesson book to guide the student from his first hieroglyphs onward.

Those of us who had learned our hieroglyphs from Erman's little 1911 *Aegyptische Grammatik* now had a far more satisfactory instrument to offer our own students. In addition, Gardiner secured the talented services of Mr. and Mrs. Davies to design a new font of hieroglyphic type. The book was not only masterly; it was also beautiful.

In Brussels the energetic Professor Jean Capart built upon the growing Belgian interest in Egyptology and particularly upon the 1923 visit of Queen Elisabeth of the Belgians to the tomb of Tut-ankh-Amon to form the Fondation Égyptologique Reine Élisabeth, an institute for research and publicity on ancient Egypt. It performed a most useful task internationally, including the publication of a spirited journal, compilations of Egyptian texts, and excavations, until the death of Capart in 1947. His mercurial enthusiasm and his special gifts in the field of Egyptian art gave the Fondation its most vigorous years of life.

The teaching of Egyptology in the United States benefited by the importation of two foreign scholars to the University of Pennsylvania, successively, Hermann Ranke from Heidelberg and Battiscombe Gunn of England. As yet, this country did not produce enough scholars to fill the few chairs in the subject.

Egyptology was not suffering from diminishing returns. Newly published inscriptions of three different kinds showed that source materials might still come to light. In 1923 Budge published a papyrus in the British Museum which contained the advice of a father to his son, and Erman immediately recognized it as a source background for much of the wisdom literature in our Bible, particularly Proverbs 22:17–24:22. This captured great interest, since it was the first really unquestionable example of textual connection between Egyptian and biblical literature.

In 1931 Alan H. Gardiner began the publication of a unified group of hieratic papyri which Chester Beatty had recently acquired in Egypt. These new texts provided a wonderful refreshment to our source material, for among them were a book for the interpretation of dreams, a mythological story in which the frivolities of the gods were recounted with bawdy irreverence, and an allegory in which the god Osiris became Truth, while his brother Seth became Falsehood.

Further, Kurt Sethe published a study in 1926 of some miserable scraps of broken pottery in the Berlin Museum. They proved to be inscribed with curses against the enemies of the Egyptian king some four thousand years ago. There must have been a solemn ceremony in which the named enemies were chanted off and the inscribed pottery was smashed, thus symbolically destroying all hostility to the throne. Later some figurines of bound captives, inscribed for the same magical purpose, turned up in the Cairo and Brussels museums. Not only was this interesting for the study of Egyptian religion, but the texts also gave a lot of historical information on foreign names and places known to the Egyptians about 1850 B.C.

No Museum, but a Papyrus

With the founding of the Oriental Institute in 1919, James H. Breasted embarked upon a busy career as the administrator of a great research institution. One of the first expeditions was a survey of field opportunities in a trip to the Near East in 1919–20, an adventurous journey in an area still recovering from the war. We have already referred to the later expansion of expeditions in the field and to the *Assyrian Dictionary* at home. In the early 1930's the Institute had thirteen major field expeditions. Another important enterprise was the publication of research projects. By the end of 1936 seventy-seven titles had appeared as reports of the Institute. So great a volume of new work has taken time for the scholars to digest.

In 1924 Breasted met with Rockefeller advisers in New York to discuss the needs of Oriental studies. For years it had been clear that the Cairo Museum was crowded and was out-of-date in its working facilities and storage space. From this meeting in New York there emerged "a $10,000,000 project to provide a magnificent new museum building (to be controlled for thirty years by an international commission, this being the period which it was estimated would be required for training a generation of young Egyptians to take over the responsibility themselves); a smaller building alongside the museum to contain administrative offices, a great scientific library and a research laboratory for the study and publication of the museum's collections; and an endowment to maintain all the foregoing."

This seemed to be enlightened generosity, planned not only to meet the physical needs of the Cairo Museum but also to train young Egyptians toward taking over the administration in their own country. The only obstacles that were foreseen were the long-standing agreement between Great Britain and France that a Frenchman should direct the Service of

Antiquities and the proposal to locate the new museum on the site of the British army barracks in Cairo, Qasr en-Nil.

The leading British journal for Egyptology hailed the Rockefeller offer as an "amazing opportunity" and as an "immense stimulus to Egyptological research." Yet the first difficulties were in London. Just at the time, the French in Syria were engaged in putting down a Druze revolt, directed against the capital in Damascus. The murder of the Sirdar was fresh in memory, and the British felt unable to give up the barracks in Cairo. The plans had to be redrawn, with the proposed museum and institute to be located on the southern end of the island, off Cairo.

In January, 1926, Breasted offered the proposal to King Fuad. His Majesty was decidedly cool to a project coming from abroad for an international control of work in Egypt. He did, however, agree that the plan be studied by his ministers. These ministers then, in the interests of national dignity, offered a number of objections to the contract as presented. For example, they objected to the composition of the international commission, since the foreigners would outnumber the Egyptians on it. The counterproposals were forwarded to Mr. Rockefeller in New York. After he and his attorneys had studied them, they accepted every one of the conditions laid down by the Egyptian authorities.

Yet the atmosphere in Egypt was becoming increasingly hostile to the offer. With the wisdom of hindsight, we can see that the diplomatic presentation had been wholly at the level of high protocol. The people who would be affected by a major change in the antiquities work in Egypt had not been consulted in advance. Naturally, since they did not know the details or atmosphere of the proposal, they permitted themselves to misunderstand it and talk against it. In particular, Pierre Lacau, Director-general of the Service of Antiquities, was, by the nature of his assignment, hostile to any change in the French supervision of archeology in Egypt. Other voices were raised against the Americans and specifically against Breasted as latecomers to the field of Egyptian antiquities who were now allegedly trying to gain a control of that field. The British were lukewarm, and Reisner, who always sympathized with Egyptian aspirations for self-rule, was cool. When Breasted brought to the Egyptian government a new contract embodying the requests which the Egyptians themselves had made, the climate had become chilly. The proposal was turned down as "infringing the sovereignty of Egypt." As in the case of political independence, no Egyptian politician dared accept anything but full and final self-rule. Mr. Rockefeller thereupon withdrew the offer.

In retrospect it still seems that a brilliant opportunity was sacrificed to bickering and petty politics. It is true that the original proposal may have carried a patronizing tone which would have been galling to patriotic Egyptians, but their objections to this had been accepted, and they might have claimed a diplomatic victory. Nearly forty years later, Egypt still has the same antiquated and crowded museum, and there is no consistent provision for training young Egyptians to become Egyptologists and administrators in the antiquities service.

Within several months Mr. Rockefeller offered Palestine $2,000,000 for a national museum. That offer was accepted, and a fine modern building arose just outside the city wall of Jerusalem.

While sitting in his room in a Cairo hotel, awaiting a response from the Egyptian government to the offer of a museum, Breasted worked away at his own research, which was the translation of and commentary on the Edwin Smith Surgical Papyrus. This was one of the two medical documents which had been the property of Edwin Smith of Luxor. It was now housed in the New-York Historical Society. Dr. Caroline Ransom Williams had rediscovered it there, and the Society had asked Breasted to publish it. The fine hieratic text carried a composite incredible to the modern understanding of science, but consistent enough in the ancient Egyptian psychology, a sober analysis of fractures and bruises presented with careful objectivity, cheek-by-jowl with religious and magical hocus-pocus. The technical competence of Breasted's publication of this papyrus offered a refutation to the gossip that he had deserted scholarship in favor of promotion. A British scholar wrote primly: "The publication is in every way exemplary." *The Edwin Smith Surgical Papyrus* set a capstone on Breasted's pyramid of great books: *Ancient Records of Egypt, A History of Egypt, Development of Religion and Thought in Ancient Egypt,* and *Ancient Times.* In his sixties and under a heavy administrative load, he was still capable of skilled and sound scholarship.

In the autumn of 1935, Breasted sailed again for Egypt. His wife Frances had died, and he had married again. This was a different honeymoon from that trip forty years earlier. Yet it was no less bursting with fervor. Breasted was full of vigor: in the Wadi Hammamat he ran up a steep slope to point out a famous inscription. He was full of good will: he arranged a luncheon in Cairo at which he and Reisner, Borchardt and Junker might be reconciled. He was full of ambition: when he returned to Chicago, he was going to begin a rewriting of his *History of Egypt.* He was full of plans: the Oriental Institute had proved its value; it should have a vigorous new life, based upon an endowment. On the ship home from Egypt he was cut down by a streptococcic infection and died after the boat had docked in New York. Happily he never learned of a heavy decision already made in the Rockefeller Foundation: the depression had made necessary a drastic refinancing of the Oriental Institute, with a severe curtailing of its far-flung activities.

WINLOCK AND THE ELEVENTH DYNASTY

The Theban headquarters of the Metropolitan Museum of Art lay within the desert bay of Deir el-Bahri. From the terrace of the expedition house, one looked across to the Eleventh Dynasty temple of Mentu-hotep II (built about 2050 B.C.) and to the Eighteenth Dynasty temple of Queen Hat-shepsut (built about 1500 B.C.). The hillside against which the house was built was honeycombed with tombs of ancient nobles. In the plain before the house lay the tremendous underground tomb of the priest Pe-di-Amen-Opet. On a shoulder off to the left was the pit where the cache of royal mummies had been found. In ancient times an annual procession had moved up the valley of Deir el-Bahri, with the god Amon coming across the Nile to visit the temple of Hat-Hor. It was a place peopled with ancient kings and queens, priests and nobles, quarrymen and stonemasons.

From the beginning of the Metropolitan concession at Thebes in 1910, the work of the Museum focused on Deir el-Bahri. The range of the evidence found was wide, but there was concentration at two points, the Eleventh and Eighteenth Dynasties. The work at Thebes was largely synonymous with the work of Herbert E. Winlock, who once called Reisner the greatest excavator of Egyptian antiquities in his day. Winlock himself had a right to the same title. Certainly few other men could bring ancient Egypt back to such vivid life in their published reports.

In 1921–22 the Metropolitan Museum Expedition made a find of amusing and fascinating material, a few family letters from the Eleventh Dynasty. Winlock's report, carrying Gunn's preliminary translation, gives us a vivid picture of the head of the house, Heka-nakht, a self-important and nagging little man who ruled his eldest son, Mersu, with a heavy rod. On the other hand, nothing was too good for the spoiled youngest son, Snefru. Through the letters we are permitted to look into the household of a small farmer and priest four thousand years ago, to hear the complaints of the family over the short rations that Heka-nakht allowed them, the bickering of the sons with the old man's concubine, the shrewd instructions on how to bargain for the rental of land, and Heka-nakht's eager indulgence to the lazy petulance of the spoiled brat Snefru.

It was not enough for Winlock to present the letters in all their unconscious comedy of situation. He felt obliged to account for their presence in somebody else's tomb high up on the desert hillside. Heka-nakht was a mortuary priest for a vizier of the period. At feast days and stated days he had to stand duty at his lord's tomb. When he was away from Thebes on business, his son Mersu would carry out the priestly function, a tedious task which consisted of merely being present. Perched up on the hillside north of Deir el-Bahri, the young man brought a batch of his father's letters. To pass the time, he sorted them and dis-carded this lot of letters and accounts. Some time later a noble was buried in a tomb nearby. When the passageway leading down to the burial pit was finally blocked up, there was still a small hole in the rubble filling. Someone picked up these discarded papyri, crammed them into the hole, dusted his hands, and went away. We are the gainers from all this in-difference to a batch of old family letters.

The expedition was excavating a huge Eleventh Dynasty tomb high up on a cliff in western Thebes in the winter of 1919–20. Previous ex-cavators had dug in the tomb twice before, but they had neglected to make a plan, and because of their summary methods, it was just barely possible that they might have overlooked a few scraps of inscription. The long corridor now yielded nothing, however. Still there were measurements to be made for the plans, and photographs had to be taken. The thorough excavator had to go to the very end, even of a failure. As the workmen were scraping up the rubbish, one of them noticed that small chips of stone were evading his hoe and trickling down into a crack in the rock flooring. The foreman summoned Winlock, who lay upon the floor and thrust an electric torch into the crack.

> The beam of light shot into a little world of four thousand years ago, and I was gazing down into the midst of a myriad of brightly painted little men going this way and that. A tall slender girl gazed across at me perfectly composed; a gang of little men with sticks in their upraised hands drove spotted oxen; rowers tugged at their oars on a fleet of boats, while one ship seemed foundering right in front of me with its bow balanced precariously in the air. And all of this busy going and coming was in uncanny silence, as though the distance back over the forty centuries I looked across was too great for even an echo to reach my ears.

They had found a hidden cache of model figures of Egyptians going about their daily occupations. The cache had been placed in the tomb of the noble Meket-Re so that he might enjoy an abundance of service throughout eternity. The gaily painted little figures showed Meket-Re inspecting his cattle and sailing on his private yacht, showed the brewery, the bakery, the butcher shop, the granary, the carpenter shops, and the women spinning and weaving. Here were an abstraction of a house and a garden, a dozen boats of different kinds and purposes, and two stately girls carrying offerings to the tomb. Never had Egyptian archeology provided so lively a picture of life on an ancient estate. It was found where other excavators had searched; it was found because of that last little ounce of care which the complete archeologist demands of himself.

The letters of Heka-nakht and the model figures of Meket-Re bring us face to face with the ancient Egyptian, not in the frozen dignity of his tombs and temples, but in the homely busyness of his kitchen and his fields.

The Eleventh Dynasty temple at Deir el-Bahri provided an excellent example of Winlock's reasoning genius in 1920–21. King Mentu-hotep of that dynasty had built a platform with a pyramid in its center and an ambulatory running around the four sides. At the rear of the platform a central-axis avenue led to a peristyle court which held the tomb of the King himself.

Fifteen years earlier the Swiss archeologist, Édouard Naville, had excavated the temple for the Egypt Exploration Society. On the rear of the great pyramid platform he had found six shrines, each built to house the funerary statue of a princess, three shrines on each side of the central axis, but somewhat off-balance with relation to that axis. For four of these shrines Naville had discovered burial pits in direct relation to the shrines, behind and below them. That is, the burial pit of princess A was immediately associated with her shrine, and the same was true for princesses B, C, and probably D. Naville found two other pits, which we shall call x and y, both empty and out of line with the shrines of princesses E and F. He assumed that they did belong to those two princesses and had been plundered in antiquity. Thus the shrines (with capital letters) and the burial pits (with lower-case letters) were on this plan.

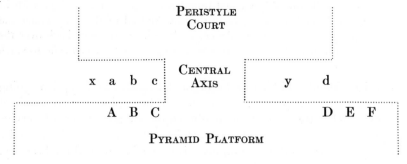

Naville had accepted the out-of-line location of his pits x and y on the argument that all six burials should lie under the peristyle court, in order to be in close association with the tomb of Mentu-hotep himself. The argument would be that when the King laid out the temple, he planned that his harem should be with him throughout eternity.

Now the Metropolitan Museum had taken over the concession at Deir el-Bahri, and Winlock was discussing Naville's reasoning with Walter Hauser. In the intervening years the tangled succession of the Eleventh Dynasty kings had become somewhat clearer. Now evidence of the royal names made it certain that the pyramid platform, with the shrines of the six princesses, had been completed before any work was done on the peristyle court. If so, the burial pits associated with the shrines should have no relation to the peristyle court. Then the empty pits x and y need have no relation to shrines E and F. If that were true, might the burial pits of shrines E and F still be found behind those two shrines?

A rereading of Naville's publication showed no evidence that he had searched behind shrines E and F, but scholars are wary about placing too much weight on theories. "Another of the interminable disappointments of a digger's life was more than we could stand." The testing of the theory was carried out with elaborate unconcern: they showed the workmen where to dig and then went off on other business. This time there was an immediate success. When the earth was cleared, an unbroken ancient pavement appeared, and it sank slightly at two points, suggesting hollow spaces below. The pavement was removed, and they found two intact burials, corresponding exactly to shrines E and F. One was of a Princess Aashait and one of a Princess Miut or "the Cat." The latter was a little girl whose relationship to King Mentu-hotep is uncertain. Aashait was a queen, somewhat more than twenty years old, "a plump little person with bobbed hair done up with innumerable plaits." She came by her plumpness honestly: her beautifully carved limestone sarcophagus, now in the Cairo Museum, shows a scene of a man milking a cow while Aashait sits on a chair, drinking milk throughout eternity.

Another adventure with the Eleventh Dynasty. A man who was excavating for an art museum might be understandably annoyed to open a tomb and find nothing but a heap of ancient corpses, strewn carelessly over the floor, with their linen wrappings torn and scattered. In fact Winlock sealed up the tomb and did not revisit it for four years, until in 1926 there came a time when the Muslim month of fast cut down on his labor force, giving a slack period to clean up postponed responsibilities. Even though a man hopes to find *objets d'art* to fill the museum cases, his scientific conscience tells him that he has to do full justice to all the evidence, no matter how disgusting some of it might be.

At first glance the sixty corpses looked as though they might have come from Christian times. The tomb itself provided not a single object. But when the linen wrappings were examined, it was discovered that they were marked in ink with names characteristic of the Eleventh Dynasty, in a handwriting that fitted the period, and carried a curious symbol which probably indicated the royal cemetery of Mentu-hotep. Since little was known about the physical type of the Thebans at that period, Dr. Douglas Derry, professor of anatomy at the Cairo University, was summoned to look the bodies over.

They had been buried with the utmost simplicity, apparently all at the same time. They had been relatively young men, their heads crowned with thick mops of hair. On the tenth body examined, an arrowhead was found sticking out of his chest. That was a lead to be followed up. In all, the searchers found a dozen arrow wounds, twenty-eight smashed heads, and six bodies which had been torn by birds of prey. These men had been soldiers, fallen upon the field of battle. Their bushy hair had been their chief armor as they fought.

Even though they were simple warriors of the rank and file, they had been accorded the honor of burial in a royal cemetery. It was a fair inference that they had been fighting on behalf of their king, Mentu-hotep, when they fell in battle. One could even reconstruct the stages of the combat. There were no wounds of the sort that hand-to-hand fighting would produce, such as cuts from swords or battle-axes. The first class of injury was an arrow wound which penetrated the body in a downward direction or a depressed fracture of the head. The soldiers had been wounded when they were assailing a fortress, and the defenders up on the ramparts had met the attack by shooting down-ward with arrows and slingshots. Mentu-hotep's forces must have been defeated, for the second type of injury was a smash on the left side of the face. When the enemy in the fortress had routed the king's soldiers, they came out onto the battlefield, jerked up the head of each fallen warrior by his heavy matted hair, which they held in the left hand, and then bashed him on the left cheek with a club. This was the *coup de grâce*, but later the vultures must have come to pick the dead bodies as they lay on the field.

Ultimately Mentu-hotep's other troops must have been successful, since they returned and were able to pick up the slain soldiers and carry them off for honorable burial. In the paintings in Egyptian tombs there had been two or three pictures showing sieges of fortresses. Here at last the grisly evidence in a hastily stacked burial provided point-by-point data for an archeological detective's reconstruction of an ancient battle.

WINLOCK, HAT-SHEPSUT, AND SEN-MUT

About 1490 B.C. the succession to the line of Eighteenth Dynasty kings was a problem. A pharaoh had died, and there was only the young son of a minor wife available to carry on the succession. The priests of Amon recognized this boy as the new divine ruler, and we call him Thut-mose III. The widowed queen, Hat-shepsut, was to act as regent during the boy's youth.

In some of her portrait statues Hat-shepsut might appear demure and feminine, but this was the soft cloak for a determined character. In about five years she stepped out of the role of regent and assumed the kingship— not ruling as queen, but as the same divinely engendered king as her ancestors. She was the female god Horus, with a beard tied to her chin. For eighteen energetic and prosperous years she was the active force in Egypt, while we hear very little about the young Thut-mose. She built extensively and restored temples which had gone to ruin. She emphasized the expansion of foreign trade. Then abruptly she disappeared from history, and Thut-mose III began a warlike and administrative career which made him one of the most famous pharaohs of Egypt.

In 1923 Winlock, digging on the two sides of the avenue leading to Hat-shepsut's Deir el-Bahri temple and going down into a deep pit on the north side, began to find fragments of statues which had been deliberately smashed. They belonged to statues of Hat-shepsut, and they ranged from tiny scraps of stone to pieces weighing a ton. Whether Hat-shepsut died a normal death or not, we do not know. We do see that when Thut-mose took the throne as sole ruler, his partisans went to this temple, dragged out her statues, smashed them into bits, and threw them into these pits.

For years the staff of the Metropolitan Museum worked a detailed game of reconstruction. Could that curiously shaped piece of granite be the elbow of the kneeling statue? Or was it a corner of a throne? The game went even further afield. In 1845 Lepsius had brought back to the Berlin Museum pieces from Deir el-Bahri. Berlin had a seated statue bearing the name of Hat-shepsut but no head. The Metropolitan Museum had found a beautiful portrait head of the queen, but no body. The material in each case seemed to be the same. Further, Berlin had a granite head of the queen which clearly had once been part of a sphinx. The Metropolitan Museum had found six smashed sphinxes. They had never succeeded in fitting a head to one of them. The two museums exchanged letters and photographs. With the amiable concurrence of the Egyptian Service of Antiquities, it ended with a friendly trade: the Berlin seated body joined the head in New York, while the Metropolitan sphinx body joined the head in Berlin. This was a fine example of enlightened co-operation, to the benefit of both sides.

The restored statues of Hat-shepsut in the Metropolitan Museum of Art make up a beautiful exhibit and are a tribute to the excavating skill of Winlock's expedition. Since Lepsius' day it should have been obvious that such fragments were buried there, but the region lay off the main line of normal digging, so three generations had worked at Deir el-Bahri without searching these pits.

Hat-shepsut had a favorite minister named Sen-Mut. Although he was an avid collector of offices and titles, one of his chief functions was the construction of monuments for his king-queen. A great triumph of this Minister of Public Works was the building of Hat-shepsut's handsome temple at Deir el-Bahri.

For the full service of worship in the temple, more than twenty little storage chapels were constructed. Each of them had an altar at the rear upon which the cult statue of a god or goddess would rest, when not carried out for some ritual. Every chapel had a door which was closed and sealed when the deity was not needed in a ceremony. Each door opened inwards, thus concealing the wall behind it.

Winlock's expedition was studying the temple in 1924–25 and noticed that upon the wall space behind each door—that is, the area concealed by the door when the chapel was opened—there had once been a carved scene and inscription. This had usually been savagely hacked out, so one could see only faint traces of a kneeling figure and a line of text. Then the staff discovered a room—eventually four rooms—where the carving had been overlooked by the ancient enemies who had been sent to destroy it. Here was Sen-Mut, facing inward toward the shrine of the god and kneeling in adoration, with an inscription which piously stated that he worshiped the god on behalf of Hat-shepsut. Surely it must have been *lèse-majesté* for this commoner to insert himself into chapels in his sovereign's temple. He succeeded in his audacity because he was the unquestioned favorite of his ruling lady. When Hat-shepsut abruptly fell from power about 1468 B.C., vengeful enemies tried to eliminate every smuggled scene of Sen-Mut in the temple. Fortunately their haste was too great for completeness.

In order to get loose stone for the embankment leading up to the temple of Deir el-Bahri, Sen-Mut had dug a deep quarry to the east and northeast of the temple. In the 1890's Naville had been clearing and copying Deir el-Bahri and had used this pit as a convenient dump. In the middle 1920's the Metropolitan Museum was trying to work out the history of the building of the temple. Foundation deposits under key locations had narrowed the date for laying out the temple plan to a span of two years. Would the quarry confirm or change this evidence?

It is tedious and probably unproductive to dig out a thirty-foot pit covered by the dump of a previous excavator, but it seemed necessary. We have already seen that the barren space produced some of the statue fragments of Hat-shepsut. At the very bottom of the quarry Winlock's men came upon a hole descending into the rock. When this was enlarged, it proved to be the entrance to a steeply descending stairway. Winlock gingerly made his way down the stairs with an electric torch. Forty-five or fifty yards down, he came into a decorated room. There on the wall was carved the bowing figure of Sen-Mut, saluting the names of Hat-shepsut written in hieroglyphs. Starting at the bottom of the quarry which he controlled and cutting at a steep angle, Sen-Mut's men had dug a long tomb shaft leading to burial rooms which lay under the front platform of the temple. Again the wily architect had tried to smuggle himself into the sacred place.

The tomb was unfinished. In part it had been carved; in part it had only been blocked out in paint. Little ink dockets on the wall showed where some foreman had inspected and approved the carving up to a certain date. The tomb had no furnishings; it had never been used. Sen-Mut and his queen must have fallen into disgrace before he could rest forever within the sacred precincts.

The crafty methods of Sen-Mut are further shown by the fact that he had a second tomb in a normal place. This, Theban Tomb 71, lies on the hillside south of Deir el-Bahri, in the conventional setting of the tombs of other Theban nobles. Perhaps he made public demonstration of the fact that he was building this acknowledged tomb in the expected place, as a cover for the insertion of a secret burial place under the Deir el-Bahri terrace. His friends may have congratulated him on the splendid location of his publicly built tomb, high over the Theban plain and enjoying the cool north wind. He could answer with smug graciousness, for he hoped for a much better location, an eternity in association with his lady, Hat-shepsut, and with the goddess Hat-Hor, Lady of the Western Mountain, whose temple was Deir el-Bahri.

His enemies had discovered him hiding behind doors up in the temple. Nearly thirty-four hundred years later the insight and persistence of Winlock discovered his secret tomb, deep down under the temple.

In the integrity of his work and in the luminous imagination which he brought to his results, Herbert E. Winlock was a great archeologist. What manner of man was he, other than this? In appearance he was tall and erect, with a dark moustache and a balding head. He looked and he was forthright. In his realistic appraisal of his fellow workers, he would describe Petrie as an authentic genius, with a lot of useless ideas; Reisner as the greatest of excavators in Egypt, but with an intriguing streak; and Sir Arthur Evans as a simple English country gentleman who was quite unscrupulous about the smuggling of antiquities. Winlock had a caustic way of deflating any show of pretension. Immediately after World War I, he returned to his excavations and received a directive from the Service of Antiquities signed "Capt. R. Engelbach." He shot back an answer signed "Maj. H. E. Winlock."

He had a mischievous way of baiting other scholars. With apparent innocence he would lead Breasted down a series of questions and receive the answers that the cylinder seal had been introduced into Egypt from Mesopotamia, the horse and chariot had been brought in by the Hyksos, the water wheel had come in with the Persians, and so on. Then he would spring his trap: "Well then, Breasted, did the Egyptians ever invent anything themselves?" Breasted, who loved his Egyptians, would sputter and then reluctantly have to accept the fact that he was being teased.

Winlock's delight was in his field work. His Egyptian workmen respected his success and relished his salty wit. But his talents were his undoing. In 1932 he was called home from Thebes to be Director of the Metropolitan Museum of Art. Although he hated to leave the field, he accepted the new post with such dedication that he suffered a stroke in 1939 and had to retire from administration. Carefully husbanding his strength over his remaining eleven years of life, he produced six books.

ARCHEOLOGY UNDER NATIONALISM

In 1923 Ahmed Kamal proposed that Egyptians be trained to understand, work in, and ultimately administer the archeology of their own land. The Director-general of the Service of Antiquities caustically remarked that with the exception of Ahmed Bey himself, few Egyptians had shown any interest in antiquity. Ahmed Kamal responded: "Ah, M. Lacau, in the sixty-five years you French have directed the Service, what opportunities have you given us?" The Egyptian government thereupon took the formal steps to inaugurate a school for the teaching of Egyptology and named Ahmed Kamal the Director. It is sad to record that he died just as the government was announcing its decision.

Nevertheless, there was formal recognition of the need for nationals to work on archeology. Under the teaching of such authorities as Golenischeff and Newberry at the University of Cairo, young Egyptians made their first steps. They were united in the enthusiasm of a new field opened for them. The best of them were sent to France, Germany, or England for advanced study. Of that first lot, five or six of them moved into responsible positions in the Service of Antiquities, the Cairo Museum, or the national university. Soon they were directing field excavations of their own. Nationalism was beginning to take over field work and administration, a process which the Rockefeller proposal for a museum and research institute had envisaged in a different way.

Of the Egyptians who became active in archeology, the most engaging and controversial of them was Selim Hassan, who held the post of Assistant Professor of Egyptology at the Cairo University. He was a man of abundant energy and a quick mind. He had shown great promise in his studies abroad. In 1928 he was assigned to spend three months on the Austrian expedition at Gizeh to receive personal training from Hermann Junker. He was then awarded his own concession in front of the Great Pyramid. Junker and Newberry gave him help and encouragement, and of course Reisner was nearby for advice. Selim Hassan enjoyed several profitable seasons, including the investigation of a curious tomb of Queen Khent-kaus, who abandoned the pyramid or mastaba form in favor of a monument shaped like a sarcophagus, and the discovery of the so-called Sports Stela, in which Amen-hotep II of the Eighteenth Dynasty gave a fascinating account of his prowess as an athlete.

Selim Hassan's excavations at Gizeh and Sakkarah ended under a cloud which cannot be dispelled. There were allegations that he had made financial profit out of his government work and other allegations that he had such political influence that he could not be prosecuted. Whatever the truth of such charges, the government continued to publish his excavation results as he wrote them up. For some years he was in and out of active service on an emergency basis, depending upon those recurrent crises which appeared from time to time when the volatile Egyptian press demanded that somebody of some experience do something about the Cairo Museum or the Service of Antiquities. It was unfortunate that politics produced controversy about the first Egyptian to achieve a wide reputation as an Egyptologist. Others were doing their work effectively and unobtrusively, so no sensational questions were raised about them. For example, the work which Professor Mustafa Amer carried out at the prehistoric settlement at Maadi enjoyed interest and respect. Now, in the 1960's, the number of Egyptian archeologists may still be small, but their work has come to international acceptance and approval.

The archeologist who is excavating for an art museum must have some assurance that he can take home materials worthy of display. Even the digger for a research institute, which theoretically is seeking information rather than objects, needs some material rewards to show his backers. The older dispensation, which the excavator thought of as the normal procedure, had been on the order of a fifty-fifty division by value. When the archeologist had sorted his season's finds into two lots, roughly equal in importance, a representative of the Egyptian government would review that assignment, probably make some changes in it, and then accept one lot for the Cairo Museum. The other lot would be assigned to the excavator, to be cleared for export abroad. Yet this procedure went beyond the law, which stipulated that all antiquities belonged to the Egyptian government. The beneficiary of a concession to dig signed a contract carrying the clause: "All the antiquities found during the entire course of the work shall be turned over to the Service of Antiquities, except for those which the said Service, in its discretion, may decide to give to the beneficiary." Under such a proviso, the excavator might be allotted everything that he found, receive a fifty-fifty division by value, a few insignificant objects, or nothing at all. As the tomb of Tut-ankh-Amon had become a controversial case, as modern communications brought new discoveries to immediate public notice, and as the atmosphere in Egypt grew increasingly hostile to "Western exploitation," the division at the end of a season became less and less rewarding. As the Service of Antiquities built up a more elaborate bureaucratic structure, the supervision of excavation in Egypt became stricter and was often responsive to antiforeign feeling expressed in the Egyptian press and parliament.

To be sure, the tightness of money under the depression was a major factor in cutting down on the number and scope of foreign expeditions in Egypt. But we have already seen that Petrie had decided to move from Egypt into Palestine in the 1920's. The retreat became general in the 1930's. The Metropolitan Museum, after twenty-four seasons at Thebes, closed down its field work in 1936. The University of Pennsylvania pulled out altogether. When the Oriental Institute ended its excavations at Medinet Habu, Chicago did not dig elsewhere in Egypt, although the Epigraphic Expedition at Luxor continued its copying work. In 1936 the Egypt Exploration Society decided to wind up its excavation at Tell el-Amarna and to move away into the Sudan for further work. The Harvard-Boston Expedition remained at Gizeh because Reisner had his publications in train, but the digging was limited to operations which might clarify Reisner's researches. After his death during World War II, Harvard Camp was also closed down. For better or for worse—and one could present arguments on both sides of the case—the old Mariette-Maspero-Petrie order of Egyptian archeology had come to an end.

THE SEQUEL

This account should not rightly close on so negative a note. In October, 1959, the governments of the United Arab Republic and the Sudan issued an appeal to nations and institutions to come into the Nile Valley and undertake archeological work. The population of Egypt had continued to rocket and now exceeded 25 million, with very little more arable land than there had been when the population was half that figure. For the economy of the land, strong measures were needed. It had been decided to build a new High Dam at Assuan, which would back up a huge lake and be greatly to Egypt's agricultural and industrial benefit. But that lake, scheduled for completion in 1965, would inundate three hundred miles of archeological territory, including more than twenty ancient temples. In this archeological crisis the two governments turned to UNESCO, which appealed to the world for help.

Nearly twenty-five years had passed with a minimum of field work. The Egyptologists had turned to other lines of research; few of them were now experienced in excavation. Further, when compared to Egypt proper, Nubia was a backward and unpromising area for digging. The preservation of the stone temples in Nubia was a job for the engineers, not the archeologists. The first reaction to the appeal was one of dismay. What could we do?

In the meantime, Egypt had undergone a revolution. The unfortunate war against Israel had been a humiliation. Anti-foreign feeling culminated in the agony of "Black Saturday," January 16, 1952, when an angry mob burned the best-known Western establishments in Cairo. There followed the peaceful *coup* of July 23, when Faruq was forced to abdicate and a military regime took over. That regime undertook the nationalization of the Suez Canal, survived an attack by Israel, France, and Great Britain, and carried through the final negotiations for the evacuation of British troops from the Suez Canal Zone. By the inauguration of its social-economic reforms, by the sheer fact of survival in a difficult world, the new regime had gained sufficient strength and self-confidence to welcome back the foreign archeologists, who had once been regarded with deep distrust. The Sudan similarly had the confidence of full independence.

The two governments offered the archeologists generous terms: at least a fifty-fifty division of the objects found, and in the case of Egypt, the future right to excavate in Egypt proper, plus the ceding of certain temples and of antiquities from the government storehouses. The atmosphere was genuinely cordial.

It is a pleasure, now that the Nubian campaign is approaching its end, to see the good performance on both sides. National and private agencies came into Nubia promptly, in great number, to take up the gigantic task of studying a vast area in a short space of time. The desolate areas of Nubia were peopled with diggers, copyists, and architects, living on dahabiyehs, because Nubia provided no other quarters. On their part, the two governments have faithfully fulfilled the promises they made when they issued the appeals. Archeologists have been helped to do the things they were asked to do; relations have been cordial; and the division of the finds has been generous.

The world of 1964 is not the world of 1864 or even of 1936. If Egyptology came of age about seventy years ago, it is now mature enough to carry out the goals of our predecessors without some of the emotional tensions of the past. The future holds great opportunity; it can be worthy of the best in the past.

BIBLIOGRAPHY

PREFACE

For the location and significance of Egyptian monuments, nothing has surpassed Baedeker's *Egypt and the Sûdân* (8th ed.; Leipzig, 1929).

A general reference book on ancient Egypt is by Georges Posener, with the assistance of Serge Sauneron and Jean Yoyotte, *Dictionary of Egyptian Civilization* (New York: Tudor Publishing Co., 1959).

The best written history of ancient Egypt, even after half a century, is still James H. Breasted, *A History of Egypt: From Earliest Times to the Persian Conquest* (2d ed.; New York: Charles Scribner's Sons, 1909). Highly authoritative is Sir Alan Gardiner, *Egypt of the Pharaohs* (Oxford: Oxford University Press, 1961).

James Baikie, *A Century of Excavation in the Land of the Pharaohs* (London, 1924), was a good popular book, without independent value.

Warren R. Dawson, *Who Was Who in Egyptology* (London, 1951), has been invaluable for personal biographies and references.

CHAPTER 1

Records of the looting of the Theban tombs are translated and studied in T. Eric Peet, *The Great Tomb Robberies of the Twentieth Egyptian Dynasty* (Oxford, 1930).

A compact summary of Egyptian later history may be found in H. Idris Bell, *Egypt from Alexander the Great to the Arab Conquest* (Oxford, 1948). On the fate of the great library, see Edward A. Parsons, *The Alexandrian Library* (Amsterdam, 1952).

Legends about the patron saint of Luxor appear in the delightful book, *Louqsor sans les pharaons: Légendes et chansons de la Haute Égypte,* by Georges Legrain (Brussels-Paris, 1914).

J. Grafton Milne wrote an article, "The Sanatorium of Dêr-el-Bahri," in the *Journal of Egyptian Archaeology*, I (1914), 96–98. Jaroslav Černý, *Ancient Egyptian Religion* ([London, 1952], pp. 124–50), has material on the late phases of the religion, including the worship of Isis at Philae. Ahmed Fakhry, *The Pyramids* ([Chicago, 1961], pp. 99–102), summarizes the late history of the Great Pyramid.

Two books on Egyptian obelisks and their later history are Sir E. A. Wallis Budge, *Cleopatra's Needles and Other Egyptian Obelisks* (London, 1926); and R. Engelbach, *The Problem of the Obelisks from a Study of the Unfinished Obelisk at Aswan* (London, 1923).

CHAPTER 2

For some of the older ideas on mummies, see Thomas J. Pettigrew, *A History of Egyptian Mummies* (London, 1834); G. Elliot Smith and Warren R. Dawson, *Egyptian Mummies* (London, 1924).

Various obsolete ideas about ancient Egypt are presented in Sir E. A. Wallis Budge, *The Mummy: A Handbook of Egyptian Funerary Archaeology* (2d ed.; Cambridge, Eng.: Cambridge University Press, 1925); and *By Nile and Tigris: A Narrative of Journeys in Egypt and Mesopotamia on Behalf of the British Museum between the Years 1886 and 1913* (2 vols.; London, 1920). An account of European misconceptions about hieroglyphs and of the ultimate decipherment is given in Erik Iversen, *The Myth of Egypt and Its Hieroglyphs in European Tradition* (Copenhagen, 1961).

On William Stukeley, see Warren R. Dawson, "An Eighteenth Century Discourse on Hieroglyphs," in *Studies presented to F. Ll. Griffith* (Oxford: Oxford University Press, 1932), pp. 465–73. Similar fantastic ideas are treated in Sir Alan Gardiner, *Egyptian Grammar* (3d ed.; Oxford: Oxford University Press, 1957), pp. 10–18. On papyrus, see James Baikie, *Egyptian Papyri and Papyrus-hunting* (London, 1925).

For Ledyard's visit to Cairo, see Jared Sparks, *Memoirs of the Life and Travels of John Ledyard, from His Journals and Correspondence* (London, 1828).

On Napoleon's expedition, there are Vivant Denon, *Voyage dans la Basse et Haute Égypte pendant les campagnes du Général Bonaparte* (Paris, 1802), which appeared in English as *Travels in Upper and Lower Egypt* (3 vols.; London, 1803); Jean-Édouard Goby, "Où vécurent les savants de Bonaparte en Égypte?" *Cahiers d'Histoire Égyptienne*, Série V (December, 1953), pp. 290–301; and Jean-Marie Carré, *Voyageurs et écrivains français en Égypte* (Cairo, 1932), Vol. I. More recent is J. Christopher Herold, *Bonaparte in Egypt* (New York: Harper & Row, 1962). The full title of the official publication is: France, Commission des Monuments d'Égypte, *Description de l'Égypte, ou, receuil des observations et des recherches qui ont été faites en Égypte pendant l'expédition de l'armée française, publié par les ordres de Sa Majesté l'empereur Napoléon le Grand* (19 vols.; Paris, 1809–28).

For the modern history in this chapter and the following, see Shafik Ghorbal, *The Beginnings of the Egyptian Question and the Rise of Mehemet Ali* (London, 1928). Alan Moorehead, *The Blue Nile* (New York: Harper & Row, 1962), deals journalistically with the period in beautifully written style.

On the Rosetta Stone there is Sir E. A. Wallis Budge, *The Rosetta Stone in the British Museum* (London, 1929).

For this chapter and the next two there is an admirable article by Caroline R. Williams, "The Place of the New-York Historical Society in the Growth of American Interest in Egyptology," in *New-York Historical Society Quarterly Bulletin*, IV (April, 1920), 3–20. On the Napoleonic statue in the United States, see John D. Cooney, "A Souvenir of Napoleon's Trip to Egypt," in *Journal of Egyptian Archaeology*, XXXV (1949), 153–57.

On the decipherment of the hieroglyphs, see the book by Iversen cited above; Budge, *The Mummy*, cited above; Gardiner, *Egyptian Grammar*, cited above; and F. Ll. Griffith, "The Decipherment of the Hieroglyphs," in the *Times Literary Supplement*, February 2, 1922, reprinted in *Journal of Egyptian Archaeology*, XXXVII (1951), 38–46.

A biography of Young is Frank Oldham, *Thomas Young, F.R.S., Philosopher and Physician* (London, 1913); a biography of Champollion is Hermine Hartleben, *Champollion, sein Leben und sein Werk* (2 vols.; Berlin, 1906).

CHAPTER 3

From the bibliography for chapter 2, the books by Shafik Ghorbal and Alan Moorehead apply to the historical setting of Mohammed Ali, and the article of Mrs. Williams to American Egyptology at that time.

Individual accounts of experiences are Frédéric Cailliaud, *Voyage à Méroé, au Fleuve Blanc* (4 vols.; Paris, 1823); J. L. Burckhardt, *Travels in Nubia* (London, 1819); and G. B. Belzoni, *Narrative of the Operations and Recent Discoveries within the Pyramids, Temples, Tombs, and Excavations, in Egypt and Nubia* (London, 1820). The removal of the Denderah zodiac was described in M. Saulnier *fils, Notice sur le voyage de M. Lelorrain en Égypte* (Paris, 1822).

Of three recent books on Belzoni, the best is by Stanley Mayes, *The Great Belzoni: Archaeologist Extraordinary* (New York: Walker and Co.,

1961). The other two are Maurice W. Disher, *Pharaoh's Fool* (London: Heinemann Publishers, 1957); and Colin Clair, *Strong Man Egyptologist* (London: Oldbourne Press, 1957).

A biography of Champollion has been noted in chapter 2. His *Monuments de l'Égypte et de la Nubie*, four massive volumes, appeared in Paris, 1835–45, with an accompanying *Notices descriptives*, based on his notes (Paris, 1844). Ippolito Rosellini, *I Monumenti dell'Egitto e della Nubia*, appeared in eleven massive volumes (Pisa, 1832–44). Lepsius, *Denkmäler aus Aegypten und Aethiopien*, was published in twelve massive volumes (Berlin, 1849–59), with five text volumes appearing later (Leipzig, 1897–1913). A more general work on his travels, translated into English, is Richard Lepsius, *Letters from Egypt, Ethiopia, and the Peninsula of Sinai* (London, 1853).

Sir John Gardner Wilkinson, *Manners and Customs of the Ancient Egyptians, Including Their Private Life, Government, Laws, Arts, Manufactures, Religion, and Early History; Derived from a Comparison of the Paintings, Sculptures, and Monuments Still Existing, with the Accounts of the Ancient Authors* (3 vols.; London, 1837), is even more useful in the second edition, revised by Samuel Birch (3 vols.; London, 1878).

A valuable article about early collectors is Jacques Tagher, "Fouilleurs et antiquaires en Égypte au XIXe siècle," *Cahiers d'Histoire Égyptienne*, Série III (November, 1950), pp. 72–86. The information about the Egyptian materials in the Peabody Museum, Salem, comes in a letter from the director, Ernest S. Dodge. Mrs. John Holt called my attention to the Egyptian elements in the Mount Auburn Cemetery, and Herbert C. Philpott, the superintendent, supplied the information. The survey of Egyptian architectural forms in America rests on an article by Claire W. Eckels, "The Egyptian Revival in America," in *Archaeology*, III (1950), 164–69. On the same subject, another article, by Clay Lancaster, appeared in the *Magazine of Art*, March, 1950. Caroline Ransom Williams wrote about the forged Menes necklace in *Gold and Silver Jewelry and Related Objects: New-York Historical Society, Catalogue of Egyptian Antiquities, Numbers 1–160* (New York, 1924). John D. Cooney reported the fabricated head from the Abbott Collection in *Brooklyn Museum Bulletin*, XI (1950), 11–26. The piece from the granite shrine at Karnak in the Boston Museum was reported by Bernard V. Bothmer in *Bulletin of the Museum of Fine Arts, Boston*, June, 1952, pp. 19–27.

Jean Capart wrote an article, "Les Fouilles américaines en Égypte," in *Revue du Cercle des Alumni de la Fondation Universitaire* (V [1934], 3–14), with reference to the earliest American interest in Egypt. An Egyptologist, Théodule Devéria, wrote about the Mormon papyri in his

Mémoires et fragments ("Bibliothèque Égyptologique," Vol. IV [Paris, 1896]), pp. 195–202.

For this chapter and subsequent chapters, a convenient reference on the archeological work in other Near Eastern lands is Jack Finegan, *Light from the Ancient Past: The Archeological Background of the Hebrew-Christian Religion* (2d ed.; Princeton, N.J.: Princeton University Press, 1959).

Gliddon's lectures were published as *Ancient Egypt: Her Monuments, Hieroglyphics, History, and Archaeology, and Other Subjects Connected with Hieroglyphical Literature* (New York, 1843). He also wrote *An Appeal to the Antiquaries of Europe on the Destruction of the Monuments of Egypt* (London, 1841).

Auguste Mariette's initial discovery was described by him in *La Sérapéum de Memphis* (Paris, 1857).

CHAPTER 4

The best biographical statement on Mariette was written by Gaston Maspero, "Mariette (1821–1881). Notice biographique," in *Auguste Mariette: Œuvres diverses* (Paris, 1904), pp. i–ccxxiv. Mariette's own excavation reports are many, and we shall note here only *Abydos* (2 vols.; Paris, 1869–80); *Dendérah* (Paris, 1870–80); *Karnak* (2 vols.; Paris, 1875); *Deir-el-Bahari* (2 vols.; Leipzig, 1877); *Catalogue général des monuments d'Abydos* (Paris, 1880); and *Les Mastaba de l'ancien empire* (Paris, 1884–85). His *Sérapéum* was noted in the bibliography for chapter 3.

Rhind's one publication was *Thebes: Its Tombs and Their Tenants, Ancient and Present, Including a Record of Excavations in the Necropolis* (London, 1862).

Piazzi Smyth's basic work is *Our Inheritance in the Great Pyramid* (London, 1864), which he followed up with two editions and three other books supporting his theories. The claim that the Great Pyramid was an instrument of prophecy was advanced in D. Davidson and H. Aldersmith, *The Great Pyramid: Its Divine Message* (London, 1924), with a later edition in 1937.

There is an appreciation of Goodwin by Warren R. Dawson, *Charles Wycliffe Goodwin, 1817–1878: A Pioneer in Egyptology* (Oxford: Oxford University Press, 1934). The humorous account of a meeting with Edwin Smith appears in A. L. Adams, *Notes of a Naturalist in the Nile Valley and Malta* (Edinburgh, 1870). Théodule Devéria, *Mémoires et fragments*, cited in the bibliography to chapter 3, tells of his meeting with Smith. The letter of an American tourist searching for memory of Smith was published in Bayard Holmes and P. Gad Kitterman, *Medicine in An-*

cient Egypt: The Hieratic Material (Cincinnati, 1914), p. 17. Ebers vigorously defended his priority claims to the Papyrus Ebers against those of Edwin Smith in a note in the *Zeitschrift für Aegyptische Sprache und Alterthumskunde* (XI [1873], 41–46); his publication of the document was *Papyros Ebers* (2 vols.; Leipzig, 1875). Breasted's publication of the other medical text is *The Edwin Smith Surgical Papyrus* (2 vols.; Chicago: University of Chicago Press, 1930). The article by Mrs. Williams, cited under chapter 2, also has an appreciation of Edwin Smith.

Some of Ebers' works were translated into English, for example, *Egypt: Descriptive, Historical, and Picturesque* (2 vols.; London, 1885); and the novels, *Uarda* and *An Egyptian Princess.*

The Report of the Committee Appointed by the Philomathean Society of the University of Pennsylvania To Translate the Inscription on the Rosetta Stone (Philadelphia, 1858, 1859), appears with the signatures of Chas. R. Hale, S. Huntington Jones, and Henry Morton.

H. H. Gorringe described the journey of the New York obelisk from Egypt in *Egyptian Obelisks* (New York, 1882).

Schliemann's raciest account of his finds appeared in *Ilios: The City and Country of the Trojans* (London, 1880).

On George Smith and the Flood Tablet, see Seton Lloyd, *Foundations in the Dust: A Story of Mesopotamian Exploration* (Oxford: Oxford University Press, 1947), pp. 164–66.

In addition to the book by Finegan, cited in the bibliography to the previous chapter, on Tischendorf's find at Mount Sinai, there is an article by Ludwig Keimer, "Les Voyageurs de langue allemande en Égypte entre 1800 et 1850," *Cahiers d'Histoire Égyptienne*, Série V (March, 1953), pp. 22–23.

The episode of the American soldiers in Egypt has been treated in William B. Hesseltine and Hazel C. Wolf, *The Blue and the Gray on the Nile* (Chicago: University of Chicago Press, 1961); certain aspects were studied by Frederick J. Cox, "Arabi and Stone: Egypt's First Military Rebellion, 1882," in *Cahiers de l'Histoire Égyptienne*, Série VIII (April, 1956), pp. 155–75. The letter from Pepi II to Har-khuf is translated in James H. Breasted, *Ancient Records of Egypt* (Chicago: University of Chicago Press, 1906), Vol. I, par. 351–54). The discovery of the dancing ivory pygmies was reported by Ambrose Lansing in *Bulletin of the Metropolitan Museum of Art*, XXIX (Supplement to November, 1934), 30–37. Charles Chaillé-Long's colorful and colored reminiscences of his mission into Africa appeared in *Central Africa: Naked Truths of Naked People* (London, 1876).

CHAPTER 5

For this chapter and the next two, a basic book is the Earl of Cromer, *Modern Egypt* (2 vols.; London, 1908). Views hostile to British policy in Egypt were expressed by Wilfrid S. Blunt, *Secret History of the British Occupation of Egypt* (London, 1922); and Pierre Crabitès, *Ismail: The Maligned Khedive* (London, 1933).

Gaston Maspero's publications are amazingly numerous. His *Histoire ancienne des peuples de l'Orient* (Paris, 1875) went through several editions, appearing in English as *The Dawn of Civilization: Egypt and Chaldaea* (London, 1894); *The Struggle of the Nations, Egypt, Syria and Assyria* (London, 1896); and *The Passing of the Empires, 850 B.C. to 330 B.C.* (London, 1900). His other titles in English are *Art in Egypt* (New York: Charles Scribner's Sons, 1912); *Manual of Egyptian Archaeology* (London, 1895); and *Guide to the Cairo Museum* (Cairo, 1895). His greatest philological achievement was the copying and translation of the texts inscribed inside the pyramids of the Fifth and Sixth Dynasties.

Two of Amelia B. Edwards' most influential books were *A Thousand Miles up the Nile* (London, 1877) and *Pharaohs, Fellahs and Explorers* (New York: Harper & Bros., 1891).

Nina Nelson, *Shepheard's Hotel* (London, 1960), is a hastily written popular book.

For this chapter and the following one, see Budge, *By Nile and Tigris* (cited in the bibliography to chapter 2); *Travels in Egypt (December 1880 to May 1891): Letters of Charles Edwin Wilbour*, edited by Jean Capart (Brooklyn Museum, 1936); A. H. Sayce, *Reminiscences* (London, 1923); Joseph Lindon Smith, *Tombs, Temples & Ancient Art*, edited by Corinna Lindon Smith (Norman, Okla.: University of Oklahoma Press, 1956); and Adolf Erman, *Mein Werden und mein Wirken* (Leipzig, 1929).

The Murch Collection in New York was noted in the *Bulletin of the Metropolitan Museum of Art*, Supplement of January, 1911; and the Murch cuneiform fragment in *American Journal of Semitic Languages and Literatures*, XXXIII (1916), 1–8.

The archeology of the Wadi Rayyân was reported by Ahmed Fakhry in *Annales du Service des Antiquités de l'Égypte*, XLVI (1947), 1–19.

For the finding of the royal mummies, there are the books by Budge, Wilbour, and Smith, listed above, and Gaston Maspero, "Les Momies royales de Déir el-Baharî," in *Mémoires de la Mission Archéologique Française au Caire*, I, No. 4 (Cairo, 1889), 511–788. A convenient English summary of the critical element of this is in Leo Deuel, *The Treasures of*

Time (Cleveland, New York: World Publishing Co., 1961). Edward L. Wilson wrote an article on the second opening of the cache, "Finding Pharaohs," in *The Century*, XXXIV (1887), 1–10.

The cited works of Budge, Wilbour, and Sayce were used in the section on the Amarna Tablets. The definitive study of the tablets is J. A. Knudtzon, *Die El-Amarna Tafeln* (2 vols.; Leipzig, 1907–15). S. A. B. Mercer, *The Tell el-Amarna Tablets* (2 vols.; Toronto, 1939), is in English, but has no other scholarly value.

Budge recounts his collecting activities in the book, *By Nile and Tigris*, cited in the bibliography to chapter 2. Appreciations of Sir Wallis Budge were made by R. Campbell Thompson in the *Journal of Egyptian Archaeology*, XXI (1935), 68–70; and by S. R. K. Glanville, *The Growth and Nature of Egyptology* (Cambridge, Eng.: Cambridge University Press, 1947).

Appreciations of Petrie were taken from the book by Smith, cited above; A. E. P. B. Weigall, *The Glory of the Pharaohs* (New York, 1933); and H. E. Winlock's obituary notice in the *Year Book of the American Philosophical Society*, 1942, pp. 358–62. His own crotchety and fascinating account of his career is *Seventy Years in Archaeology* (London, 1931).

CHAPTER 6

Sayce's *Reminiscences* were cited in the bibliography to chapter 5. An appreciation of him by F. Ll. Griffith appeared in the *Journal of Egyptian Archaeology*, XIX (1933), 65–66.

The chief source on Wilbour is his correspondence, published in *Travels in Egypt*, cited in the bibliography to chapter 5. Further brief biographical material appeared in the *Catalogue of the Egyptological Library . . . of . . . Charles Edwin Wilbour*, compiled by W. B. Cook, Jr. (Brooklyn Museum, 1924). John D. Cooney reported the fabricated head in the Wilbour collection in the *Brooklyn Museum Bulletin*, XI (1950), 16–17. Information about Wilbour's relation to the Tweed Ring appeared in the *Providence Journal*, e.g., reminiscences by David Patten, July 25, 1937; July 25, 1958; and February 24, 1960. The Aramaic papyri purchased by Wilbour were published as *The Brooklyn Museum Aramaic Papyri: New Documents from the Jewish Colony of Elephantine*, edited by Emil G. Kraeling (New Haven, Conn.: Yale University Press, 1953).

The German works cited are Adolf Erman's *Neuägyptische Grammatik* (Leipzig, 1880); *Aegyptische Grammatik mit Schrifttafel, Literatur, Lesestücken und Wörterverzeichnis* (Berlin, 1894); and *Aegypten und ägyptisches Leben im Altertum* (Tübingen, 1885), which was translated into English as *Life in Ancient Egypt* (London, 1894); and the first edition of Eduard Meyer's *Geschichte des Alterthums* (5 vols.; Stuttgart, 1884–1902). The episode in the feud between Sethe and Naville was recounted in J. L. Smith, *Tombs, Temples & Ancient Art*, cited in the bibliography to chapter 5.

Some of the implications of the theory of evolution and Higher Criticism were discussed by William F. Albright, *From the Stone Age to Christianity: Monotheism and the Historical Process* (2d ed.; Baltimore: Johns Hopkins Press, 1946), particularly pp. 51–60.

The Israel Stela is translated in *Ancient Near Eastern Texts Relating to the Old Testament*, edited by James B. Pritchard (2d ed.; Princeton, N.J.: Princeton University Press, 1955), pp. 376–78. Two chief publications on the Aramaic papyri are A. E. Cowley, *Aramaic Papyri of the Fifth Century B.C.* (Oxford: Oxford University Press, 1923); and the work edited by Kraeling cited above. A popular account which deals with Greco-Roman papyri is James Baikie, *Egyptian Papyri and Papyrus-hunting* (London, 1925); see also the chapter by C. H. Roberts in *The Legacy of Egypt*, edited by S. R. K. Glanville (Oxford: Clarendon Press, 1942), pp. 249–82. The problem of preserving Egyptian monuments against subsurface water is treated in Somers Clarke and R. Engelbach, *Ancient Egyptian Masonry: The Building Craft* (Oxford: Oxford University Press, 1930), pp. 69–77.

Publications of the work of Theodore M. Davis include *The Tomb of Iouiya and Touiyou*, by Davis, Maspero, and Newberry (London, 1907); *The Tomb of Queen Tîyi*, by Davis, Maspero, G. E. Smith, Ayrton, and Daressy (London, 1910); and *The Tombs of Harmhabi and Touatânkhamanou*, by Davis, Maspero, and Daressy (London, 1912). Elliot Smith's judgment on the mummy in the so-called tomb of Tiy was delivered in his *The Royal Mummies* ("Catalogue Général . . . du Musée du Caire," LIX [Cairo, 1912]), 51–54. Some accounts of Davis' work are drawn from J. L. Smith's book, cited in the bibliography to chapter 5. Winlock's report on one of Davis' finds is Herbert E. Winlock, *Materials Used at the Embalming of King Tūt-ʿankh-Amūn* ("Metropolitan Museum Papers," No. 10 [New York, 1941]).

CHAPTER 7

For the rise of nationalism in Egypt, see H. A. R. Gibb, *Modern Trends in Islam* (Chicago: University of Chicago Press, 1947); and articles in *The Encyclopaedia of Islam* (Leyden, 1913–24). For the recapture of the Sudan, see Cromer, *Modern Egypt*, cited in the bibliography to chapter 5. Pierre Crabitès, *The Winning of the Sudan* (London, 1934), is anti-

British. More objective is P. M. Holt, *The Mahdist State in the Sudan, 1881–1898: A Study of Its Origins, Development, and Overthrow* (Oxford: Oxford University Press, 1958).

A popular book including material on the Assuan Dam is H. E. Hurst, *The Nile* (London, 1952). Pierre Loti's lament over the loss of temples was *La Mort de Philae* (Paris, 1908). Henry G. Lyons wrote *A Report on the Temples of Philae* (Cairo, 1908).

The intact tomb at the Turin Museum was published by Ernesto Schiaparelli, *La Tomba intatta dell'architetto Cha nella necropoli di Tebe* ("Relazione sui lavori della Missione Archeologica Italiana in Egitto— anni 1903–1920," Vol. II [Turin, 1927]).

Petrie gave his principles for excavation in *Methods and Aims in Archaeology* (London, 1904). An appreciation of F. Ll. Griffith appears in the *Journal of Egyptian Archaeology*, XX (1934), 71–77; of N. de G. Davies in the *Journal of Egyptian Archaeology*, XXVIII (1942), 59–60.

The Berlin Dictionary of hieroglyphic was published in five volumes, with six supplementary volumes, by Adolf Erman and Hermann Grapow, *Wörterbuch der ägyptischen Sprache* (Leipzig, 1925–50). The history of the Dictionary was given by Grapow in the *Vorträge und Schriften* of the Deutsche Akademie der Wissenschaften zu Berlin, Vol. LI (1953).

Pier published the Stela of Tjetji as "A New Historical Stela of the Intefs," *American Journal of Semitic Languages and Literatures*, XXI (1904–5), 159–62. Budge's part in the affair was given in his *By Nile and Tigris* (II, 363 ff.), cited in the bibliography to chapter 2.

Much of the material on Breasted comes from the book by his son, Charles Breasted, *Pioneer to the Past: The Story of James Henry Breasted, Archaeologist* (New York: Charles Scribner's Sons, 1943). Appreciations of Breasted appeared in the *Journal of Egyptian Archaeology*, XXI (1935), 249–50; the *Journal of the American Oriental Society*, LVI (1936), 113–20; and *The American Scholar*, V (1936), 287–99. Material on the two Nubian expeditions was published by Breasted: "The Temples of Lower Nubia," *American Journal of Semitic Languages and Literatures*, XXIII (1906–7), 1–64; and "The Monuments of Sudanese Nubia," *American Journal of Semitic Languages and Literatures*, XXV (1908–9), 1–110. I also had access to copies of Breasted's field journals. The copies of scenes and inscriptions made by these expeditions were never published as a whole.

For the legend of a lost oasis, see Ralph A. Bagnold, *Libyan Sands: Travels in a Dead World* (London, 1935), pp. 327 ff.

Breasted published the philosophical text in the British Museum in *Zeitschrift für ägyptische Sprache*, XXXIX (1901), 1–16. His books included *A History of Egypt* (New York: Charles Scribner's Sons, 1905); *Ancient Records of Egypt* (5 vol.; Chicago: University of Chicago Press, 1906); *Development of Religion and Thought in Ancient Egypt* (New York: Charles Scribner's Sons, 1912; "Harper Torchbooks" paperback [New York: Harper & Bros., 1959]); and *Ancient Times: A History of the Early World* (Boston: Ginn & Co., 1916). The latter was reviewed by Theodore Roosevelt in *The Outlook*, February 14, 1917.

CHAPTER 8

On Reisner, G. Steindorff wrote an appreciation in the *Bulletin of the Museum of Fine Arts*, XL (1942), 92–93; and Winlock gave his estimate in the *Year Book of the American Philosophical Society*, 1942, pp. 369–74. Material on Reisner and his expedition appears in Dows Dunham, *The Egyptian Department and Its Excavations* (Boston: Museum of Fine Arts, 1958).

Of Reisner's many publications we may mention *The Hearst Medical Papyrus* (Leipzig, 1905); *Mycerinus, the Temples of the Third Pyramid at Giza* (Cambridge, Mass.: Harvard University Press, 1931); *Excavations at Kerma* ("Harvard African Studies," Vols. V–VI [Cambridge, Mass.: Harvard University Press, 1923]); *The Development of the Egyptian Tomb down to the Accession of Cheops* (Cambridge, Mass.: Harvard University Press, 1936); and *History of the Giza Necropolis* (2 vols.; Cambridge, Mass.: Harvard University Press, 1942–55, the second volume of which was completed by W. S. Smith). The quotation about the burial mound at Kerma is taken from Reisner's preliminary account of the excavation, in the *Bulletin of the Museum of Fine Arts*, XII (1915), 72.

The structure of the Napatan and Meroitic dynasties was given by Dows Dunham, "Notes on the History of Kush, 850 B.C.–A.D. 350," *American Journal of Archaeology*, L (1946), 378–88.

Griffith's most influential work in demotic was *Catalogue of the Demotic Papyri in the John Rylands Library, Manchester* (3 vols.; Manchester, Eng.: Manchester University Press, 1909). His pioneering work in Meroitic was *Karanòg: The Meroitic Inscriptions of Shablûl and Karanòg* (Philadelphia, 1911).

An obituary notice on T. Eric Peet appeared in the *Journal of Egyptian Archaeology*, XX (1934), 66–70; one on Somers Clarke in the *Journal of Egyptian Archaeology*, XII (1927), 80.

The "Tytus Memorial Fund Series," published by the Metropolitan Museum of Art (New York, 1917–27), consisted of five volumes of copies of Theban tombs by N. de G. Davies.

The Earl of Carnarvon and Howard Carter published their earlier work under the title, *Five Years' Exploration at Thebes: A Record of Work Done 1907–11* (London, 1912).

Joseph Lindon Smith's reminiscences were cited in the bibliography to chapter 5. Corinna Lindon Smith published her autobiography as *Interesting People: Eighty Years with the Great and Near-Great* (Norman, Okla.: University of Oklahoma Press, 1962).

Edgar J. Banks' popular account of his work in Mesopotamia was *Bismya or the Lost City of Adab* (New York, 1912). For the story of the discovery of the Hittites see O. R. Gurney, *The Hittites* (Penguin Books, 1952); or, more popularly, C. W. Ceram, *The Secret of the Hittites* (New York, 1956). The survey of Sinai was reported by Leonard Woolley and T. E. Lawrence, *The Wilderness of Zin (Archaeological Report)* (London, 1915). For Palestine a book covering knowledge up to the period of this chapter was R. A. S. Macalister, *A Century of Excavation in Palestine* (New York, 1925). Sir Arthur Evans' definitive publication was *The Palace of Minos: A Comparative Account of the Successive Stages of the Early Cretan Civilization as Illustrated by the Discoveries at Knossos* (4 vols.; London, 1921–35).

Ludwig Borchardt published the first description of the head of Nefertiti in *Porträts der Königin Nofret-ete aus den Grabungen 1912–13 in Tell el-Amarna* ("Deutsche Orient-Gesellschaft: Wissenschaftliche Veröffentlichen," Heft XLIV [Leipzig, 1923]).

CHAPTER 9

George Ambrose Lord Lloyd, British High Commissioner for Egypt and the Sudan, 1925–29, wrote *Egypt since Cromer* (2 vols.; London, 1933–34).

The basic publication of the tomb of Tut-ankh-Amon is Howard Carter, *The Tomb of Tut.ankh.Amen* (3 vols.; London, 1923–33). The first volume was done with the collaboration of A. C. Mace. A choice selection of objects is in Penelope Fox, *Tutankhamun's Treasure* (London, 1951). Christiane Desroches Noblecourt, *Life and Death of a Pharaoh: Tutankhamen* (Paris, 1963), is beautifully illustrated. Discussion of the alleged curse and of Carter's difficulties with Egyptian authorities appears in Charles Breasted's book, cited in the bibliography to chapter 7, and in Joseph Lindon Smith's book, cited in the bibliography to chapter 5.

Obituary notices on Lord Carnarvon appeared in the Carter book, cited above (Vol. I), and in the *Journal of Egyptian Archaeology*, IX (1923), 114–15. Notices on Howard Carter are in the *Journal of Egyptian Archaeology*, XXV (1939), 67–69; on Arthur C. Mace in the *Journal of Egyptian Archaeology*, XV (1929), 105–6; on Alfred Lucas in *Annales du Service des Antiquités de l'Égypte*, XLVIII (1947), 1–6; and on Harry Burton in the *Bulletin of the Metropolitan Museum of Art*, XXXV (1940), 165. Lucas' most used publication is *Ancient Egyptian Materials and Industries*, revised and enlarged by J. R. Harris (4th ed.; London, 1962).

The story of the finding of the tomb of Hetep-heres is told in Dows Dunham's book, cited in the bibliography to chapter 8. The definitive publication of the tomb is G. A. Reisner, *The Tomb of Hetep-heres, the Mother of Cheops*, completed and revised by William Stevenson Smith (*A History of the Giza Necropolis, Vol. II* [Cambridge, Mass.: Harvard University Press, 1955]). Reisner's theory on the reburial was given in the *Bulletin of the Museum of Fine Arts*, XXVI (1928), 76–88, and in Joseph Lindon Smith's book, cited in the bibliography to chapter 5.

John Pendlebury, *Tell el-Amarna* (London, 1935), is a popular account of the British work at that site. An amusing and partly fictional book on the work is Mary A. Chubb, *Nefertiti Lived Here* (London, 1954).

Analysis of the newly found primitive cultures appears in Elise J. Baumgartel, *The Cultures of Prehistoric Egypt* (2 vols.; London, 1947–60). For the discoveries at Tanis, see Pierre Montet, *Tanis, douze années de fouilles dans une capitale oubliée du delta égyptien* (Paris, 1942).

The developing work of the Oriental Institute in Egypt and western Asia was presented in James H. Breasted, *The Oriental Institute* ("University of Chicago Survey," Vol. XII) (Chicago: University of Chicago Press, 1933). I forbear to list here all of the Oriental Institute publications resulting from these operations.

For Palestinian archeology see W. F. Albright, *The Archaeology of Palestine* (rev. ed.; Penguin Books, 1960); and his *Recent Discoveries in Bible Lands* (New York: Biblical Colloquium, 1955); and *The Bible and the Ancient Near East: Essays in Honor of William Foxwell Albright*, edited by G. Ernest Wright (New York: Doubleday & Co., 1961), especially the chapter by Wright himself.

For Garstang's view on Jericho, see John Garstang and J. B. E. Garstang, *The Story of Jericho* (rev. ed.; London, 1948); also John Garstang, *The Foundations of Bible History: Joshua, Judges* (London, 1937). One report on the work at Beth Shan was Alan Rowe, *The Topography and History of Beth-Shan* (Philadelphia, Pa.: University of Pennsylvania Press, 1930).

Two reports on the French work at Byblos are Pierre Montet, *Byblos et l'Égypte: Quatre campagnes de fouilles à Gebeil, 1921–1922–1923–1924* (2 vols.; Paris, 1928–29); and Maurice Dunand, *Fouilles de Byblos* (2 vols.; Paris, 1937–54). Claude Frédéric Armand Schaeffer reported on his excavations at Ras Shamra in *Ugaritica* (4 vols.; Paris, 1939–62). A selection of translations of the Ugaritic epics by H. L. Ginsberg appears in *Ancient Near Eastern Texts Relating to the Old Testament,* edited by James B. Pritchard (2d ed.; Princeton, N.J.: Princeton University Press, 1955), pp. 129–55.

James H. Breasted wrote about the wall paintings at Salihiyeh in *Oriental Forerunners of Byzantine Painting: First-Century Wall Paintings from the Fortress at Dura on the Middle Euphrates* (Chicago: University of Chicago Press, 1924). Two publications on Dura-Europos are M. I. Rostovtzev, *Dura-Europos and Its Art* (Oxford: Oxford University Press, 1938); and Carl H. Kraeling, *The Synagogue,* Part I of *The Excavations at Dura-Europos, Final Report* (New Haven, Conn.: Yale University Press, 1956).

Two good little books on Mesopotamian archeology are Seton Lloyd, *Mesopotamia: Excavations on Sumerian Sites* (London, 1936); and *Foundations in the Dust: A Story of Mesopotamian Exploration* (Oxford: Oxford University Press, 1947). The University of Pennsylvania Press published *Excavations at Tepe Gawra,* Vol. I by E. A. Speiser, 1935; and Vol. II by A. J. Tobler, 1950. For Sir Leonard Woolley's account of his work at Ur, see his *Excavations at Ur: A Record of Twelve Years' Work* (London, 1954). Woolley gave highlights of his career in *Spadework: Adventures in Archeology* (London, 1953).

The Indus Valley cultures may be studied in brief in Stuart Piggott, *Prehistoric India to 1000 B.C.* (Penguin Books, 1950).

Again I refrain from listing Oriental Institute publications on specific operations. An amusing and popular account of the expedition at Tell Asmar is Mary A. Chubb, *City in the Sand* (New York: Thomas Y. Crowell Co., 1957). A statement on the changing philosophy of the Institute was made by Thorkild Jacobsen and John A. Wilson, "The Oriental Institute: Thirty Years and the Present," in the *Journal of Near Eastern Studies,* VIII (1949), 236–47.

CHAPTER 10

The Cambridge Ancient History was issued by the Cambridge University Press in twelve volumes, 1923–39. A new edition is now appearing in separate chapters. Two Americans thus far have appeared as authors,

William Stevenson Smith of the Boston Museum of Fine Arts and the late William C. Hayes of the Metropolitan Museum of Art.

The three dictionaries mentioned are Adolf Erman and Hermann Grapow, *Wörterbuch der Aegyptischen Sprache* (5 vols.; Leipzig, 1925–50); W. E. Crum, *A Coptic Dictionary* (Oxford: Oxford University Press, 1929–39); and the Oriental Institute, *The Assyrian Dictionary*, edited by I. J. Gelb, Th. Jacobsen, B. Landsberger, and A. L. Oppenheim (Chicago: University of Chicago Press, 1956—).

Alan H. Gardiner, *Egyptian Grammar: Being an Introduction to the Study of Hieroglyphs* (Oxford: Oxford University Press, 1927), attained a third edition in 1957. The evaluation of the *Grammar* quoted was from Thomas O. Lambdin in *The Bible and the Ancient Near East: Essays in Honor of William Foxwell Albright*, edited by G. Ernest Wright (New York: Doubleday & Co., 1961), p. 280.

Sir Alan Gardiner left his scholarly reminiscences to be published after his death, *My Working Years* (London: Coronet Press, 1964).

An obituary notice on Jean Capart appeared in *Chronique d'Égypte*, XXII (1947), 181–215.

References to the three new bodies of texts may be found in *Ancient Near Eastern Texts Relating to the Old Testament*, edited by James B. Pritchard (2d ed.; Princeton, N.J.: Princeton University Press, 1955—) on the wisdom text, p. 421; on the Chester Beatty papyri, pp. 14, 495; and on the cursing texts, p. 328.

The story of the offer of a museum to Egypt is told in Charles Breasted's book, cited in the bibliography to chapter 7. The medical text was published by James H. Breasted, *The Edwin Smith Surgical Papyrus* (2 vols.; Chicago: University of Chicago Press, 1930).

The accounts of Winlock's discoveries were taken from his preliminary reports, as they appeared in the *Bulletin of the Metropolitan Museum of Art*. These were assembled and rewritten in H. E. Winlock, *Excavations at Deir el Baḥri, 1911–1931* (New York: Macmillan Co., 1942). The Eleventh Dynasty family letters were published by T. G. H. James, *The Ḥekanakhte Papers and Other Early Middle Kingdom Documents* (New York: Metropolitan Museum, 1962). Winlock published the model figures in *Models of Daily Life in Ancient Egypt from the Tomb of Meket-Rēꜥ at Thebes* (Cambridge, Mass.: Harvard University Press, 1955); and the buried soldiers in *The Slain Soldiers of Neb-ḥepet-Rēꜥ Mentu-ḥotpe* (New York: Metropolitan Museum, 1945).

A notice on the death of Herbert E. Winlock appeared in the *Bulletin of the Metropolitan Museum of Art*, IX (1950), 7–9. He was the subject of a lively profile in the *New Yorker,* July 23, 1933. Winlock's appraisal of some other scholars appeared in *Year Book of the American Philosophical Society:* on Evans in 1941, pp. 372–76; on Petrie in 1942, pp. 358–62; and on Reisner in 1942, pp. 369–74.

An obituary notice on Selim Hassan appeared in *Archiv für Orientforschung,* XX (1963), 310.

On the new High Dam and the Nubian archeological emergency, see issues of the UNESCO *Courier* for February, 1960, and October, 1961; Leslie Greener, *High Dam over Nubia* (New York: Viking Press, 1962); and Walter A. Fairservis, Jr., *The Ancient Kingdoms of the Nile and the Doomed Monuments of Nubia* (Mentor Books, 1962).

BIOGRAPHICAL NOTES

Most Arabic names appear under the first of two or more names. Thus Mohammed Ali is alphabetized as M and Ahmed Kamal as A. The Arabic article *al-* or *el-* and the European *de* or *d'* have been ignored in the alphabetical listings.

Abbas II Hilmi (1874–1944), son of Taufik and Khedive of Egypt, 1892–1914; still very young when he succeeded to rule. Always a reluctant collaborator with the British, he was in Istanbul when World War I broke out and was deposed on December 19, 1914.

"Dr." Henry *Abbott* (1812–59), British physician (not an M.D.); practiced in Cairo, 1830–52; exhibited his collection in New York, 1853–54; had to leave it there against his debts; returned to the practice in Egypt.

The *Abd er-Rasul* family of Thebes came into prominence in the 1880's, when it became apparent that Abd er-Rasul Ahmed had found a hiding place of royal mummies. The brothers were in the service of Mustafa Agha, the British consular agent. The elder brother, Mohammed Abd er-Rasul, confessed the family activity in 1881 and was rewarded with cash and a government job. In 1891 Mohammed pointed out to the government a second great find at Deir el-Bahri, with over one hundred mummies. Some of these mummies were exhibited at the Columbian Exposition in Chicago in 1893.

Andrew Leith *Adams* (1820–82), British army surgeon and naturalist; made a study trip in Egypt in 1862–63 in the company of Rhind and published his observations.

Jamal-ed-Din *al-Afghani* (about 1838–97); born in Iran or Afghanistan; lectured in Istanbul about 1870 but was attacked for lack of orthodoxy; came to Cairo about a year later. His fiery rejection of past and present made him unacceptable to Western and Eastern authorities. He left Egypt in 1879 and died in Istanbul. A most influential apostle of nationalism.

Ahmed Kamal (1849–1923), Egyptian Egyptologist, student of Heinrich Brugsch, with the Service of Antiquities for about thirty-five years.

He was the first Egyptian to undertake scholarly work in Egyptology and published extensively. Just before his death, he successfully proposed a school in Cairo to teach Egyptians the ancient history of their country.

Ali Murad, American consular agent at Luxor in the 1880's and 1890's. I have no data on him, except as he appears in Wilbour's letters.

Émile *Amèlineau* (1850–1916), French cleric; studied under Maspero; excavated badly at Abydos, 1894–98; sold his finds in Paris, 1904. He was Professor of the History of Religions at the École des Hautes Études in Paris.

William Amhurst Tyssen-Amherst, first Baron *Amherst* of Hackney (1835–1909), collector of antiquities and manuscripts, patron of excavation in Egypt. Papyri from his collections were acquired by the Morgan Library in New York in 1913; most of his collection was auctioned in 1921.

Ahmed *Arabi* Pasha (about 1839–1911); called *"al-Misri,"* or "the Egyptian"; born a fellah; commissioned in the Egyptian army, 1862; headed a protest against economies in the Army in 1878 and demonstrations against the government in February and September, 1881. Became a pasha and Minister of War, February, 1882; his influence toward independence provoked the British occupation and his own defeat at Tell el-Kebir on September 13. He was exiled to Ceylon for life but allowed to return in 1901. A soldier rather than an idealist, he was a national hero.

Giovanni *d'Athanasi* (1799–after 1837), originally a Greek named Yanni Athanasiou; served Salt, British Consul-general; excavated at Thebes and traded in antiquities. His personal collection was auctioned in London in 1837.

Edward Russell *Ayrton* (1882–1914), British archeologist; started work in Egypt with Petrie, 1902; with Davis at Thebes, 1905–8.

William John *Bankes* (before 1800–1855), British Member of Parliament; traveled extensively in the East. Four years before Champollion's decipherment, Bankes gave a clue to the reading of royal names in hieroglyphic.

Giovanni Battista *Belzoni* (1772–1823), Italian adventurer; came to England at the age of twenty-five and performed as a strong man; went to Egypt in 1815 to be a technician for Mohammed Ali, but instead collected antiquities for Henry Salt and others. He discovered the tomb of Seti I at Thebes and found the entrance to the Second Pyramid at Gizeh. He died of dysentery on a trip to Timbuktu.

William Berman Sedgwick *Berend* (1855–84), New York banker; studied with Maspero in Paris; published a little; and left a fortune which rumor set at four million francs.

Samuel *Birch* (1813–85), British Egyptologist and Sinologist; served the British Museum, 1836–85; helped found the Society of Biblical Archaeology in 1872. At that time he was the leading British figure in Egyptology.

Ludwig *Borchardt* (1863–1938), German Egyptologist; studied under Erman; to Egypt in 1895, working with Lyons at Philae. With Maspero he began the official *Catalogue* of the Cairo Museum. He specialized in archeology and architecture and excavated at several points, notably at Tell el-Amarna, where he found the famous head of Nefert-iti. Forced out of Germany by the Nazis, he and his wife founded the Swiss Institute in Cairo.

Urbain *Bouriant* (1849–1903), French Egyptologist; studied under Maspero; lived in Egypt 1881–98 and worked in the Service of Antiquities or with the French archeological mission.

Luther *Bradish* (1783–1863), Massachusetts lawyer; followed his journey to Istanbul on a trade mission with visits to Syria, Palestine, and Egypt. In 1820–21 he was a member of the military expedition sent by Mohammed Ali to conquer the Sudan.

James Henry *Breasted* (1865–1935), American Egyptologist; born in Rockford, Illinois, August 27, 1865; studied under Erman, collaborated on the Berlin Dictionary of hieroglyphic; made an epigraphic survey of Nubia and the Sudan, 1905–6, 1906–7. From 1895 he held the first chair of Egyptology in the United States, at the University of Chicago, and was Director of the Oriental Institute from its beginning in 1919. Because he wrote brilliantly, his works were translated into eight other languages. His books and textbooks had great popular appeal. He died in New York, December 2, 1935. Breasted was one of the great American voices on the past.

Emil *Brugsch* (1842–1930), German archeological administrator, younger brother of Heinrich Brugsch; was a photographer and lithographer; assisted his brother, Mariette, and Maspero; was responsible for clearing the cache of royal mummies in 1881. He had a reputation as an intriguer; with one hand he worked for the Service of Antiquities, with the other did secret business with antiquity dealers.

Karl Heinrich *Brugsch* (1827–94), German Egyptologist; sent to Egypt in 1853 and was frequently there; head of the Khedive's school of Egyptology in Cairo, 1870–79; Professor of Egyptology at Göttingen, 1868. A vigorous writer in geography, lexicography, and demotic, he was the chief German scholar in the period between Lepsius and Erman.

Guy *Brunton* (1878–1948), British archeologist; worked with Petrie

1913; later excavated on his own, notably on the Badarian stage of pre-dynastic culture; was with the Cairo Museum from 1931.

Adriaan *de Buck* (1892–1959), Dutch Egyptologist, a clergyman; studied with Sethe at Göttingen; charged with the responsibility of copying and publishing the Coffin texts in 1924; continued this task to his death. He was appointed to the chair of Egyptology at the University of Leyden in 1939. A modest, able, and respected figure.

Sir Ernest Alfred Wallis *Budge* (1857–1934), British scholar and museum official; educated at Cambridge; very successful collector of antiquities for the British Museum in Egypt and Mesopotamia, as he recounts in his scandalous *By Nile and Tigris*. He was a prodigious editor of texts in a great range of Oriental languages, although his accuracy was often questioned. A titanic figure, both praised and disliked.

John Lewis *Burckhardt* (1784–1817), Swiss traveler; educated at Leipzig, Göttingen, and Cambridge; journeyed as "Sheikh Ibrahim," an itinerant Muslim scholar from India. His travels in Arabia are even more famous than those in Nubia, and he visited both Mecca and Medina in 1814–15. His untimely death robbed scholarship of an admirable observer.

Harry *Burton* (1879–1940), British photographer; worked on excavations with Theodore M. Davis; joined the Metropolitan Museum in 1914 as a photographer, developing high technical skill; loaned to Carter and Carnarvon for photography on the tomb of Tut-ankh-Amon in 1923.

Frédéric *Cailliaud* (1787–1869), French mineralogist; employed by Egypt from 1815 to find ores; became a gifted describer of ancient monuments. His assignment to find minerals took him not only to the Sudan but also to the Red Sea and the oases, and he published his observations.

Amice M. *Calverley* (1896–1959), British-born Canadian artist, musician; encouraged by Woolley to take up archeological copying; began to copy at Abydos in the temple of Seti I for the Egypt Exploration Society, 1927. Her last copying there was in 1949.

Jean *Capart* (1877–1947), Belgian Egyptologist; studied under Wiedemann at Bonn; directed the Royal Museum in Brussels; created the Fondation Égyptologique Reine Élisabeth to promote interest in Egyptology; excavated in Egypt; made several trips to the United States; served the Brooklyn Museum as adviser. Capart specialized in Egyptian art and published handsome portfolios of little-known pieces. A volatile enthusiast and brilliant showman, he did much to bring ancient Egypt to modern notice.

George Edward Stanhope Molyneux Herbert, fifth Earl of *Carnarvon* (1866–1923), British patron of archeology. Ill-health directed him to the climate of Egypt, where he began an archeological career and was associated with Howard Carter from 1907. Their work was crowned by the discovery of the tomb of Tut-ankh-Amon in 1922. Carnarvon was a collector of great taste, and his fine collection of Egyptian art objects went to the Metropolitan Museum of Art in 1926.

Howard *Carter* (1873–1939), British artist and archeologist; went to Egypt in 1891 to copy for the Archaeological Survey of Egypt; learned excavation under Petrie in 1892; copied in temple of Deir el-Bahri under Naville; was Inspector of Antiquities for the Egyptian government, 1899–1902; with Theodore M. Davis in 1902; with Lord Carnarvon from 1907. Carter was responsible for the admirable clearance of the tomb of Tut-ankh-Amon, 1922–32. Although he was a man of high individuality who found it difficult to work harmoniously with others, his contributions to Egyptology in art and excavation were great.

Giovanni Battista *Caviglia* (1770–1845), Italian sailor; employed by Salt, British Consul-general, from 1816 on to investigate the pyramids and sphinx at Gizeh, which he did skillfully and ingeniously.

Jean François *Champollion*, "le Jeune" (1790–1832); educated by his brother, Champollion-Figeac; read a paper on Coptic before a learned society at the age of sixteen. His letter on the decipherment of the hieroglyphs was presented to the Académie des Inscriptions et Belles-Lettres at Paris on September 29, 1822. At first a professor at Grenoble, he went to the Collège de France in Paris in 1831. In 1828–29, with the Italian Rosellini, he undertook an expedition to Egypt to copy the monuments.

Somers *Clarke* (1841–1926), British architect; worked with Quibell and others on excavations at el-Kab in the 1890's; built his own house at el-Kab and retired to it in 1902; worked on architectural history, and posthumously aided by Engelbach, produced an admirable book, *Ancient Egyptian Masonry: The Building Craft* (Oxford: Oxford University Press, 1930).

Col. Mendes Israel *Cohen* (about 1790–1847), American officer of Portuguese origin; received American citizenship for his services in the War of 1812; resided in Baltimore. He made his own collection on a trip up the Nile in 1832; added to it in 1835 by purchases in London from an auction of Henry Salt's objects; and loaned it to George Gliddon for the latter's 1842–44 lectures. The collection is now in the Johns Hopkins University.

Eckley B. *Coxe*, Jr. (1872–1916), American businessman; joined the Egypt Exploration Society in 1895; financed excavations by the University of Pennsylvania in Nubia and Egypt.

Evelyn Baring, First Earl of *Cromer* (1841–1917), British diplomat and administrator; knighted, 1892; received earldom, 1901. An artillery officer with service in India, he became Commissioner of the Public Debt in Egypt, 1877–79. From 1883 to his retirement in 1907, he was British Agent and Consul-general in Egypt, the effective ruler of the land. His constant goal was the financial stability which would make Egypt a steady country in Western terms. His 1908 publication, *Modern Egypt*, gives his philosophy of administration; he was a brilliantly successful exponent of nineteenth-century paternalistic guidance of Afro-Asian lands.

Walter Ewing *Crum* (1865–1944), British Egyptologist; studied under Maspero and Erman; held no academic post; spent the major part of his life compiling a Coptic dictionary.

Norman de Garis *Davies* (1865–1941), British artist, formerly a clergyman; worked with Petrie in 1898. Davies was the foremost copyist of Egyptian tombs, which he published meticulously. He was assisted by his wife, Nina, also a gifted artist.

Theodore Monroe *Davis* (1837–1915), American businessman and patron of archeology; became interested in Egypt in 1899; financed excavations in the Valley of the Kings, 1903–12, with remarkably successful results, most of which are in the Cairo Museum. Most of his private collection went to the Metropolitan Museum.

Baron Dominique Vivant *Denon* (1747–1825), patron of arts and letters. Although of the old regime, he accepted the French Revolution. Denon was the most articulate chronicler of the cultural side of Napoleon's expedition to Egypt and was Director-general of the Museums of France, 1804–15. His collections, sold after his death, went chiefly to French provincial museums.

Étienne M. F. *Drioton* (1889–1961), French clergyman (a Canon) and Egyptologist; with the Louvre Museum from 1926; was Director-general of the Service of Antiquities in Egypt from 1936 to 1952, at which time the Egyptians took over the directorship; was a professor at the Collège de France from 1957. Drioton specialized in religious, magical, and cryptographic texts. Amiable and supple, he was a devout clergyman.

Bernardino *Drovetti* (1775–1852), Italian-born, French citizen and military officer; was French Consul-general in Cairo, 1802–14 and 1820–29; explored the Egyptian oases, but is chiefly noted for the collections which his agents assembled, which were ultimately sold to the Turin, Louvre, and Berlin museums. A passionate and lawless fighter for his own interests.

Lady Lucie *Duff-Gordon* (1821–69), lived in the Maison de France at Luxor, 1863–69, because of ill-health; wrote delightful "Letters from Egypt."

Georg Moritz *Ebers* (1837–98), German Egyptologist; studied under Lepsius at Berlin; was Professor of Egyptology at Leipzig; bought a medical papyrus, which now bears his name, from Edwin Smith at Luxor in 1872. In addition to his scholarly works, his popular writings had great influence; among them were the well-illustrated *Aegypten in Wort und Bild*, an admirably edited Baedeker for Egypt (1878), and some highly popular novels.

Amelia Blanford *Edwards* (1831–92), British writer, a successful novelist; first visited Egypt 1873–74; took it over as her province of interest. Her *A Thousand Miles up the Nile* (1877) was extraordinarily influential. She was the prime force in founding the Egypt Exploration Fund in England in 1882. Her American lectures, 1889–90, were published as *Pharaohs, Fellahs and Explorers*. Friend of all the Egyptologists of the day, by her will she established a chair in Egyptology at the University of London for Petrie, 1894.

Auguste *Eisenlohr* (1832–1902), German Egyptologist; studied under Lepsius; was Professor of Egyptology at Heidelberg, 1872–85.

Reginald *Engelbach* (1888–1946), British engineer and archeologist; with Petrie in 1911; at Cairo Museum, 1920–46. His most important publications were on architecture, especially obelisks.

George Bethune *English* (1787–1828), American adventurer, Harvard graduate, clergyman, newspaper editor, officer in the Marines; became a Muslim and served in the campaign against the Sudan; wrote *A Narrative of the Expedition to Dongola and Sennaar* (Boston, 1882).

Johann Peter Adolf *Erman* (1854–1937), German Egyptologist, studied under Ebers; was Professor of Egyptology and head of the Egyptian section of the Berlin Museum, 1884–1923; a brilliant grammarian and genial translator. His philological studies revolutionized the study of the Egyptian language. He also wrote books on the life, religion, and literature of ancient Egypt which were fundamental in the science. In the 1890's he started the great Berlin Dictionary of the Egyptian language, on which publication began in 1926. The introduction to this monumental dictionary carried thanks to three Americans—James H. Breasted, Mrs. Caroline Ransom Williams, and John D. Rockefeller, Jr.—for making possible a publication which had been initiated under government auspices. Erman was one of the greatest figures in Egyptology.

Marie-*Eugénie*-Ignace-Augustine de Montije (1826–1920), Empress of France as wife of Napoleon III, Spanish-born, with a maternal grandfather who had been a naturalized American of Scottish birth; famed for her beauty and elegance. (Louis) Napoleon III lived, 1808–73; was Emperor of France, 1852–70. After the collapse of the Empire, they lived in exile in England.

Sir Arthur *Evans* (1851–1914), British archeologist; studied at Oxford and Göttingen; imprisoned for involvement in a Balkan revolutionary movement. After Crete broke out of the Turkish Empire, Evans excavated there, with brilliant results. He published the sumptuous volumes, *The Palace of Minos*, an exciting restoration of a forgotten culture. A man who always went his own way.

Clarence S. *Fisher* (1876–1941), American archeologist; worked for the University of Pennsylvania at Nippur, Mesopotamia, 1898–1900; later served with Reisner in Egypt; was Curator of Egyptian Antiquities at the University Museum, Pennsylvania, 1915–25; excavated in Egypt, notably at Memphis; excavated for Pennsylvania in Palestine at Beth Shan, for Chicago at Megiddo. His later years were spent in Jerusalem, working on a corpus of Palestinian pottery and devoting his time and resources to the care of poor children.

Charles Lang *Freer* (1856–1915), American businessman and art collector; presented the American government with the Freer Gallery to house his fine collections, particularly from the Far East.

Sir Alan Henderson *Gardiner* (1879–1963), British Egyptologist; read Egyptian with Griffith; studied in Paris, in Berlin with Erman; collaborated in the work of the Berlin Dictionary. Of independent means, he left the university chairs to others, although he held readerships. From his early scholarship onward, he produced an extraordinary volume of admirable studies of Egyptian texts. Two culminations of his work were his *Egyptian Grammar* (1927) and his *Egypt of the Pharaohs* (1961). He and Griffith were the two great philologists of the ancient Egyptian language in England. He is given a respect which verges on awe.

John *Garstang* (1876–1956), British archeologist; worked under Petrie at Abydos in 1899; at University of Liverpool, was Reader in Egyptian Archaeology from 1902, Professor of Archaeology from 1907; excavated at Meroë, 1910–14. In 1919 he became Director of Antiquities in Palestine and Director of the British School of Archaeology in Jerusalem; he excavated Jericho in Palestine, later at Mersin in Turkey. From 1948 he was Director of the British School of Archaeology in Ankara. One of the older school of excavators.

George Robins *Gliddon* (1809–57), British-born American citizen. His father was a merchant and the first American Consul in Egypt, and he also became a Consul there. He published an appeal for the preservation of the Egyptian monuments in 1841; gave public lectures in the United States, 1842–44. An enlightened man in an age of greed.

Vladimir Samionovich *Golenischeff* (1856–1947), Russian Egyptologist, wealthy member of Tsarist nobility; in frequent visits to Egypt brought back to Russia antiquities which are now in the Moscow Museum and literary papyri which are in the Hermitage in Leningrad; left Russia after the revolution and lived in France and Cairo. The leading Russian in the field.

Charles Wycliffe *Goodwin* (1817–78), British lawyer, justice, and Egyptologist, able student of Egyptian language and literature, judge in the Far East from 1865; visited Egypt on his way east.

William Henry *Goodyear* (1846–1923), American museum official and writer on art; studied in Germany; was a curator in the Metropolitan Museum of Art, 1881–88; of the Brooklyn Museum, 1899–1923.

Charles George *Gordon* (1833–85), "Chinese Gordon," British soldier and administrator; made his first fame by service in China from 1860. Commissioned in the Egyptian army, 1873, his services were chiefly in equatorial provinces, with courageous exploration until 1876. As Governor-general of the Sudan, 1877–79, he fought against the slave trade. After an interlude, during which he studied biblical history and archeology in Palestine, he returned to Egypt in 1884 and was sent to evacuate the Sudan of British and Egyptian forces, in the face of the Mahdist uprising. It is not clear whether he disobeyed instructions or was trapped at Khartum. He recognized the rule of the Mahdi in Kordofan; he permitted the slave trade to resume, and he assisted refugees to escape the Sudan. When a relieving force was only three days away, he was killed in the Mahdist taking of Khartum, January 25, 1885.

Henry Honeychurch *Gorringe* (1841–85), American naval officer; brought the New York obelisk from Alexandria, 1880–81; made a small collection of Egyptian antiquities.

Sir J. Eldon *Gorst* (1861–1911), British diplomat, financial adviser to the Egyptian government, 1898–1904; succeeded Cromer as British Agent and Consul-general, 1907–11. The Liberal government in England had him carry out a policy of withdrawal from firm political control. He was blamed by the British as too precipitate, by the Egyptians as too slow.

Eugène *Grébaut* (1846–1915), French Egyptologist; studied under Maspero; was Director-general of the Service of Antiquities, 1886–92, a post for which his rigid and unimaginative nature did not fit him; from 1892, was a lecturer on ancient history at the Sorbonne.

Bernard Pyne *Grenfell* (1869–1926), British papyrologist; was Professor of Papyrology at Oxford from 1916; the leading excavator of Greco-Roman documents in Egypt from 1897.

Francis Llewellyn *Griffith* (1862–1934), British Egyptologist; was Reader in Egyptology, 1901–24, and Professor of Egyptology, 1924–32, at Oxford; with Petrie, 1884–88. A brilliant linguist, he had high achievement in demotic texts and did pioneer work in Meroitic. Griffith was the foremost British linguist of the Egyptian languages in his day. By his will he endowed Oxford with an Egyptological Institute which included a building, library, and manuscripts.

William N. *Groff* (1857–1901), American student under Maspero in Paris; published more than a dozen articles, chiefly in French journals.

Battiscombe George *Gunn* (1883–1950), British Egyptologist, an amateur of Egyptology, he was encouraged by Gardiner to enter the field professionally and joined an expedition in Egypt under Engelbach in 1913. From 1924 to 1931, he worked for the Service of Antiquities and the Cairo Museum; he went to the University of Pennsylvania in 1931, and was named to the professorship of Egyptology at Oxford in 1934. His highly original mind contributed richly to the understanding of the Egyptian language and literature.

Harry Reginald Holland *Hall* (1873–1930), British archeologist; educated at Oxford; became Assistant Keeper of Egyptian and Assyrian Antiquities at the British Museum in 1896; and became Keeper when Budge retired in 1924; he specialized in Egyptian and Aegean archeology and participated in excavations in Egypt and Mesopotamia. His influential *The Ancient History of the Near East* (1913) went into ten successive editions.

Anthony C. *Harris* (1790–1869), a British merchant at Alexandria and a notably successful collector, particularly of papyri; published a few studies and was once President of the Egyptological Society of Cairo. His adopted daughter, Selima (died 1895), a Negress, was a highly cultivated woman; she inherited his collection and sold it to the British Museum in 1872.

Robert *Hay* (1799–1863), British copyist and collector, frequently in Egypt, 1824–38, where he copied admirably and formed a large collection. His manuscripts and part of his collection are in the British Museum, with the remainder of his collection in the Boston Museum of Fine Arts.

Mrs. Phoebe Apperson *Hearst* (1842–1919), Californian, widow of a mining magnate, mother of William Randolph Hearst; financed the University of California expeditions in Egypt, under Reisner's directorship. He named a medical papyrus in her honor.

William Randolph *Hearst* (1863–1951), American newspaper publisher. The bulk of his Egyptian collection was auctioned in London in 1939; many smaller pieces were on sale at Gimbel's in New York.

Uvo *Hölscher* (1878–1963), German architect and engineer; was a professor at the Technische Hochschule at Hannover; before World War I, worked on the architectural history of the Second Pyramid temple at Gizeh and of a gate at Medinet Habu; from 1926 to 1932, directed the excavations of the Architectural Survey of the Oriental Institute at Medinet Habu.

Arthur Surridge *Hunt* (1871–1934), British papyrologist; was Professor of Papyrology at Oxford from 1913; collaborated with Grenfell in excavations and publication.

Jan Herman *Insinger* (1854–1918), Dutch resident in Egypt. Poor and tubercular, he lived by buying and selling antiquities, lending money, and working for Egyptologists. A demotic papyrus bears his name because he was instrumental in buying it.

Ismail (1830–95), son of Mohammed Ali's adopted son, Ibrahim Pasha; was Pasha of Egypt, 1863–67; Khedive, 1867–79; deposed in 1879 on the intervention of England and France; famed for the completion of the Suez Canal during his regime. He strove mightily to build Egypt into a modern nation, but his lack of financial understanding brought such a heavy national debt that the Western powers felt obliged to take control of the economy of the land in 1877.

Hermann *Junker* (1877–1962), German Austrian Egyptologist, a priest; from 1910, was Professor of Egyptology at Vienna; conducted excavations in all parts of Egypt, covering all periods. A most versatile philologist, he had high ability in the language of all periods. From 1929 he was Director of the German Archaeological Institute in Cairo, in which capacity he did his best to serve the German interests of the day. A highly respected scholar.

Horatio Herbert Kitchener, First Earl *Kitchener* of Khartum (1850–1916), British general and administrator. An army engineer, he made surveys in Cyprus and Palestine. He was attached to the Egyptian army from 1883; Sirdar in 1892; conducted the campaign against the Mahdists in the Sudan, 1896–98. After service in the Boer War and India, he became British Agent and Consul-general in Egypt, 1911–14, where he promoted reforms on behalf of the fellahin. He was recalled to England to head the War Office at the beginning of World War I and lost his life when a ship struck a mine in 1916. His Egyptian collection sold at auction in 1938.

Pierre *Lacau* (1873–1963), French Egyptologist; was Director-general of the Service of Antiquities in Egypt, 1914–35, a period of difficult adjustment for the French control of archeology. A very able copyist and philologist.

Rev. Gulian *Lansing*, D.D. (1825–92), the most scholarly of the American missionaries in Egypt; served in Damascus, 1850–56, and in Egypt, 1856–92. His son Joseph served as a physician in Egypt, and his grandson Ambrose became an Egyptologist, working for the Metropolitan Museum.

John *Ledyard* (1751–88), American adventurer and explorer; born in

Groton, Connecticut; attended Dartmouth for training as a missionary, but left and went to sea; found service with Captain Cook on the voyage around the world, 1776–80; explored in Siberia in 1787; discussed with Thomas Jefferson the exploration of the American northwest, but instead was commissioned by the African Association in London to ascend the Nile, cross Africa, and descend the Niger. He died in Cairo before the journey started.

Georges *Legrain* (1865–1917), French Egyptologist; turned from philological studies to conservation in 1895, when he was made responsible for the preservation of the temple at Karnak; made rich discovery of statues at that temple in 1903; took great interest in the workers, their songs, and stories.

Karl Richard *Lepsius* (1810–84), German Egyptologist; studied at German universities; afterward switched from general European archeology to Egyptology and became a leading authority on the Egyptian language and monuments; led a copying expedition to Egypt and the Sudan, 1842–45, followed by magnificent publication; became Curator of the Egyptian collections in Berlin in 1865. A strong advocate of the painstakingly analytical German method of research, as opposed to the more esthetically sensitive French method.

Ferdinand *de Lesseps* (1805–94), French diplomat, engineer, and idealist; was French Consul in Egypt, 1833–37, where he formed a friendship with Said. When Said became Pasha, he recalled de Lesseps to Egypt and gave him a concession to cut a canal across Suez. Against formidable opposition and obstacles, the project was pushed through to an 1869 success. It is illustrative of his grandiose dreaming that he insisted that the controlling company for the Suez Canal be called "Universal." His 1879–88 attempt to cut a canal across the isthmus of Panama ended in failure.

Alfred *Lucas* (1867–1945), British chemist; went to Egypt to head the chemical laboratory of the Survey Department; became an expert on chemistry for legal purposes, an authority on poisons, ballistics, and handwriting; retired from this service in 1923 and became chemist to the Service of Antiquities; among his accomplishments was an admirable performance on the materials from the tomb of Tut-ankh-Amon. The leading authority on the chemistry and use of ancient Egyptian materials.

Sir Henry George *Lyons* (1864–1944), British army engineer; rose to rank of colonel; was in Egypt or the Sudan from 1890, excavating or surveying temples; surveyed Philae before construction of the Assuan Dam; directed the first Archaeological Survey of Nubia 1907–9.

Albert M. *Lythgoe* (1868–1934), American Egyptologist; graduated from Harvard; studied with Wiedemann at Bonn; participated in the California excavations at Naga ed-Deir and elsewhere with Reisner, 1899–1904; went to the Metropolitan Museum of Art in 1906 for work at Lisht and the Khargeh Oasis; was Curator of Egyptian antiquities at the Museum, 1906–29. He deserves major credit for building up the Metropolitan Museum's Egyptian collections and furthering the career of Winlock, while he himself stayed modestly in the background.

Arthur Cruttenden *Mace* (1874–1928), British archeologist, cousin of Petrie; worked with him, 1897–1901; with Reisner, 1901–6; with Metropolitan Museum, 1906–12, 1919–22; loaned to the work on the tomb of Tut-ankh-Amon, 1922–24, but thereafter his health failed.

Mohammed Ahmed, self-proclaimed *Mahdi* ("Guide") (died 1885), a Dongolese; united the aggrieved Muslims of the Sudan against the Egyptians and British, with decisive military successes, 1883–85; succeeded by his Khalifah ("Successor"), Abdullah, of the Baggara tribes, who was defeated by Kitchener at the Battle of Omdurman, September 2, 1898. The Mahdist movement collapsed within the following two years.

Auguste Ferdinand François *Mariette* (1821–81), French Egyptologist; was a professor at Boulogne, 1841; attached to the Louvre, 1849; came to Egypt in 1850 and discovered the Serapeum at Sakkarah; excavated for the Louvre. In 1858 he was appointed Conservator of Egyptian Monuments and served until his death. He opened up many important monuments, but the position he held forced him to please his ruler with some new sensation every year. His excavation methods were still primitive, but his one-man control of antiquities did check the unbridled plundering which had gone on before his regime. One of the famous figures in Egyptology.

Gaston Camille Charles *Maspero* (1846–1916), French Egyptologist; was Director-general of the Service of Antiquities in Egypt, 1881–86, 1899–1914; was Professor of Egyptology in Paris from 1869 and member of the French Academy from 1883; knighted by the King of England, 1909. A gifted philologist, brilliant historian, prodigious writer. He and Erman of Berlin and Petrie of England stand out as the three leading Egyptologists at the end of the nineteenth century.

Eduard *Meyer* (1855–1930), German historian; was a professor at the University of Berlin. In addition to his *Geschichte des Alterthums*, he published important studies on phases of Egyptian life, particularly chronology.

Mohammed Abduh (1849–1905), Egyptian religious and political reformer; born a fellah; studied at al-Azhar; became a teacher and religious editor, 1879–80; banished from Egypt for political activity, 1882–89; became state mufti, 1899; reformed the teaching at al-Azhar. A sincere reformer and fervent patriot.

Mohammed (or Mehemet) *Ali* (1769–1849), Balkan soldier of fortune and founder of a ruling line in Egypt; born at Kavalla in Thrace; came to Egypt in 1799 with the Turkish troops to fight the French; by 1806, acknowledged as Pasha of Egypt. With tyrannical zeal, he worked to better Egyptian agriculture and to introduce some industry. His armies were successful in Arabia and the Sudan. In Asia Minor the military skill of his son, Ibrahim Pasha, even threatened the Ottoman Empire, but the Western powers did not want to see Turkey disappear, and Europe intervened in 1833 and 1841 to restrain Mohammed Ali. He lost his incentive and then his reason. A year before his death, his son Ibrahim took over the pashalik.

Mohammed Mohassib Bey (1843–1928), antiquities dealer at Luxor from about 1880. Lady Duff-Gordon was his first mentor. Although he was attacked by Grébaut for his traffic in antiquities in the late 1880's, he was one of the most reliable dealers in Egypt.

Sir Robert Ludwig *Mond* (1867–1938), British chemical industrialist and patron of archeology; from 1901 on financed excavation in Egypt, particularly the clearance of Theban tombs.

Jacques Jean Marie *de Morgan* (1857–1924), French archeologist; worked in Egypt particularly on prehistoric materials; was Director-general of the Service of Antiquities, 1892–97; began the French work at Susa in Iran.

Rev. Chauncey *Murch* (1856–1907), American missionary at Luxor, a collector and a dealer in antiquities. Sales were made from his collections to the British Museum and to the Art Institute of Chicago; the bulk of his collection was presented to the Metropolitan Museum of Art, New York, in 1910.

Mustafa Agha Ayat (died 1887), British, Belgian, and Russian consular agent in Egypt, posts which he held for over fifty years, a Muslim. Many early travelers expressed their indebtedness to his helpfulness and to his lavish hospitality. He used his diplomatic position to secure immunity in his flourishing antiquities trade, but after the discovery of the royal mummies, Belgium dropped him as consular agent. An accomplished linguist and a person of charm.

Henri Édouard *Naville* (1844–1926), Swiss Egyptologist; studied under Lepsius; excavated for the Egypt Exploration Fund, 1883–1913. Old-fashioned in manners and ideas, he carried on a running feud with the "Berlin school" until his death.

Harold Hayden *Nelson* (1878–1954), American Egyptologist; studied under Breasted; went from Instructor to Professor of History at the American University of Beirut, 1904–24; from 1924 to 1947, was Director of the Epigraphic Survey of the Oriental Institute at Luxor and Professor of Egyptology at the University of Chicago. A modest and genial man, a devoted follower of Breasted.

Percy Edward *Newberry* (1869–1949), British Egyptologist; was Professor of Egyptology at Liverpool, 1906–19 and Professor of Ancient History and Archeology at Cairo, 1929–32; began work with Petrie in 1888 as a botanist; copied tombs and excavated from 1890; was a specialist on scarabs. He was always concerned with accompanying influential visitors around Egypt to interest them in the field.

William George Spencer Scott Compton, Fifth Marquis of *Northampton* (1851–1913), British nobleman; was patron of excavations at Thebes, 1898–99.

Thomas Eric *Peet* (1882–1934), British Egyptologist; was first a mathematician, then a classical scholar; excavated in Italy, 1906; went over to Egyptian excavation with success; read hieroglyphs with Gardiner in 1911; was Lecturer in Egyptology at the University of Manchester, 1913–28; Professor of Egyptology at Liverpool, 1920–33; and Professor of Egyptology at Oxford, 1933–34. He happily combined high linguistic ability with competence in field archeology and published translations from hieratic texts, a mathematical papyrus, and records from the end of the New Kingdom.

Sir William Matthew Flinders *Petrie* (1853–1942), British Egyptologist, largely self-taught; began work in Egypt in 1880 and continued there nearly every year, until he moved his British School of Archaeology in Egypt over into Palestine in 1927. Since Petrie published his results almost at once, his books are very many. His quarrels were many also, and it is greatly to the credit of Amelia B. Edwards that she ignored his outspoken criticism and set up the Edwards Professorship of Egyptology at the University of London specifically for him. By his insistence that excavation was a serious business, he was one of the greatest forces in archeology anywhere.

Garrett Chatfield *Pier* (1875–1943), American museum official; studied in Europe and Egypt; with Breasted at Chicago in 1906; served the Metropolitan Museum, 1907–14; formed a collection of Egyptian antiquities.

James Edward *Quibell* (1867–1935), British archeologist; worked first with Petrie; later worked in the Service of Antiquities and at the Cairo Museum; is best known for his excavations at Sakkarah.

Hermann *Ranke* (1878–1953), German Egyptologist; from 1910 was

Professor of Egyptology at Heidelberg, with interim services at the University of Wisconsin and the University of Pennsylvania.

George Andrew *Reisner* (1867–1942), American Egyptologist; born in Indianapolis, November 5, 1867; studied at Harvard, Göttingen, and Berlin; changed from cuneiform studies to Egyptology. In 1897 he went to Cairo to publish certain categories of objects in the Museum; directed the Hearst Expedition for the University of California, 1899–1904; from 1905 headed the Harvard-Boston Expedition at the pyramids, in Nubia, and in the Sudan; also spent two seasons at Samaria in Palestine and two seasons directing the Archaeological Survey in Nubia; was Curator of Egyptian Antiquities at the Boston Museum of Fine Arts from 1910 and Professor of Egyptology at Harvard from 1914. He was blessed with success in every enterprise, chiefly because of his exacting methodology. His Harvard Camp at the pyramids always promoted good work. He was a devoted friend of the Egyptians, high and low. Although he approached blindness in his latter years, he continued to work on publication. The finest of excavators, he died at Gizeh, June 6, 1942.

Sir Peter Le Page *Renouf* (1822–97), British Egyptologist; was a professor at the Catholic University, Dublin; with the British Museum, 1885–91; chiefly known for a translation of the Book of the Dead.

Alexander Henry *Rhind* (1833–63), Scottish lawyer whom ill-health forced to live in a mild climate; excavated at Thebes, 1855–56 and 1856–57; visited Egypt again in 1862–63. His collection went to the National Museum of Antiquities, Edinburgh. Several important papyri are associated with his name. A careful excavator.

The Marquis Maxence du Chalvet *de Rochemonteix* (1849–91), French Egyptologist, student of Maspero; came to Egypt in 1875; served in the Egyptian government 1879–85; began the copying of the temple of Edfu.

Niccolo Franceso Ippolito Baldessare *Rosellini* (1800–43), Italian Egyptologist; accompanied Champollion on a copying mission in 1828–29; was Professor of Oriental Languages at Pisa.

Mikhail Ivanovitch *Rostovtzev* (1870–1952), Russian-born American historian and archeologist; was a professor at the University of St. Petersburg 1903, a specialist on Russian connections with the Hellenistic Orient; to Oxford in 1918, to the University of Wisconsin in 1920, and to Yale in 1925. Two of his most influential books were *The Social and Economic History of the Roman Empire* (1926) and *The Social and Economic History of the Hellenistic World* (1941). A book in more popular vein was *Caravan Cities* (1932). From 1928 he directed the joint expedition of the

French Academy and Yale University at Dura-Europos. He made Yale an outstanding place to study the Hellenistic Orient.

Said (died 1863), one of the younger sons of Mohammed Ali; was Pasha of Egypt, 1854–63. Noted for his huge size, he was a Francophile and the ruler who began the Suez Canal.

Henry *Salt* (1780–1827), British painter; was taken on trips to Asia and Africa as an illustrator; was British Consul-general in Cairo, 1816–27. He himself excavated at Thebes, but chiefly, like Drovetti, employed others to gather antiquities for him, Belzoni among them. His collections were purchased by the British Museum, the French government, and others.

Ernest *de Sarzec* (1836–1901), French Consul at Bosrah; discovered the Sumerian civilization in his 1877 excavations at Telloh.

Sebastien Louis *Saulnier* (1790–1835), French prefect and collector. After his death, most of his collection of Egyptian antiquities went to Berlin by purchase.

Rev. Archibald Henry *Sayce* (1845–1933), British Assyriologist; educated at Oxford; was Professor of Assyriology at Oxford, 1891–1919; discovered the empire of the Hittites; served on committees to revise the translation of the Old Testament; published extensively, including semipopular works. From 1879 to 1908 he spent most of his winters on the Nile, writing and copying texts.

Johannes Heinrich *Schaefer* (1868–1957), German Egyptologist; studied under Erman; was first a philologist, but an early appointment to the Berlin Museum (Curator from 1907 on) shifted his specialty to art; became the leading analyst of the principles and practices of ancient Egyptian art. His *Von Aegyptischer Kunst* is a classic in the field.

Ernesto *Schiaparelli* (1868–1938), Italian Egyptologist; studied under Maspero; excavated in Egypt, 1903–20; was director of the Turin Museum.

Heinrich *Schliemann* (1822–90), German-born; acquired a fortune in Russia as a military contractor at the time of the Crimean War; became an American citizen in California in 1850; retired in 1866; traveled; and studied in Paris; first tested the mound of Hissarlik (Troy) in 1870; began authorized digging in 1871; found "the treasure of Priam" in May, 1873; from 1871 to 1890 worked also on the Greek mainland. The German excavator Dörpfeld later corrected his findings at Troy. A brilliant, opinionated, and magnetic personality.

Selim Hassan (1887–1961), Egyptian Egyptologist; studied in Paris and Vienna; with the Cairo Museum, 1920–29; in 1928, became Assistant Professor of Egyptology at the Cairo University and began excavations, first at Gizeh, later also at Sakkarah; was Sub-director of the Service of

Antiquities, 1936–39. His excavations were marked with continual success, but he became involved in controversy arising out of Egyptian politics and his later years were spent in a struggle for reinstatement.

Kurt Heinrich *Sethe* (1869–1934), German Egyptologist; studied under Erman; was Professor of Egyptology at Göttingen and later in Berlin; was a brilliant philologist and editor of texts. In his prime he was unrivaled at work on texts, but he had little interest in art and archeology.

Gustav *Seyffarth* (1796–1885), German-born scholar; was Professor of Archaeology at the University of Leipzig, 1825–54; migrated to the United States in 1854; became professor at Concordia College, St. Louis.

Edwin *Smith* (1822–1906), American adventurer; born in Connecticut; lived in Egypt, 1858–76, chiefly at Thebes; was dealer in antiquities and money-lender. He was a good decipherer of hieratic; owned and sold the Ebers Medical Papyrus to Ebers in 1872; owned and kept the Edwin Smith Surgical Papyrus, which his daughter presented to the New-York Historical Society in 1906. He lived in Italy his last thirty years. An equivocal figure.

George *Smith* (1840–76), British Assyriologist; had been a bank-note engraver; did cleaning and repairing work at the British Museum; made his sensational discovery about the cuneiform Flood Tablet in 1872; excavated at Nineveh in 1874–76.

Sir Grafton Elliot *Smith* (1871–1937), Bitish anatomist; Professor of Anatomy at the School of Medicine in Cairo, 1900–1909; examined thousands of mummies and became a leading authority on the process of mummification. A prominent exponent of a theory that ancient Egypt was a genetic center for civilization all over the world, including the Americas.

Joseph Lindon *Smith* (1863–1950), American artist; studied in Paris, 1883–84; visited Egypt, 1898; soon developed a style of copying the ancient carved scenes which became famous and which he applied successfully in Greece, Syria, Iran, the Far East, and Central America. His visits to Egypt were regular, and he was called in to assist in archeological work by Davis in Thebes, by Quibell in Sakkarah, and by Reisner at Gizeh; he was formally appointed to the Harvard-Boston staff in 1912. His book, *Tombs, Temples & Ancient Art* (see the bibliography to chapter 5), gives an interesting personal view of Egypt over half a century.

Charles Piazzi *Smyth* (1819–1900), Scottish astronomer; propounded extraordinary theories on the construction and measurements of the Great Pyramid, which he surveyed in 1865. Smyth was a controversial figure, particularly when his fanciful ideas were under discussion.

Georg *Steindorff* (1861–1951), German Egyptologist and Erman's first student; had a forty-year teaching career at the University of Leipzig, until the Nazis forced his emigration to the United States in 1938; excavated near the pyramids, in Upper Egypt, and in Nubia; traveled extensively in the interests of his editorship of Baedeker's *Egypt and the Sudan*, was long an editor of the leading Egyptological journal in Germany; was the author of a Coptic grammar and wrote an attractive book on the Egyptian New Kingdom, which now, with the collaboration of Keith C. Seele, appears in English as *When Egypt Ruled the East*. In his later years in California, he revised his Coptic grammar and published the Egyptian sculpture in the Walters Art Gallery in Baltimore. He was respected and loved as "Uncle George" by his younger colleagues.

William *Stukeley* (1687–1765), British physician, one of the founders of the Society of Antiquaries and its Secretary, 1718–27; entered the church, 1729; student of Druidism.

Nicolas *Tano* (died 1924), Greek antiquities dealer in Cairo; was relatively able and reliable.

Taufik (or Tewfik) (1852–92), son of Ismail and Khedive of Egypt 1879–92. By nature a quiet and pious family man, he showed courageous devotion to his post during the Arabi revolt of 1882. For most of his rule, he obediently followed Cromer's advice.

Lobegott Friederich Konstantin *Tischendorf* (1815–74), German biblical scholar; was a professor at Leipzig; discovered the biblical manuscript, the Codex Sinaiticus, at the monastery on Mount Sinai, 1844–59.

Todros (Tawadrus) *Boulos* (died 1887), also called Theodore, a Copt; was Prussian consular agent at Luxor, later the German consular agent. He was an antiquities dealer, originally trained as a silversmith, and was skilled at forgery. He knew no foreign language, but his son Mohareb Todros (about 1847–1937), who succeeded him, learned German and English.

Robb de Peyster *Tytus* (1876–1913), American archeological volunteer; graduated from Yale; assisted on Egyptian digs, as with Newberry on the palace of Amen-hotep III in southern Thebes, 1901–2. His mother financed the "Tytus Memorial Series" of fine copies of Theban tombs by Davies.

Col. Richard William Howard-*Vyse* (1784–1853), British officer; with the British engineer, Perring, excavated and measured the pyramids of Gizeh from 1835 on. Their descriptions and measurements were of great value, but Vyse's direct method of forcing his way through obdurate stone was violent. "Little progress was made, until quarrymen arrived from the Mokattam, who understood their business, and could use gun-

232 — BIOGRAPHICAL NOTES

powder." His expedition penetrated the Third Pyramid and discovered the fine basalt sarcophagus of Men-ku-Re. On the way to England, this piece was lost at sea when the ship went down off Spain in 1838.

Arthur Edward Pearse Brome *Weigall* (1880–1934), British archeologist; worked first with Petrie, 1901; with Service of Antiquities, 1905–14; published several popular books on ancient Egypt, many of them over-effusive.

Frederic Cope *Whitehouse* (1842–1911), American lawyer; studied in Europe; wrote several articles on Lake Moeris and the pyramids.

Charles Edwin *Wilbour* (1833–96), American journalist and Egyptologist; studied at Brown University; became court reporter and then journalist in New York. Because of his relationship to the Tweed Ring, he left a prosperous career in New York in 1874 and went to live in France and studied in Paris and Heidelberg; from 1880 on, he spent his winters in Egypt, with some summers in New England. A very able copyist, he communicated his studies to others and never sought to publish. The letters to his family from 1880 to 1891 give a vivid picture of Egypt in that period. He collected a number of antiquities, and his collection and his library went to the Brooklyn Museum. In his memory his daughter Theodora established the Wilbour Professorship of Egyptology and an institute for study in that field at Brown University.

Sir John Gardner *Wilkinson* (1797–1875), British Egyptologist; lived in Egypt, 1821–33; had a house built above the tombs of the nobles in Thebes. A copyist with a skilled eye, his *Manners and Customs of the Ancient Egyptians* (1837) was handier and more analytical than the massive collections of the Napoleonic expedition, the works of Champollion, or those of Lepsius; therefore he had great influence on the understanding of ancient Egypt.

Edward Livingstone *Wilson* (1838–1903), American photographer; went to Egypt to photograph monuments and was invited to attend the second opening of the cache for royal mummies in 1882.

Sir Francis Reginald *Wingate* (1861–1953), British general and administrator; after Indian service, was with Egyptian army from 1883; was Governor-general of the Sudan and Sirdar of the Egyptian army, 1899–1916, and British High Commissioner in Egypt, 1916–19; had excellent command of Arabic. Wingate took great interest in the monuments of the Sudan.

Herbert Eustis *Winlock* (1884–1950), American Egyptologist; born in Washington D.C.; after graduation from Harvard in 1906, immediately joined the Metropolitan Museum's Egyptian expedition, under Lythgoe; from 1906 to 1931, excavated at Lisht, the Khargeh Oasis, and Thebes;

from 1928, was the Director of the field expedition; was Curator of
Egyptian Collections at the Metropolitan Museum, 1929–39; in 1932,
called home to New York to become Director of the Metropolitan
Museum of Art, a post he held until illness forced his retirement in 1939.
A brilliantly successful excavator, he had a gift for presenting his reports
as exciting detective stories. One of the finest products of American
scholarship in the Oriental field.

Sir (Clarence) Leonard *Woolley* (1880–1960), British archeologist;
started at the Ashmolean Museum with Arthur Evans; went to Egypt to
dig for the University of Pennsylvania, to Carchemish on the Euphrates
for the British Museum in 1912. A delightful account of these experiences
appears in his *Dead Towns and Living Men* (1920). Held as a prisoner
of war in Turkey in World War I, he returned briefly to Egypt to dig
at Tell el-Amarna, then in 1922 began his famous excavation at Ur in
Iraq. In 1936 he started a new site in northern Syria at Tell Atchana,
which proved to be the ancient capital Alalakh. At the time of his death
he had completed the volume on the ancient Orient for the UNESCO
World History. A charming storyteller and an uncannily successful excavator, he had a gift for giving his admirable results the widest publicity.

Thomas *Young* (1773–1829), British physician and physicist; was
best known for his work in optics; successfully recognized the character
of Egyptian writing about 1814 but did not follow through; established
an Egyptological society in London in 1819.

Saad *Zaghlul* Pasha (1860–1927), Egyptian nationalist; born a fellah;
started a career in law; became cabinet minister in 1906, but was forced
by Kitchener in 1912 to resign because of his outspokenness; founded the
Wafd party to work for Egyptian independence; exiled, 1919–21, and
again, 1921–23; formed a ministry in 1924, but was forced to resign
after the assassination of Sir Lee Stack, the Sirdar. For fifteen years, he
was the spearhead of the nationalist movement in Egypt.

INDEX

Plate numbers follow the page references. Place names are followed by (P). For ancient Egypt, names of gods are followed by (G), of kings by (K), of queens by (Q), and of nobles by (N).

Institutions are normally listed under place; e.g., "British Museum" under "London."

Most Arabic names appear under the first of two or more names. Thus Mohammed Ali is alphabetized as M and Ahmed Kamal as A. The Arabic article al- or el- and the European de or d' have been ignored in the alphabetical listings.

Among the page numbers, references to the biographical notes on persons are given first and in italics.